A COMPLETE BOOK ON HEALTH AND NUTRITION

A COMPLETE BOOK ON HEALTH AND NUTRITION

C.S. JAIN

CYBER TECH PUBLICATIONS
4264/3, Ansari Road, Daryaganj, New Delhi-110002 (India)
Ph.: 011-23244078. Fax: 011-23280028
E-Mail: cyberpublicationsdelhi@yahoo.com

A Complete Book on Health and Nutrition

First Edition 2009

Reprint 2025

Published by G.S. Rawat

For Cyber Tech Publications

4264/3, Ansari Road, Daryaganj, New Delhi - 110 002

E-mail : cyberpublicationsdelhi@yahoo.com

Phone : 011-23244078,

Fax : 011-23280028

Printed at

PREFACE

Health aspects of food is not longer confined to "health food types" and those on medically restricted diets. The book provides separate lists of foods, which could prevent and positively effect various body conditions such as Diabetes, Asthma, Arthritis, Stomach conditions etc..

Health and Nutrition is that the body is made of food and must be repaired withfood when necessary, as a wall of brick and mortar. An introduction to Nutrition and Health is compiled and edited primarily for undergraduate students. It is not, however, an elementary text and presupposes knowledge of biology upto junior college level. The inclusion of the greater detail is usually found in texts of undergraduate level is deliberate.

The uniqueness of this text is greatly due to the blending of the editor's many years of teaching experience in health and Nutrition.

—*Editor*

CONTENTS

1
CHAPTER

HEALTH AND NUTRITION

Human body has two main mechanisms, one which nourishes the body and the other which cleanses he body by eliminating the remaining refuse. Nature has made the body such a perfect machine in itself that it has got computers which decide as to which acids and other chemicals are required for digesting the food you have eat. Then in the body itself there are chemical factories in the form of glands etc. which produce the required juices and chemicals. When due to various reasons, some part of the body becomes unhealthy, then the decisions abut the process to be followed. For restoring health to that part are also taken within the body. And action starts within those factories for producing various elements for improving that situation. But if you continue to put more and more load on you body machine and your body parts do not get enough time to do all those jobs, then what can the poor nature do! It is, therefore, necessary that you do not so overload you body systems that your life force is left with no time to pay attention to restoring health to your unhealthy parts.

While discussing nutrition and nutritive diets it will, therefore, be always necessary that the factories located in the body are not put under such a pressure which they can not cope with.

Food which has not been cooked on fire has a great importance for your diet. Their vitamins are not destroyed and their enzymes also remain intact. The supporters of uncooked food ask as to which animal other than man eats it food after cooking it on fire. None! Then why should man do so? They repeat the English proverb "God sends food and the Devil sends cooks". There is great force in what they say. But if some body presses, in the present day world, that all threat you eat must not be cooked on fire, then that person must be expecting too much! Almost all the fruits are eaten raw. Cucumber, gourd, and tomatoes, though vegetables, are used like fruits. Dried fruits, nuts, kernels of fruits and seeds of various types are also eaten without cooking. After this, dried seeds of sour pomegranate, mint, coriander, tamarind, amla etc. are eaten in the form of chutnees. Carrot, radish, cabbage, turnip, beet, sweet potato and onion etc can be eaten raw in salads. Then, out of the remaining vegetables, soa, bathua, pumpkin, and swuash etc are very tasty when grated and taken in curd. Now for vegetarians, the question remains about some vegetables, pulses and cereals. Out of these, wheat, gram, mung, peanut (ground nut), methic (fenugreek) and alfalfa etc can be sprouted and eaten. If in this way, from the above mentioned foods and from milk and yogurt you can meet three fourth of your requirements, then what is the harm in eating unpolished cooked rice, bread made of whole wheat from which bran has not been removed, unfried food and vegetables, steamed or cooked with very little oil as part of the remaining one fourth of your diet? Cooking while playing havoc with vitamins, enzymes and some mineral salts has, no doubt, some advantages as well. It increases the palatability and digestibility of food. It eliminates harmful organisms found in food. It even makes alteration in the nutritional value of some foods. Starch foods like potatoes and beans are made more digestible by cooking.

Despite some of the above mentioned advantages accruing

form cooking, it must be conceded that uncooked food is much better for healthy living. The American medical researcher Francis Pottenger compared cats which had been fed raw food with cats which had been fed cooked food. "The cats which were given raw meat and raw milk grew, bred and lived their lives with every sign of good health. Mother cats gave birth to an verge of five kittens a time which they suckled normally. The other cats which were fed cooked meats, did not do so well." Cooking should preferably be done in earthern ware or stoneware utensils. Enamelled vessels come next. Brass or copper vessles which have been properly tined may be a good third. Aluminium foil should not be allowed to come in contact with liquid food. It has not yet been firmly established if stainless steel utensils are safe for cooking.

Steaming, boiling and baking are acceptable forms of cooking. Roasting is bad, if the colour of the roasted thing changes. Frying is the worst. It makes the fried food indigestible because the oil penetrates the food through and through. Digestion of he fried food cannot start until the whole of the oil soaked by that food has been digested. "High temperature-short time" methods of cooking are considered better. Steam pressure cooking even preserves nutrients better. For minimizing nutrient losses during cooking, choose fresh foods which are not cut or bruised. If the peel or outer layer is not unpalatable, cook the food whole without cutting. If cutting is necessary, then kept the pieces large and cut just before cooking. In case of boiling, add food to the boiling water which should be the minimal in quantity and could possible be used as gravey or soup. Cook at high temperatures for the shortest time possible using a tight fitting lid.

The cooked food should preferably go directly from the fire to the table. Bacteria do not enter the cooked food straight away. It takes them a while to realise and to get going. Microbiologists call this the "lag Phase"-generally estimated at about an hour and a half. So if you never leave food to cool for longer than ninety minutes, the bacteria never reach their attack phase. Bacteria can multiply rapidly at any temperature between 5°C and 63°C. So the strategy should be never to leave the food between these two temperatures for more than 90 minutes at a time. While heating the food, temperature of more than 75°C must be reached to ensure that all bacteria are killed. This will also destroy most of the enzymes that may have by any chance been left in that food. Admitted that the enzymes of foods cooked at temperatures higher than 60°C ordinarily get destroyed but then this is also scientifically proven that if the food is such as does not tempt you, then your glands do not release that juicy substance and other digestive elements which help transform those foods into life force. Under these circumstances, if one fourth of you food is cooked, but tempting, you glands will make available digestive chemicals in large quantities.

Daily ration of sprouted beans. Sprouts relatively contain the largest amount of nutrients per unit of any food known to man. Sprouts produce a fountain of power for chemical changes. Enzymes are produced. Starch gets converted into glucose. Protein is transformed into amino acids. Vitamin value increases. In fact a new explosion of life force takes place. According to Dr. bailey of the University of Minnesota U.S.A., the vitamin C value of wheat increases 600 percent in the early sprouting period. Dr. Ernest Krebs has reported that vitamin B increases over 1000 percent in the spouted seed. Dr. C.R. Shaw of the university of Taxas Cancer Centre found that cancer was inhibited upto 90 per cent when healthy bacteria were exposed to a cancer causing substance in the presence of a juice made from whet sprouts.

Enzymes which initiate and control almost every chemical reaction in our bodies, are greatly activated in the sprouting process. Enzymes spark the entire digestive system to synthesize the nutrients in our food into blood. They are they key to longevity. Enzymes are immobilized at temperatures below zero degree Celsius (32°F and begin to die at temperatures above 50°C. For this reason, cooked food is devoid of its life giving properties. Sprouts are so alive that they are still growing when you are eating them.

All live food has vibratory electrical life energy. Sprouts are nutritionally complete, economically sound and for survival a great food. Alfafa sprouts are an excellent and soft food. They are easily digested and assimilated even by infants and the elderly. They contain every known vitamin in perfect balance, necessary for the human body.

Some Important guidelines for Sprouting

Sprouting moisture and warmth are needed. The procedure for sprouting is very simple and easy, as explained below:

1. Clean the seeds thoroughly and weed out the defective ones as also tiny pieces of hard substances.

2. Wash the seeds with water several times to ensure that no dirt remains.

3. Soak these washed seeds in water, preferably in an earthen pot. The water should be 5 to 7 centimeters (two to three inches) above the seeds.

4. The seeds should remain soaked in water for six to ten hours. Some harder seeds, such as soyabeans, will require more time, while others will require less time. Ten hours is the maximum time because after that they will begin to rot. By soaking, the seeds absorb sufficient moisture necessary for bringing them into life. This purpose is fully served in six to ten hours. The best course is to soak the seeds before going to bed and take them out in the morning.

5. After taking out the soaked seeds from the water, wash them several times with fresh water.

6. Take a thick piece of cotton cloth of a size according to the quantity of the sprouts to be made. Soaked and washed seeds should be put into this piece of cloth and loosely tied. This small bundle may be hung on a peg or kept some where. It may be useful to expose this bundle to the morning sun for an hour or so.

7. After 10 to 14 hours, the seeds will germinate. Tiny sprouts will poke their way out and begin to grow. The time will vary according to season. In hot season the germination takes less time than in cold season.

8. During the period of the seeds are kept tied in the cloth, it should be ensured that this bundle does not go dry. Water is to be sprinkled over it several times during the day especially in hot season to keep it always wet. Twice or thrice during the day the seeds are to be flushed with water several times to remove the shine that generally accumulates on them.

9. Soyabean or similar other hard seeds require more time for sprouting. They require more warmth also. Such seeds, after being tied in cloth, should be fully covered with some woolen piece all around and kept some where, with heavy weight placed on them. Let remain there for ten or fifteen hours and they will sprout. The time required will be more or less, according to season.

10. After the seeds sprout, they are ready for use. If the sprouting is allowed to continue longer, the nutritional value increases tremendously.

11. If the sprouts are exposed to indirect sunlight for the

last two hours before consumption, they will become green and attractive.

12. After sprouting and before consumption, remove all the defective and hard seeds which have not sprouted. This picking has to be necessarily done in the case of soyabean, pulses like moth and moong otherwise while eating if any hard seed comes under your teeth, the whole taste is spoiled. A little time spent in weeding out defective seeds will make you relish the sprouts more.

13. It is best to wash and rinse the sprouts before eating. Afterwards they should be placed in a thick dry cloth and tied tightly to remove excess moisture. You will relish more if the sprouts have less moisture.

14. After the seeds have sprouted, they can be placed in a covered container and kept in the refrigerator. They can last for several days without spoiling. Please remember to keep them covered. They will not spoil even when kept outside the refrigerator also but must be washed and then their extra moisture removed as explained earlier.

15. Each sprouted seed can be eaten by itself without the addition of salt or any other condiments. They have there own delicious taste, why spoil it with any additions? However, to create variety and taste, mix several sprouts such as moong, moth, kidney bean, gram and alfalfa. In the beginning take sprouts in a small quantity and after pounding or grinding them in a blender or otherwise. When they are easily digested, increase their proportion in your diet.

Sprouts are enjoyed more when they are fresh. Lemon juice can make the sprouts more tasty. Crated coconut and carrots or dates in small pieces can be mixed with the sprouts. These become more tasty by begin taken with green coriander or *methi* (fenugreek). Sprouted seeds are greatly enjoyed as part of salads or mixed with yogurt as '*raita*'. A mixture of honey and lemon or of thick curd can be used as a dressing for sprouts. Mix sprouts with other foods according to your taste and enjoy eating them. But eat them you must, everyday, with every meal! You will soon realize that making sprouts a part of your diet has a dramatic effect on your health. With this live food, all the cells of your body will become active. You will feel so active and agile that you yourself will be astonished.

Health and Natural Food

Food produced on fertile land without the use of chemical fertilizers, pesticides, or other chemicals is known as natural food. Pasturized milk does not remain a natural food, nor is white wheat flour. The whole wheat flour has very good proteins, natural oil, minerals, other elements and vitamins B and E in good quantities but in the production of white whet flour most of them are lost. Fresh fruits and vegetables are not only good to taste but also have nutritive elements in large quantities. If fresh vegetables are left in an open room for one day, almost half of their vitamin C is lost. Many people cut vegetables long before cooking. By doing this they provide greater outer surface for some of their nutritive elements to evaporate. Fruits and vegetables which are frozen in the deep freeze lose most of their vitamins B1 and B2. All the enzymes of milk are destroyed in pasturization. Food on which pesticides have been sprinkled, should be thoroughly washed before use. Wash them before cutting.

These days some of the pesticides and chemicals sprayed are such as would not be washed away with cold water. Therefore use luke warm water for washing such food. Those of you who have your own land for agriculture, should grow your vegetables on that land which has been fertilized with natural compost only and where no pesticides or chemicals have been used. And pluck such vegetables or fruits just a little before use. Those are the best natural food.

Health agencies dietitians and the dietary department play a leading role in assuring that quality nutritional care is provided. The focus of nutritional care in health agencies is on providing clients with appropriate kinds and amounts of food and nutrients, on promoting the client's comfort, and on providing education for clients. Since the severity and frequency of malnutrition (that is, malnutrition resulting from acts or omissions of health care providers) has beer; recognized, health professionals are directing more attention toward maintaining or improving the nutritional status of their clients. Providing for the client's nutritional health is the mutual responsibility of physicians, dietitians, nurses, and others.

When foods are selected carefully, they can provide all of the essential nutrients needed for normal functioning of the human body. In this context, food is necessary to provide energy, to provide structural components for building and repairing body tissues, and to regulate body processes.

Nutrient Requirements are essential nutrients (carbohydrates, fats, proteins, minerals, vitamins, and water) that have specific functions in the human body. When the energy-yielding nutrients, that is, carbohydrates, fats, and proteins, are oxidized in the body, energy is captured in a chemical compound known as adenosinetri-phosphate (ATP), which will then release the energy slowly so that it can be used for physical activity (work), heat production, and metabolic processes. Enzymes, vitamins, and minerals, as well as water, are needed in order for these oxidation reactions to take place. Energy requirements are expressed in terms of kilocalories (kcal), Calories (Cal), or kilojoules (kJ). Fats and carbohydrates contain only h elements carbon, oxygen, and hydrogen. Since fats contain less oxygen than carbohydrates, they have greater potential for oxidation and thus provide more energy per gram than carbohydrates. Proteins also contain nitrogen, out this does not contribute substantially to the energy value. The physiological fuel value, or the amount of energy generated in the body, of 1 gram of protein is 4 kcal (17 kJ); carbohydrate, 4 kcal (17 kJ); fat 9 kcal (38 kJ). Many fats, carbohydrates (glucose and glycogen particularly), and proteins are synthesized in the body, but certain compounds as well as minerals and vitamins that are considered dietary essentials must be provided by the food supply. There are also vitamins and minerals that are essential to bodily functions.

Proteins

The word protein comes from a greek word meaning "first in importance". Proteins are formed by a combinaiton of oxygen, nitrogen, carbon, phosphorus and sulphur etc. Proteins are extremely important for body development. If proteins are in short supply, your body "eats" its own muscles in order ot keep vital organs working. Proteins provide the building blocks needed for growth, repair and maintenance of body tissues and organs. They are composed of more than sevent amino acids: For assimilation of proteins, body releses enzymes into the intestinal tract. Enzymes break the protein down into amino acids. tehse acids are absorbed into your bloodstream. About ten amino acids are essential for good nutrition. Proteins which have a fair balance of these essential amino acids are known as high quality proteins. Proteins of milk, almonds, nuts, soyabean, eggs, and meat are of high quality. Cereals, pulses, peas, and seeds have some of the essential amino acids in short supply. Their proteins are, nevertheless, of good quaity. Mixing some of these foods gives teh same results as a high quality protein. Deficiency in the proteins of cereals is made up by the proteins of the pulses. It is consequentlyappropriate to take pulses with cereals. Muscles, skin,ensymes and hormones are all made of amino acids. Their needs are continuousso your need for proteins is also contstant. due to shortage of proeinsyoufeel weak and tired. If proteins are takenin excess, the blood getsvitiated and rotting startsinside the intestines. Need for proteins depends upon the body weight. For every kilogram of body weight, one gram of protein is required per day. According to one school of thought if you are taking sufficinet calories in your food, there willnot be any shortage of proteins becase nature has kept appropriate proportions of these two essential requirements of the body in various food items. You have, however, to pay attention to the quality of protein in the food.

Functions of Essential Nutrition

Large teaching hospitals and medical centers an administrative dietitian usually manages the dietary department. She is assisted by clinical dietitians who are responsible for assessing clients nutritional status and needs, planning nutritional care, and giving nutrition counseling. Clinical dietitians are also responsible for planning food and menu selections that are appealing and palatable to the client while providing nutritious food. Large teaching hospitals and medical centres are likely to have a multidisciplinary nutritional support service whose function is to serve clients who have special nutritional needs. The goals of a nutritional support service often include:

(1) monitoring the nutritional status of clients in a health agency,

(2) consulting,

(3) supervising the implementation of nutritional support in selected clients, and

(4) providing a multidisciplinary approach to nutritional care.

Nurses, dietitians, and physicians consult with the nutritional support team when they suspect a client has a serious nutritional problem or when they need assistance in handling a client's nutrition related needs. A protocol may describe the services a nutritional support team provides and criteria for determining if the services of the team should be requested.

Functions of Essential Nutrients

Functions	*Nutrients Involved*
Energy	Carbohydrates, fats, proteins
Structure	Proteins, minerals
Regulation of body processes	Minerals, vitamins, water
Dietary essentials in each nutrient group	
Fat	Linoleic acid, arachidonic acid
Protein	Essential amino acids: histidine, leucine, isoleucine, lysine, methionine, phenylalanine, threonine, tryptophan
Menerals	Calcium, phosphorus, sodium, potassium, sulfur, chlorine, magnesium, iron, selenium, zinc, manganese, cobalt, copper, molybdenum, iodine, chromium, fluorine, vanadium, tin, nickel, silicon, arsenic.
Vitamins	Fat-soluble: A, D, E, K Water-soluble: thiamin, riboflavin, niacin, B-6, folate, B-12, pantothenic acid, biotin, C (ascorbic acid)

Food Functions

The study of nutrition involves the identification of individual nutrients essential for growth and for the maintenance of individual organisms; it includes the determination of interrelationships among nutrients within individual organisms, as well as the evaluation of the quantitative requirements of organisms for specific nutrients under various environmental conditions. Treated in this article are the identification and determination of the requirements of nutrients, the ways in which they vary from one organism to another, and the ways in which requirements for certain of them arose. Food serves three functions in most living organisms. First, it provides materials that are metabolized either by oxidative or by fermentative processes to supply the energy required for the absorption and translocation of nutrients, for the synthesis of cell materials, for motility and locomotion, for excretion of waste products, and for all other activities of the organism. Second, food supplies the electron donors (reducing agents) required for the formation of the reduced coenzymes (enzyme components) necessary for the synthetic processes that occur within the cell. Third, food provides the materials from which all of the structural and catalytic components of the living cell can be assembled by processes sometimes called *anabolism*. The three roles of food are not mutually exclusive; energy-yielding substances in many organisms may function in all three ways, and essential nutrients, if present in excess, may frequently be metabolized to supply energy. The essential precursors (i.e., the substances from which other substances are formed) of cell materials can be divided into two groups-nonessential nutrients, which can be synthesized by the cell from other materials, and essential nutrients, which, because they cannot be synthesized by the cell, must be supplied in foods. All of the inorganic materials required for growth, together with an assortment of organic compounds whose number may vary from one to 30 or more, depending on the organism, fall into the latter category. Although organisms are able to synthesize nonessential nutrients, such nutrients are frequently utilized directly if present in food, thereby saving the organism the need to expend the energy required to synthesize them.

One method of classifying living organisms on a nutritional basis centres on the way in which the functions of food are carried out. Thus, organisms such as green plants and some bacteria that need only inorganic compounds for growth are called *autotrophic* organisms; and organisms, including all animals, fungi, and most bacteria, that require both inorganic and organic compounds for growth are called *heterotrophic*. Although these general terms are widely employed, the classification has been broadened to describe various nutritional patterns that have been observed. In one scheme, organisms are classified according to the energy source they utilize. Phototrophic, or photosynthetic, organisms trap light energy and convert it to chemical energy in the form of an energy-rich compound, adenosine triphosphate (ATP); chemoautotrophic, or chemosyntheti, organisms utilize inorganic or organic compounds to supply their ATP requirements. An additional method of differentiation is based on the type of electron-donor material utilized to form the reduced coenzymes required for synthesis of cell constituents.

If the electron-donor material consists of inorganic compounds, the organism is said to be lithotrophic; if organic, the organism is organotrophc. Combinations of these patterns may also be used to describe organism; higher plants, for example, are photolithotrophic; i.e., they utilize light energy, with the inorganic compound water serving as the ultimate electron donor. Certain photosynthetic bacteria that cannot utilize water as the electron donor and require organic compounds for this purpose are called photo-organotrophs. Animals, by this classification, are chemoorganotrophs; i.e., they utilize chemical compounds to supply ATP and organic compounds as electron donors. Despite wide variations in the nature of the external energy source utilized by various organisms, all organisms form from the external energy source the immediate intracellular source of energy, ATP, which is common to all cells. Through the breaking of the high-energy phosphate bonds of ATP and thus by its conversion to a less energy-rich compound, adenosine diphosphate (ADP), ATP provides the energy for the chemical and mechanical work required by an organism. The energy requirements of the organism can be measured in either joules or calories; the need for cell-precursor materials cannot be.

All animals, fungi, and most bacteria are chemoorganotrophs (i.e., organic compounds supply both ATP and serve as electron donors). In these organisms the multiple roles played by foodstuffs are partially obscured because the carbon-containing compounds that serve as energy sources also serve as electron donors and provide intermediate compounds from which many cell materials are synthesized. Similarly, essential organic nutrients, when present in excess, may be utilized in part to provide the energy needs of the organisms.

Evolution of Organisms

Nucleic acids, proteins, carbohydrates, and fats, which are present in all living cells, are formed by specific reaction sequences from a limited number of smaller compounds, most of which are common to all living organism and, according to current theories, were available on Earth before life arose. Since less complex metabolic organization and less energy are required to synthesize cellular proteins form preformed amino acids than from carbondioxide and other precursors, it is assumed that the simplest early forms of life were heterotrophic organisms requiring many organic nutrients for growth and that they selected such nutrients from their surroundings. As the supply of these preformed substances was exhausted the organisms presumably developed the capacity to synthesize these preformed substances from simpler (precursor) materials Present in the environment; in some organism, this synthesizing capacity eventually evolved to the extent that carbon from carbon dioxide could be utilized to synthesize organic compounds. At this point, autotrophy, as it now is known, became possible; autotrophy, in fact, may have evolved as a result of the exhaustion of the supply of preformed organic materials in the environment and the consequent necessity of organisms to synthesize the requirements themselves in order to survive. Implicit in this theory is the demonstrable assumption that autotrophic cells contain the most complex biosynthetic organization found in living things and that heterophic cells are simpler in that certain biosynthetic pathways do not occur. After the evolution of photosynthesis, a constantly renewable source o the organic compounds necessary for heterotrophic cell growth became available. It became feasible that those organisms whose environments provided a constantly available supply of a given compound could lose, through changes in their genetic material (mutations), the ability to sun the size that compound and still survive. Entire biosynthetic path ways may have been lost in this way; as long as such mutant organisms remained in an environment that supplied the necessary compound, the simplification in cellular organization and the energy saved by using preformed cell components would have given them a competitive advantage over the more complex parents from which they were derived and permitted stabilization of the mutation within the cell type. A theory that the requirements of modern organisms for essential organic nutrients arose through the loss of synthetic abilities present in more complex parent organisms as confirmed between 1940 and 1950 by the discovery that artificially produced mutant offspring of microorganisms can be readily obtained and may require the presence of one or more preformed organic compounds, which the parent microorganisms could synthesize.

Foodstuffs of chemoorganotrophs are composed chiefly of large molecules, such as nucleic acids, proteins, lipids, and carbohydrates, which are derived from other organisms. When these materials are eaten as food, they usually must be broken down into the low-molecular-weight substances from which they were formed (e.g., purine and pyrimidine bases from nucleic acids, amino acids from proteins, fatty acids from fats, and simply sugars from carbohydrates) before they can be absorbed and utilized. The breakdown process is generally accomplished outside the cells (extracellularly) of both unicellular and multicellular organisms through hydrolysis (breakdown involving water), catalyzed by specific enzymes secreted for this purpose. Some unicellular organisms (e.g., the protozoan genus Amoeba), however, engulf particulate matter and hydrolyze it intracellularly. The organic products ofdigestion produced extracellularly, together with essential inorganic nutrients, must cross one or more cell membranes before they can be utilized for growth. When nutrient concentrations are high, some materials may diffuse through the cell membrane to enter the cell. Absorption of some materials can occur from an extracellular solution containing small quantities of the nutrients to an intracellular solution containing large quantities (active transport) and is catalyzed within the cell membrane by systems that are specific for the type of compound being transported. Those catalysts best characterized involve either specific proteins with high affinity for the nutrient substance being transferred or enzymes that chemically modify the nutrient during its passage through the membrane or both.

Essential Requirements of Determination

Estimated that the approximate quantities of chemical elements in the human body (in percent of wet weight) are oxygen, 65; carbon, 18; hydrogen, 10; nitrogen, 3; calcium, 2; phosphorus, 1.1; sulfur, 0.25; potassium, 0.20; sodium, 0.15; chlorine, 0.15; magnesium, 0.05; iron, 0.004; copper, o.00015; manganese, 0.00013; and iodine, 0.00004. Also present are traces of about 20 other elements—e.g., zinc, cobalt, silicon, molybdenum, selenium, aluminum, arsenic, barium, boron, o mine, cadmium, chromium. Analytical figures such as those for humans given above serve to distinguish between chemical elements that occur in relatively large amounts—oxygen, carbon, nitrogen, sulfur, and phosphorus—and the so-called trace elements, an obsolescent term applied to elements that are present in small amounts and that in the past could be detected in tissues but not analyzed accurately. The methods used to determine the pure substances necessary for growth are similar in principle for all organisms. Occasionally, crude diets lacking only one or a few nutrients result in some naturally occurring deficiency disease; the substance that cures such a condition can be determined directly by adding it to the diet. Certain vitamins were recognized in this way. In the absence of a deficiency condition, a crude nutrient medium (or diet) adequate for growth is selected for the organism to be studied, and attempts are then made to replace the various ingredients of the medium with purified materials and, finally, with substances of known *composition*. If replacement with substances of known *composition permits growth*, the added materials can be determined with relative ease; if the pure substances do not allow growth, however, chemical testing must be carried out to isolate and identify the substances in crude materials that permit growth. Detailed nutritional requirements of many organisms are known, and essentially all of the organic nutrients are available as pure compounds, so determination of the nutrient requirements of a previously unstudied organism is a comparatively easy task. Elucidation of trace-element requirements remains troublesome, however, because these substances occur commonly as contaminants in other materials.

Nutritional Guidelines

Food and Nutrition Board of the National Research Council establishes recommended dietary intakes for nutrients, that is, the quantities of certain nutrients that are thought to be adequate to meet the known nutritional needs of practically all healthy persons. The Recommended Dietary Allowances (RDAs) are recommended amounts of each nutrient, and these must be translated into food plans to help individuals select adequate diets. The Food Guide Pyramid was developed by federal government agencies to help consumers make food choices to maintain good health. The guidelines suggest eating patterns based on a substantial number of servings of cereal-based foods and of fruits and vegetables; smaller amounts of animal products (meats, eggs, dairy) are recommended than in earlier published guidelines. The National Research Council suggests that consumption of diets rich in plant foods lowers the risk of chronic diseases, such as cancer, diabetes, and cardiovascular disease. A reduction in fat consumption, particularly saturated fats, is also recommended; fat consumption should not exceed 30% of caloric intake. The Nutrition Labeling and Education Act of 1990 requires nutritional labeling for almost all foods to aid in selection; requirements for terms used to describe nutrient content are specified.

Carbohydrates

Chemically, Carbohydrates are compounds of carbon, hydrogen and oxygen. this element in food provides us both the heat and the energy. Commonest carbohydrtes in human food are starch and sugar. Both of these are found in green plants. Starch causes fat to ccumulate on the body . Digestion of sarch puts a great strain on the liver. Shortage of carbohydrates produces listlessness and weakness. Its exess produces obesity. reserves of carbohydrates are found in the form of glycogen in your liver and in your muscles. These reserves are handy during fasting periods. An Ordinary person requires 160 to 240 gms of carbohydrates per day. The quantity of carbohydrates in various food items is given Table 1.1.

Carbohydrate-rich Foods

Plants synthesize carbohydrates by the process of photosynthesis and store them in the form of starch (a complex carbohydrate) or simpler sugars, such as glucose, fructose, or

Table 1.1: Minerals, Trace Elements, and Acid base balance values given per 100 gms of Edible Portion

Food stuff	*Mag-nesium mg*	*Sodi-um mg*	*Pota-ssium mg*	*Copper mg*	*Sulphur mg*	*Chlori ne mg*	*acid base ml Acid*	*Balance Oin base*
Bajra	125	10.9	307	0.55	147	39	87	-
Barley	127	16.1	253	0.34	130	91	57	-
Dhal	185	39.8	800	0.72	174	9	-	91
Corn(Maize)	144	15.9	186	0.19	114	33	102	-
Green Gram	171	28.0	843	0.97	188	12	-	99
Mothi Beans	225	29.5	1096	0.85	180	9	-	316
Peas, Dry	124	20.4	725	0.85	189	59	-	7
Rice, Milled	48	8.0	70	0.72	53	7	72	-
Sorghum	140	7.3	131	1.78	54	44	25	-
Wheat, whole	138	17.1	284	0.49	128	47	77	-
Wheat Flour	55	20.0	315	0.49	122	29	76	-
Refined	42	9.3	130	0.19	115	47	80	-
Amaranth	247	230.0	341	0.33	61	88	-	472
Bamboo Shoots	32	91.0	-	0.19	-	76	-	-
Beet Root	9	59.8	43	0.20	14	24	-	93
Bitter Groud	21	2.4	171	0.19	21	8	19	-
Brinjal	16	3.0	200	0.17	44	52	-	14
Brussel Sprouts	26	7.9	477	0.07	212	22	23	-
Broad beans	33	43.5	39	0.17	53	43	5	-
Cabbage	10	14.1	114	0.08	67	12	-	111

(Table Continued)

Food stuff	*Mag-nesium mg*	*Sodi-um mg*	*Pota-ssium mg*	*Copper mg*	*Sulphur mg*	*Chlori ne mg*	*acid base ml Acid*	*Balance Oin base*
Carrot	20	53.0	138	0.05	231	34	99	-
Cauliflower	20	53.0	138	0.05	231	34	99	-
Cucumber	11	10.2	50	0.10	17	15	0	0
Drum Stick	24	-	259	0.60	137	423	-	-
Lady Fingers	43	6.9	103	0.19	30	41	-	31
Lettuce	30	58.0	33	0.08	27	23	-	41
Mango Green	21	43.0	83	0.24	15	2	-	40
Mint	-	-	-	-	84	34	-	-
Neem Leaves	127	72.7	254	0.06	96	26	-	75
Onion	-	4.0	127	-	-	-	-	-
Peas	34	7.8	79	0.23	95	20	93	-
Potato	20	11.0	247	0.20	37	16	-	36
Pumpkin	14	5.6	139	0.20	16	4	-	24
Radish	-	33.0	138	-	-	-	-	-
Spniach	84	58.5	206	0.01	30	54	-	134
Tomato	12	12.9	146	0.14	11	6	-	55
Amla	-	5.0	225	0.18	-	-	-	-
Apple	7	28.0	75	0.13	7	1	-	24
Banana	34	36.6	88	0.40	7	8	-	45
Coconut Meal deoiled	355	72.5	2003	-	431	374	-	99
Gauva	8	5.5	91	0.34	14	4	-	9
Jack Froot	27	41.11	191	0.23	69	9	-	27

(Table Continued)

Food stuff	Magnesium mg	Sodium mg	Potassium mg	Copper mg	Sulphur mg	Chlorine mg	acid base ml Acid	Balance Oin base
Jabul	35	26.2	55	0.23	13	8	-	41
Lemon	-	-	270	0.16	-	-	-	-
Lichi	10	124.9	159	0.30	19	3	-	73
Mango	27	26.0	205	0.20	17	3	-	73
Musk Melon	31	104.6	341	0.03	32	80	-	135
Water Melon	13	27.3	160	0.05	42	21	-	135
Orange	9	4.5	93	0.58		5	-	29
Papaya	11	6.0	69	0.20	11	-	-	40
Peach	21	2.0	453	0.06	26	0	-	18
Pineapple	20	34.7	37	0.36	20	13	-	21
Pomegranate	12	0.9	133	0.17	12	2	-	29
Chillies Dry	-	14.0	530	-	-	-	-	-
Chillies Green	24	6.5	217	1.55	34	15	-	16
Coriander	-	32.0	990	-	-	-	-	-
Cumin	-	126.0	980	-	-	-	-	-
Ferugreek seeds	-	19.0	530	-	-	-	-	-
Beef	-	52.0	214	-	-	-	-	-
Fish Prawan	-	66.0	262	-	-	-	-	-
Fish rohu	13	101.0	288	0.13	103	3	-	275
Liver	-	73.0	166	-	-	-	-	-
Mutton	-	3.0	270	-	-	-	-	-
Milk Buffalo's	-	19.0	90	-	-	-	-	-
Milk cow's	-	16.0	140	-	-	15	-	

sucrose. The structural components of plants include cellulose (a glucose polymer that the human body cannot digest), hemicellulose, and pectin. These, together with other complex carbohydrates (such as gums) produced by plants and bacteria, are classified as dietary fiber. Desirable dietary fiber intakes can be achieved most satisfactorily by consumption of fruits, vegetables, legumes, and whole grain cereals. In most of the world, about 80% of the calories consumed are carbohydrates, primarily from cereal-based foods. (Carbohydrates supply only about half of the calories in the United States.) In addition to being goods sources of energy and fiber, whole grains supply B vitamins and minerals and contain small amounts of protein. The most common cereal grains consumed on a worldwide basis are wheat, rice, and corn (maize). Some grains such as rice, oats, barley, and buckwheat are consumed s whole, cracked, or polished grains. Others, such as corn and wheat, undergo a series of mechanical disintegrations that reduce the grain to grits or flour. While or cracked grains can be consumed directly as cereals, while grits and flours are baked into bread products, made into pastas, or processed into ready-to-eat cereals. Each processing step adds to the convenience and cost of the final product. Enrichment of cereal-based foods (thiamin, niacin, riboflavin, and iron are required for product to be labeled as enriched; calcium and vitamin D are options) restores some of the nutrients lost during milling. It is estimated that 90% of the flour sold in the United States is enriched.

The effects of certain mineral deficiencies on the development of higher plants and animals are illustrated by several photographs. Naturally occur in deficiencies of a number of different trace elements occur in various parts of the world in special types of soils and are therefore of tremendous economic and agricultural importance. Several examples of specialized mineral requirements are demonstrated to be required for the growth of many—perhaps all—higher plants but has not been implicated as an essential element in the nutrition of either microorganisms or animals. Trace amounts of fluorine (as fluoride) are certainly beneficial, and perhaps essential, for proper to the formation in higher animals, but no essential role for fluorine in other organisms has been found. Similarly, iodine (as iodide) is required in animals for formation of thyroxine, the active component of an important regulatory hormone; it plays no known role in other organisms. Silicon (as silicate) is a prominent component of the outer skeletons of diatomaceous protozoans and similar organisms and is required in them for normal growth. In higher animals, the requirement for silicon is much smaller. A less obvious example of a specialized mineral requirement is provided by calcium, which is required by higher animals in comparatively large amounts because it plays a role in the formation of bone and eggshells (in birds); for organisms, calcium is an essential nutrient but only as a trace element. Several additional examples of specialized requirements are evident. Mineral elements in wide variety are present in trace amounts in almost all foodstuffs. It cannot be assumed that, because a given mineral element is nonessential, it plays no useful role in metabolism. Important antagonistic relationships between certain mineral nutrients also are known. A large excess of rubidium, for example, interferes with the utilization of potassium in some lactic-acid bacteria; zinc can also interfere with manganese utilization in the same organism. In animal nutrition, excessive molybdenum or zinc (both of which are essential minerals) interferes with the utilization of copper, another essential mineral, and, in higher plants, excessive zinc can lead to a disorder that is known s *iron chlorosis*. Proper nutrient growth media for microorganisms and plants or diets for animals, therefore, require not only that the essential mineral elements be provided in sufficient amounts but also that they be used in the proper ratios to each other.

Essential Organic Nutrients

Considered in this section is the nature of the essential

organic nutrients, necessary building blocks of various cell components that certain organisms can o longer synthesize and therefore must be supplied to them preformed. These essential compounds include certain amino acids, which are the precursors of protein; purine and pyrimidine bases or their derivatives, which are the precursors of nucleic acids; fatty acids, which are precursors of fats and phospholipids; and, occasionally (in mutant organisms), simple sugars (e.g., glucose). Other essential organic nutrients include the vitamins, which are required in small amounts (relative to, for example, the amino acids), because of either the catalytic role or the regulatory role they play in metabolism.

Proteins usually contain about 20 different amino acids or their derivatives, and there are organism that require none, several, or most of them for growth. Many yeasts and bacteria (*e.g., Escherichia coli*) are able to synthesize all of their amino acids from other compounds (glucose and ammonium salts). Animals may require up to nine or 10 different amino acids in their diets. Species of lactic-acid bacteria have been identified as requiring none (*Streptococcus bovis*), a few (*Lactobacillus plantarum*), or as many as 17 amino acids (*Streptococcus equines*).

Fats:

Fats are required both as a concentrated source of energy and for providing some essential fatty acids for lubricating various types of operations within the human body. Mostly the pure fats and oils supply the need in this behalf but food stuffs rich in fats like nuts, soyabean and some oil seeds consumed as such as also contribute to these needs. Cereals, pulses and vegetables also contain very all amounts of fat. Their contribution is however, valuable because of the quality of the fatty acids of those foods. As the "essential" fatty acids are mostly supplied by vegetable based oils, a percentage of such oils will also have to be included in the diet, whatever their other short-comings may be.

All fats and oils have three types of fatty acids i.e. saturated, mono unsaturated and poly unsaturated. Saturated fatty acids cause considerable rise in the levels of blood cholesterol when taken in large quantities. Poly unsaturated fatty acids donot raise cholesterol levels and mono saturated acids on the one hand lower blood cholesterol levels and on the other, they raise HDL proportion. It is consequently necessary to know the ratio of these types of fatty acids in the various fats and oils before deciding which fats to use the most. These are given in the table below:

Table 1.2: Types of fatty acids in the various fats and oils

Type of Fat	*Percentage of saturated fatty acids*	*Percentage of mono un-saturated fatty acids*	*Percentage of Poly un-saturated fatty acids*
Butter oil	65	31	4
Coconut oil	91	6	3
Corn oil	13	26	61
Cotton seed oil	28	19	53
Lard	43	45	12
Olive oil	14	77	9
Palm oil	53	37	10
Peanut oil	18	49	33
saflower oil	11	12	77
Sesme oil	16	41	43
Soyabean oil	16	24	60
Sunflower oil	11	22	67

These percentages are approximate and will depend on the actual samples.

Various types of hydrogenated oils (vanaspati ghee) also have very high percentage of saturated fatty acids depending upon the base and the processing involved. Poly unsaturated fatty acids in some other edible oils and fats are: Mustard oil 25%, Rice bran oil 25% vanaspati 6%. quantity off at required for a well balanced diet cannot be indicted with any precision. It will, however, do no harm if 25 to 35 gms of fat is consumed daily by a normal adult person of 70 kgs body weight. Nutritionists are, however, agreed that not more than 30 percent of the total calories consumed should be derived from fat and saturated fatty acids should not account for more tan one fourth thereof. A minimum of 50 per cent of all fats consumed should be vegetable based to ensure the supply of sufficient "essential" fatty acids to the body. The above requirements are for a normal person but those who do heavy work or strenuous exercise need more fat. Their increased needs of fat are generally proportionate to their calory needs. Mode of consumption of fat also effects cholesterol levels. Consumption of large amounts of fat at one time raises cholesterol levels more than if the same quantity and quality of fat is taken in small dozes. Fats produce nearly twice as much heat as the same weight of carbohydrates in the process of their oxidation. That energy is transformed into muscular work and body heat.

Persons who have a heart condition or high blood pressure should avoid saturated fatty acids. They should, therefore, try to avoid whole milk, cream, butter, butter oil, coconut oil, lard, palm oil, etc. they should use skimmed milk and its products instead.

Lipids Related Compounds

Lipids general name for the class of compounds to which fats and oils belong. Fats, chemically known as *triglycerides*, are composed of fatty aids attached to glycerol. A fatty acid molecule is composed of an even-numbered carbon chain (4-22 carbons), which can be completely filled with hydrogen (saturated) or can contain some unfilled carbon-to-carbon double bounds (unsaturated). The fatty acid composition of triglycerides in fats or oils is characteristic of the source of the material. All foods contain some lipids, even fruits and vegetables. In fats from animal sources the majority of the fatty acids are saturated (for example, stearic and palmitic acid), but in vegetable fats the fatty acids may be mono-, di-, or polyunsaturated. Cholesterol, an important component of cell membranes and precursor for steroid hormones and bile acids, is present only in foods from animal sources.

Phospholipids are essential components of all cell membranes. Those organisms that have lost the ability to synthesize certain lipids (since they are supplied in their diets), require them as essential nutrients. Essential fatty acids for rats (and most vertebrates) include linoleic and arachidonic acids and, perhaps, linolenic acid as welt. For many bacteria (e.g., Erysipelothrix rhusiopathiae, several species of lactic-acid bacteria), oleic acid is essential for growth, although it can be replaced in most cases by linoleic acid and by an unusual fatty acid called *lactobacillic acid.*

Choline, a nitrogen-containing compound found in the phospholipid lectithin, is usually listed among the nutrients required by rats, although it can be synthesized by them if sufficient vitamin B_{12} is present. Cholineis also required for growth of certain pneumococcal bacteria. Inositol, another structural component of certain lipids, is an essential nutrient for many yeasts but appears to be synthesized by most animals. Finally, the steroid cholesterol is an essential nutrient for a wide variety of protozoans and for the bacteria-like organisms known as *mycoplasmas*. Higher animals are able to synthesize this important cell constituent; it is not present in most bacteria.

Saturated fats such as butter, lard, and tallow are solids at room temperature; polyunsaturated fats (oils) are liquids at room temperature. Saturated fats generally have low smoke points (the temperature at which the fat begins to break down) and are to as useful for frying; oils have higher smoke points. The most common vegetable oils in the United States are extracted from soybeas, cottonseed, corn, sunflower, canola (from rapeseed), and safflower, which all have a high proportion of polyunsaturated fatty acids. More than half of the dietary fat in the United States comes from animal sources; the remainder is from vegetable oils. Slightly less than 40% of the calories in the American diet are from fats and oils.

Vegetable oils can be partially or fully hydrogenated to make solid or plastic fats. For example, in making margarines, some liquid oil is added to hydrogenated fat, as well as color, flavoring, and liquid (usually milk) to emulate the consistency, flavour, and cooking characteristics of butter. The amount of fat or oil in a margarine spread can be reduced slightly (from 80% fat to about 68%) without changing its cooking properties. Reduced-calorie spreads can be made by diluting the fat with water or incorporating air to make a whipped product. Shortening, for baking and frying, can be made from hydrogenated vegetable oils alone or can be blended with animal fat. Supergly cerinated shortenings have mono-and diglycerides added to improve backing and emulsifying properties.

Vitamins

Vitamins are organic chemical compounds that are required in the dietinonly very small amounts but are vital for normal growth and health. The early differentiation of vitamins was by letters of the alphabet, but as chemical identification has become clear, the tendency is to use the chemical name instead. Vitamins are primarily regulatory substances. As a group they promote growth and the maintenance of health and vigor. They bring about thee effects usually by their roles as catalysts in chemical reactions throughout the body. This helps to explain why vitamins are needed in such very small amounts and yet are vital to life. If they are lacking completely or are very deficient in the diet, definite dietary-deficiency diseases result. Less pronounced deficiencies may cause vague and less easily recognized conditions that may be responsible for a lack of optimum growth, health, and vigor. Many vitamins are available in concentrated forms, but for a normal, healthy individual a variety of foods remains the recommended source of vitamins. With the very concentrated vitamin capsules available it is possible to get too much of certain fat soluble vitamins, such as vitamins A and D, which results in toxic effects in the body.

Vitamins may be defined as nutritionally essential organic substances that play a catalytic role within the cell, usually a components of coenzymes or other groups associated with enzymes. More than half of the water-soluble vitamins required by humans were discovered when they were found to be growth factors for microorganisms. Vitamin requirements are specific for each organism, and their deficiency may cause disease. Vitamin deficiencies in young animals usually result in growth failure, various symptoms whose nature depends on the vitamin, and eventual death. Certain vitamins (retinol, calciferol, tocopherol, and ascorbic acid) do not a appear to play an essential role in unicellular organisms. Para-aminobenzoic acid is a vitamin for several bacteria only becaue it is an essential precursor of the vitamin folic acid, which, since it is unable to cross the bacterial cell memberane, must be synthesized from paraaminobenzoic acid. Heme and lipoic acid are typical vitamins for organisms that cannot synthesize them, but they have a catalytic role in all organisms; they are synthesized by higher animals. A few bacteria have lost the ability to convert certain vitamins to their functional forms, the coenzymes; the preformed coenzymes (or intermediates in their synthesis) thus are vitamins for such organisms.

Some Functions of Essential Vitamins

Vitamins	*Functions*
Fat-Soluble	
Vitamin A (retinoids, carotenes)	Night vision (Preformed vitamin A); antioxidants (carotenoids); growth, reproduction, immune system integrity
Vitamin D (calciferol)	Promotes absorption and use of calcium and phosphorus; rickets prevention
Vitamin E (tocopherols)	Antioxidant, membrane integrity, heme synthesis
Vitamin K	Formation of proteins, particularly for blood clotting.
Water-soluble	
Thiamin (B-1)	Coenzyme in energy metabolism, particularly from carbohydrates; antiberiberifactor
Riboflavin (B-2)	Coenzyme in energy metabolism, protein metabolism
Niacin	Coenzyme in energy metabolism, antipellagra factor
Vitamin B-6 (pyridoxine, Pyridoxal, Pyridoxamine)	Coenzyme in amino acid and protein metabolism
Folate	Coenxyme in DNA and RNA metabolism; single carbontransfers, red blood cell formation
Panthothenic acid	Coenzyme in energy metabolism

Vitamin B-12	Coenzyme in DNA and RNA
	(cobalamin) metabolism; single
carbontransfers; red	blood cell formation
Biotin	Coenzyme in fatty acid and carbohydrate metabolism
Vitamin	Collagen formation; antioxidant; C (ascorbic
acid)	detoxification; scurvy-preventive vitamin

Vitamin A

Vitamin a is an alcohol that can be formed in the bodies of animals from yellow and orange pigments, known as carotenes and xanthophylls, which are found in plants. The vitamin A value of foods includes the vitamin as such plus any pigments that are precursors of the vitamin. Plants contain the precursors rather than the preformed vitamin. In animal foods such as whole milk and butterfat both substances may be present. In plant tissues, the intensity of yellow or green colour indicates the presence of carotenes and, therefore, the vitamin A value. In green-coloured vegetables carotenes are always present although chlorophyll (green pigment) may mask their presence. Vitamin A and carotenes are ft soluble, and hence are not dissolved in cooking waters to any appreciable degree. In most cooking processes they are relatively stable but may be destroyed by oxidation in the presence of air. Vitamin A is important in human nutrition for the maintenance of sound epithelial tissues which aid in resistance to infection; for the synthesis of visual purple, the pigment that is deficient in night blindness, and the maintenance of normal vision; for growth; and for normal tooth development. Vitamin A is stored in the body so that symptoms from its deficiency usually develop rather slowly. Important animal sources of vitamin A are liver, butterfat, and egg yolk. It is usually added to margarine. Important plant sources of vitamin A value are the deep green and yellow vegetables.

B Complex Vitamins

Thiamin (vitamin B1) belongs to the water-soluble vitamin B complex. It is widely distributed in both plant and animal foods but often in low concentration. Fresh fruits, vegetables, and milk, although not rich sources of thiamin, may contribute important amounts if eaten in the quantities recommended for good nutrition. Enriched and whole grains, organ meats, pork, legumes, eggs, and nuts are important sources of thiamin in the diet. Because thiamin is water soluble it tends to be dissolved in cooking waters. It also tends to be destroyed in an alkaline medium. The longer the time of heating and the greater the alkalinity, the greater is the extent of inactivation. Nutritionally, thiamin prevents or cures *beriberi*, a multiple neuritis. It is essential for maintaining healthy nerve tissue, helps keep a normal appetite, and aids digestive functions, including good muscle tone and motility in the digestive tract. As with most members of the B complex group, thiamin plays an important role as part of a coenzyme in cell metabolism. It is essential for the utilization of carbohydrates for energy in the body. Riboflavin (vitamin B_2) is a greenish-yellow, fluorescent, somewhat water-soluble vitamin of the B complex. Its stability is greatly affected by light, but it is much more resistant to destruction by heat than is thiamin. It may be destroyed by being heated in an alkaline solution, however. Riboflavin is widely distributed in plant and animal tissue. A Because it is formed in the leaves of plants, green leafy vegetables are a good source of the vitamin. Seeds are rather low in riboflavin. Milk, when consumed in the recommended amounts, supplies a substantial part of the daily riboflavin allowance. Other important food sources are eggs, enriched and whole grain cereals, lean meat, and cheese. Riboflavin is part of several coenzymes that are active in energy metabolism in living cells, so it is essential for general health at all ages. It is necessary for growth and reproduction. A deficiency of riboflavin may result in *cheilosis* (fissures and cracks in the angles of the mouth), in skin lesions, and in burning and sensitivity of the eyes. Deficiency symptomsin, man have been found to be less specific than in many animals.

Niacin is also a member of the B complex and is water soluble but very resistant to heat and oxidation. Little is lot in cooing unless the cooking water is discarded. It was discovered in 1937 that niacin prevents or cures pellagra, a disease characterized by a severe skin rash, diarrhea, and nervous disorders. The amino acid tryptophan is a precursor of niacin because the body can change it into niacin. Recommended dietary allowances for niacin are expressed in terms of niacin equivalents, which include tryptopha. Animal protein foods of high biological value (that is, those that contain adequate amounts of essential amino acids) contain tryptophan. Lean meat, fish, and poultry are good sources of both niacin and tryptophan. Enriched or whole grains, legumes, and nuts are also important sources of niacin. Niacin is part of a coenzyme that plays an essential role in oxidation-reduction reactions of living cells.

Other B complex vitamins include vitamin B6 (pyridoxine), pantothenic acid, folacin, and vitamin B12 (combalamin). Vitamin B6 is important in a number of enzyme systems in the body. Pantothenic acid is part of coenzyme A, a most important substance in body metabolism. Lack of folacin in man result sin gastrointestinal disturbances and a macrocytic anemia, an anemia characterized by the presence of many large immature red blood cells. Vitamin B12 is effective in the treatment of pernicious anemia.

Vitamin D

Vitamin D is necessary for the normal calcification of bones and teeth. It is essential for calcium absorption and utilization. Severe deficiency of this vitamin results in the disease rickets in infants and children. The vitamin is fat soluble and is little affected by ordinary food processing. Few foods are significant sources of the vitamin; however, certain sterols (fatlike substances) in the skin may be changed into active vitamin D by exposure to ultraviolet light. Hence, this vitamin has been called the "*sunshine vitamin*." Milk is usually fortified with Vitamin D.

Vitamin E

Vitamin E refers to a group of compounds called *tocopherols*. It is fat soluble and is required for normal reproduction in rats and for the prevention of muscular dystrophy in several animals. All of the functions of vitamin E in the human body have not been fully determined. Humans do require the vitamin for the prevention of certain blood disorders. Vitamin E appears to act in the body as an antioxidant, controlling unwanted oxidation in the cells. It also acts as an antioxidant foods such as vegetable oils where it is nature ally present.

Vegetable and Fruits

These foods constitute major sources of provitamin A carotenoids, ascorbic acid and many minerals, as well as digestible carbohydrates and fiber. Vegetables include a variety of edible parts of plants (leaves, stems, flowers, roots, tubers, pods, and seeds) and are usually eaten cooked or raw. Fruits of certain plants (tomatoes, eggpalnt, squash, and peppers) are grouped with the vegetables. Fruits generally contain more sugar than vegetables. Supplies of fresh fruits and vegetables were at one time limited by their seasonal nature, but the development and refinement of transportation, packaging, and canning and freezing technologies extended the availability. Freezing or canning of frits and vegetables is done as soon after harvesting as possible, usually within hours, to help preserve optimum quality and nutritional value in the finished product. Modified and controlled atmosphere storage extend the shelf-life of fresh produce.

Although it is unlikely that any individual food or combination of foods can provide complete disease protection, risk of chronic disease can be reduced by increased consumption of plant-based foods and decreased consumption of fats. Food formulations that are described as fat-free, low in fat, or reduced calorie depend on the use of fat substitutes and mimetics, as well as high-intensity sweeteners. Small amounts of high-intensity artificial sweeteners, such as saccharin, aspartame, and acesulfame-K, are used in tabletop sweeteners, beverages, candies, dessert mixes, and dairy products. When these sweeteners replace sugar in food products, bulking agents (such as sorbitol, polydextrose, fewer calories than fat, because they are partially absorbed or nonabsorbed in the intestinal tract. They provide sensory characteristics in foods similar to those imparted by ats. Carbohydrate-based fat substitutes, such as cellulose, gums, dextrins, modified starhes, and polydextrose, can be found in a variety of foods, including dairy products, frozen desserts, and salad deressings. Microparticulated protein is made from egg white or milk proteins. The spherical particles produced by the processes are so small that the tongue perceives them as fluid, with a smooth cream texture. Microparticulated protein cannot be used in cooked foods because it forms a gel when heated. Sucrose polyesters are composed of six to eight fatty acids bound to a sucrosemolecule; these fat substitutes are heat stable and have potential for use in backed and fried foods.

2

CHAPTER

FOOD QUALITY AND NUTRITION

Eating brings us mental satisfaction. Eating also helps in building our social relations specially when we sit with others and eat. But these are not the only functions of food. It fulfills some physiological functions too. When we work and play our body requires energy. Food provides this energy. Our body is constantly at work even when we are at rest. We reach, digest and utilize food, pump blood, excrete waste material. A regular supply of energy is required to perform these and similar functions and food is the source of this energy. There is growth and repair in our body. Energy and body building materials are necessary for this growth, repair and replacement of damaged cells and tissues. Our body is open to the attacks of the disease causing germs. Energy and some essential substances are needed to fight these attacks and keep the body in good health. Food is the source of these essential materials and the energy required for each one of these functions. Food provides energy for various voluntary and unvoluntary tasks. It provides materials for growth, repair and replacement. It provides materials to fight against diseases and regulate organ-systems.

Food serves three functions in most living organisms. First, it provides materials that are metabolized either by oxidative or by fermentative processes to supply the energy required for the absorption and translation of nutrients, for the synthesis of cell materials, for motility and locomotion, for excretion of waste products, and for all other activities of the organism. Second, food supplies the electron donors (reducing agents0 required for the formation of the reduced coenzymes (enzyme components) necessary for the synthetic processes that occur within the cell. Third, food provides the materials from which all of the structural and catalytic components of the living cell can be assembled by processes sometimes called *anabolism.* The three roles of food are not mutually exclusive; energy-yielding substances in many organisms may function in all three ways, and essential nutrients, if present in excess, may frequently be metabolized to supply energy. The essential precursors (i.e., the substances from which other substances are formed) or cell materials can be divided into two groups-nonessential nutrients, which can be synthesized by the cell from other materials, and essential nutrients, which, because they cannot be synthesized by the cell, must be supplied in foods. All of the inorganic materials required for growth, together with an assortment of organic compounds whose number may vary from one to 30 or more, depending on the organism fall into the latter category. Although organisms are able to synthesize nonessential nutrients, such nutrients are frequently utilized directly if present in food, thereby saving the organism the need to expend the energy required to synthesize them.

The recorded history of mankind demonstrates repeatedly the close association between war, pestilence, famine and death. St John describes this association in his allegory of he Four Horsemen of the Apocalypse. Unfortunately it must be admitted that the factual evidence supporting a causal relationship between poor diets and susceptibility to infectious diseases is far from satisfactory. However, there is nodoubt that malnourished patients often have a low resistance to an infection once it is established. The role of infectious diseases in precipitating nutritional disorders, such as kwashiorkor, beriberi and keratomalacia, by increasing the needs for essential nutrients is now realized to be very important. Before considering these problems a brief summary of the defences of the body against infections.

Humans, as biological beings, require food to sustain life. Humans eat to satisfy hunger and to meet a basic drive for food. But a person is also a social being. Humans have learned to live and work together and have organized themselves into societies. As human infants grow and develop they are incorporated into this society through varied experiences, and some of these experiences involve food. The pattern begins with the family and is modified as a child grows into adult-hood and travels in ever-widening circles of contact with others. Contrary to the popular belief that dietary patterns are very stable and unyielding to change, patterns of eating by individuals and families an, in a dynamic, continuous process of change as their economic, social, and technological environments change. The term culture is used to describe a way of life in which there are common customs or rules for behaviour and in which there is a common understanding among members of the group. The culture in which one develops determines, to a large extent, one's food patterns or habits. Foods are eaten in combination with other foods ill ways that are determined and continued by the culture. Food patterns may markedly differ from one culture to another. Grasshoppers, backed mouse, or roast do may be delicacies in some parts of the world, whereas it would be unthinkable for humans to consume them in other areas. Eggs may be a staple breakfast food in certain cultures, whereas in others it, is taboo for at least some members of the group to eat them. Not everyone in a cultural group eats exactly alike, however. Within a culture, individual preferences differ and subgroups develop. Families tend to develop their own distinctive food patterns, and even individuals within a family have personal food preferences. Differences both between and among cultural groups may be found in not only what specific foods are eaten but in the number of meals eaten each day, the way the food is served, and the utensils used in the service. Each culture passes on its food habits and patterns through training children from infancy so that each child knows what is acceptable and not acceptable and patterns become familiar. The geography of an area and variations in climate influence the types of food that are usually grown and are readily available. This, in turn, affects the eating patterns of people in this area. Examples are the widespread use of pinto beans and chili peppers in the southwestern United States and the extensive use of seafood in costal areas. The influence of diverse ethnic groups, such as Mexican, Chinese, Italian, Scandinavian, and others, is also seen in geographical areas where these groups have predominated. Each group has developed a cuisine with its distinctive combination of flavourings for basic foodstuffs. Economics can be a powerful factor in changing dietary patterns although these changes may be transitory in some cases. When family food budgets are restricted because of financial problems, less expensive foods must make up a larger share of the menus offered. Knowledge of nutrition and the effects of various diets on health encourages many of those responsible for food purchasing and preparation to adjust food patterns in accordance with suggestions from various govern-mental and professional agencies. Dietary guidelines have been suggested by the U.S. Departments of Agriculture and Health and Human Services. These guidelines recommend that fewer fats, fewer sugars, and less salt be consumed and that more starch and fiber-containing foods be added to the diet. Food also has significance in relation to religious beliefs and practices. The types of foods chosen, the complete omission of certain foods, and Frequency of eating other Foods may be dictated by religious preferences. The growth of the food industry and technological developments that keep an ever-increasing supply of convenience-type foods on the market affect the purchasing habits of the consumer and the types of family meals served.

Advertising through the media of television, radio, newspapers, and magazines makes sure that the consumer knows about new types of foods that are available and is enticed to try them.

The development of technological expertise in food preservation extends the seasons of food availability. Refrigeration and freezing processing within the home make possible patterns of eating that cannot exist in a technologically developing society in which methods for keeping fresh foods are not available. The type of equipment available for food preparation, such as modern rangers and microwave ovens, markedly affects patterns of eating. The proliferation of food vending machines in technologically developed countries also helps to mold food habits. The ready availability of fast-food restaurants is changing the eating patterns of many individuals. An increasingly larger share of the U.S. consumer food dollar is being spend for meals away from home.

Much of modern society has become oriented toward science of nutrition has increased our confidence in the ability to provide foods that supply adequate nutrients foe health. Developments in food technology may influence even the social aspects of food as they decrease individual family members' reliance on each other for providing prepared food to eat. Perhaps the impact of technology has had an influence in stimulating the "back to nature" movement in food. Organic home gardening is becoming popular among some groups in which so-called natural or unprocessed foods are emphasized. With all of these technological influences, it is important that tile meanings of food, other than merely the biological ones, be considered. Food means security. Infants learn about security when mothers respond to their crying by giving them food. Familiar foods bring back memories of home family and make one feel secure.

Certain foods show status. Beefsteak has status in the United States. Polished white rice has status over brown rice in some countries. Foods commonly eaten by blacks in the southern United States—collards, turnip greens, fat pork, and certain fish—were for s long time not acceptable to whites because of status. Now this has changed, and "soul food" is served in prestigious restaurants. The study of foods should help one to appreciate the food patterns of other cultures and to gain understanding of them. Fascinating experiences await the adventure who learns to enjoy the foods of many different ethnic or cultural groups.

Thousands of favour sensations are experienced in a lifetime. Flabour is a complex quality, involving an integration of sensations from the olfactory center in the nasal cavity, the taste bunds on the tongue, and various pressure and movement sensors in the mouth. In a broad sense, the appearance of a food and even the sound of crunching such crisp foods as raw carrots and celery may be part of the overall flabour complex. Sometimes the words flabour and taste are used synonymously. It is generally accepted, however, that there are only four primary taste sensations involving the taste buds on the tongue: sweet, sour, bitter, and salty. Taste buds are founding small elevations, called papillae, on the surface of the tongue. The actual taste sensations are produced when bitter, salty, sweet, or acid substances in solution contact taste receptors in the taste pore leading to the taste bud. Much of what we call taste is a combination of odor and taste sensations. Some foods with an intense aroma, such as well-prepared coffee or fresh, ripe pineapple, may affect the olfactory center more than the taste receptors. In order to stimulate the olfactory centre, substances must be in gaseous form.

The gaseous molecules enter the nose as food is placed in the mouth and are drawn toward the olfactory centre where they stimulate nerve endings. Nerve impulses are thus sent to the brain to be interpreted. The sense of smell is estimated to be about ten thousand times as sensitive as the sense of taste in detecting minute concentrations and it can differentiate hundreds, or possibly thousands, of distinct odors. Temperature may affect the blending of primary tastes as well as other factors contributing to flavour. Within the temperature range at which most food is eaten, from ice cream to hot chocolate, there are marked changes in the apparent intensity of some of the primary tastes. At higher temperatures the same amount of sugar will seem sweeter than at lower temperatures. Just the reverse seems to be true of salty tastes.

A substance such as menthol feels cool; it, sensitizes certain receptors in the mouth and throat so that they exaggerate the feeling of coolness. Other substances in foods such as hot peppers irritate the mucous membranes liming the mouth and give a biting or hot sensation. Countless numbers of molecules contribute to our perception of odor or aroma and taste. Many of the odorous substances in food may occur in such vanishingly small concentrations that it is difficult, to show, that they are even present. With the development of analytical tools such as the gas chromatograph the chemist has been bale to separate, isolate, and identify many of the molecules that are responsible for aroma and taste in such foods as onions, strawberries, and beef. However, continuing research in the field of flavour is necessary to learn more about flavour molecules and how the flavour of food is perceived by the human. The aroma and taste of food seem to be the complex results of many simultaneous responses to odor and taste stimuli. Some flavours occur preformed in foods as they are served. For example, strawberries, peaches, and other fresh fruits each contain a unique flavour bouquet composed of many volatile substances that stimulate the nasal olfactory center in combination with sweet and acid components that stimulate the taste buds. Raw vegetables, meats, and fish also present characteristic flavours the flavour of raw meat and fish is appreciated by some, whereas others prefer the change in flavour that occurs when these products are cooked. Cooked flavour is often formed from non-flavourful substances, sometimes called precursors, that are present in the raw food.

The chemical changes that occur during heating in the presence of air may be very complex and are not completely understood for most foods. Different flavours are produced when foods such as meat, are cooked in water that when they are roasted in an oven where they are surrounded by dry heat. Some cooked flavour precursors are present in the lean portion of meats such as beef, pork, and lamb, whereas other precurosors are resent in that fat. The tantalizing odors developed during the banking of bread are additional examples of flavor substances produced by heating. Many of the volatile substances that waft from the oven where bread is baking are initially the products of yeast fermentation. Crust formation occurs as the outer layers of the bread are dehydrated and subjected to very high temperatures. Browning of the crust contributes to both a pleasing appearance and a pleasant flavour. A knowledge of flavour chemistry and ways of simulating natural flavours is especially important as the world population increases and new protein foods are required.

The protein may be derived from soybeans, fish meal, or algae, but it will have no nutritional value if it is not eaten by the people who need it. It must be flavoured so that it will be acceptable and sought after. The flavour chemist, in order to successfully apply the science of flavour to the development, of new products and the improvement of old ones, must know what substances are responsible for the acceptable flavour and the mechanism by which people eating the food will experience flavour.

The physical properties of foods, including texture, consistency, and shape, involve the sense of touch of feeling. This is called the tactile sense. When food is contacted, pressure and movement receptors on the skin and muscles of the mouth and tongue are stimulated. Sensations of smoothness, stickiness, graininess, brittleness, fibrous qualities, or lumpy characteristics may be detected. The eye appeal of foods is contributed by such qualities as colour, form, size, and arrangement or design. Without an attractive appearance, many foods are rejected without being tasted. The commercial vendor of prepared foods regards appearance as being extremely important. The proper use of seasonings and flavouring materials greatly enhances the natural flavours of other foods. The appeal to the senses from a prepared dish entices one to eat and enjoy it. Flavourful food therefore, is always the ultimate goal of the cook. Salt and pepper are basic seasoning substances that should be used to heighten the taste of a food without changing it or adding their own flavours. Optimal amounts to be added will vary with the food product being prepared and with the preferences of the persons who will consume the food. For most cooked dishes, the seasonings should be added in small increments, with a tasting after each addition, until the most desirable taste is achieved.

Salt is a crystalling substance with the chemical name of sodium chloride (NaCl). It is obtained from salt beds or extracted from bring and is purified before being marketed for food use. An anticaking agent may be added to it and it may be iodized for nutritional purposes. The usual amount of salt consumed varies from one population to another as well as from one individual to another. Because of the possible relationships between a high sodium intake and hypertension (high blood pressure), governmental and professional organizations have encouraged Americans to reduced their intakes of salt. A number of individuals are following low sodium diets for specific health purposes. The judicious use of herbs and spices, as well as fresh lemon juice, may make foods acceptable with little or no added salt as the reduction of dietary sodium becomes necessary or desirable. Black pepper is the dried unripe berry of a climbing vine. White pepper is the kernel of ripe berry. Red peppers, native to the Americas, come from crushed red pepper pods and include cayenne pepper. Red peppers are "hot" but also have their own distinctive flavours. Peppers in the ground form are often used to season food without altering the natural flavour of the food. However, certain cuisines use peppers in amounts large enough to convey their own distinctive flavours. Monosodium glutamate (MSG) is a crytalling material that looks something like salt. It occurs naturally in a variety of foods and may be produced from hat gluten or corn protein and also from sugar beet molasses in a fermentation process. MSG has come into general use, both commercially and in the home, as a seasoning substance.

Although this substance is generally considered to be a flavour enhancer or intensified, bringing out the flavours of other foods, it may also add its own flavour to foods when used in sufficiently large amounts. A group of compounds called 5' *–ribonucleotides* has been reported to act synergistically with MSG. Synergism refers to cooperative action among two or more substances so that the total effect of the mixture is greater than the sum of the individual effects. Even a very small amount of the ribonucleotides increases the flavour-enhancing properties of MSG. Some of the 5'- ribonucleotides have been recommended as flavour enhancers by themselves and are being used commercially in Japan. In the past, there has been controversy over the safety of the widespread use of MSG in foods. Extensive study of its effects oil a variety of animal species, however, has lead to the conclusion that, in the amounts commonly used, there is no hazard to the public health. Probably 1 to 2 large doses of MSG with symptoms such as tingling, warmth, and a feeling of pressure in the upper part of the body. Although MSG is commonly used in a number of manufactured, food products, processed foods marketed primarily for babies and small children do not now include this flavour substance as an ingredient. The history of the use of spices and herbs is a fascinating one. In ancient times, spices were valued for many nonfood purposes, such as ingredients in ointments, cosmetics, embalming preservatives, and medicines.

After the first century A.D. spices were increasingly utilized as condiments in food. Spices were so important, costly, and scarce that wars were fought for them. The term spice is often used to cover a wide variety of dried aromatic vegetable products that are used in building the flavours of prepared Foods. True spices are defined as parts of aromatic plants, such as bark, roots, buds, flowers, fruits, and seeds, that are grown in the tropics. Examples of spies include all spice, anise, caraway, cardamom, cayenne pepper, cinnamon, cloves, cumin, ginger, mace, nutmeg, paprika, pepper, and tumeric. Some spices are sweet, some are spicy sweet, and some are "hot." Herbs are usually leaves of' plants that grow in a temperate climate. Examples of herbs are *basil, bay leaves, marjoram, mint, oregano, rosemary, sage, savory, tarragon*, and *thyme*. Seeds used in cooking may sometimes be classified separately since they come from plants cultivated in both tropical and temperate regions.

Examples of seeds include caraway, celery, and dill, Spice blends are mixtures of several true spices, herbs, seeds, and dehydrated vegetables for use in food preparation. They include curry power, chili power, poultry seasoning, and mixed pickling spice. In practical use it is difficult to separate spices and herbs. They are both commonly used as flavour builders in the cooking process so that their separate flavours merge indistinguishably with the total flavour as it develops. Some herbs, and spices, however, have very distinctive flavours and, when used in quantities large enough to taste, become major flavours for prepared foods rather than blending into the total flavour. These special flavoured spices and herbs include basil, which has a war sweet flavour that blends well with tomato dishes; oregano, with a strong bittersweet taste commonly associated with spaghetti sauce; tarragon and its licorice-like flavour; and sage, with a pungent, fragrant flavour that permeates many stuffings for poultry or meat. Spices are sold whole or in ground forms. Flavour strength and quality are quite well preserved in the whole spice but are gradually lost during long storage. Flavourits much more readily lost form the ground spices. Herbs also tend to lose flavour during storage. Neither ground spices nor herbs should be purchased in quantity for usual use. Both spices and herbs should be stored in a cool, dry place in airtight containers. Under favourable conditions they should keep their aroma and flavour for several months. Since ground spices release their flavour immediately when added to prepared dishes, they should usually be used near the end of the cooking period. Whole spices are added at the beginning of long cooking periods so that their full flavour can be extracted. They may be tied in a cheese cloth bag so that they can be easily removed. Whole herbs should be crumbled before use to release flavour. Extracts and essential oils from aromatic plants, dissolved in alcohol, are often used in the flavouring of baked products, puddings, sauces, and confections. These include extracts of vanilla, lemon, orange, and almond and oils such as peppermint and wintergreen. These are used in small amounts but add their own distinctive flavours to the final products.

These flavourings should be stored in tightly closed containers and put in a cool place to avoid loss of volatile substances.

Several types of browning that may occur during food preparation affect palatability. Some of the changes associated with browning are detrimental to the quality of the food while others are beneficial. A type of browning or darkening that is undersirable is that which occurs on the cut surfaces of such fresh fruits and vegetables as bananas, apples, peaches, and potatoes when they are exposed to air. This type of darkening is sometimes called *enzymatic oxidative browning* for it requires oxygen from the air and enzymes, which are present ill the plant tissue itself. The enzymes catalyze (increase the speed at which the reaction occurs) the addition of oxygen to certain substances already present in the plant tissue, producing brown colored compounds. Another type of browning that occurs in a variety of food products involves neither enzymes nor oxygen from the air and, therefore, is sometimes called *nonezymatic nonoxidative browning*. This process has also been named, after the Frenchman who first described it, the *Maillard reaction*. The browning of baked products such as bread has been attributed chiefly to the Mailard reaction. The brown color of caramel candy is also the result of a browning reaction of the Mailard type. Browning is encouraged in baked products and in caramels and is desirable for both flavour and appearance. Examples of' products in which the Maillar reaction is undesirable are the browning of dried milk and eggs stored for relatively long periods of time. When browning occurs in these products, they not only become less attractive but they are more difficult to rehydrate and the nutritive value of their protein is decreased. The Maillard or nonenzymatic browning reaction involves, as a first step, the combination of a sugar with the amino group of a protein. A series of additional complex chemical reactions then follows and ventually a brown colour results. Thus, any food that contains both sugars, such as glucose, and proteins may be susceptible to browning of the Maillard type if it is stored for long periods of time or is subjected to very high temperatures. Table sugar, or sucrose, does not participate in the Maillard reaction. However, browning is produced in yet another way when table sugar is heated to high temperatures. When the quality of a food is judged or evaluated by the use of the senses (taste, smell, sight, touch, and hearing), it is said to be a sensory or subjective or organoleptic evaluation. Since food is prepared for the primary purpose of being eaten and enjoyed through the senses, sensory evaluation is most appropriate.

Nutritional Evolution of Organisms

Nucleic acids, proteins, carbohydrates, and fats, which are present in all living cells, are formed by specific reaction sequences from a limited number of smaller compounds most of which are common to all living organisms and, according to current theories, were available on Earth before life arose. Since less complex metabolic organisation and less energy are required to synthesize cellular proteins from preformed amino acids than from carbon dioxide and other precursors, it is assumed that the simplest early forms of life were heterotrophic organisms requiring many organic nutrients for growth and that they selected such nutrients from their surroundings. As the supply of these preformed substances was exhausted the organisms presumably developed the capacity to synthesize these preformed substances from simpler materials present in the environment; in some organisms, this synthesizing capacity eventually evolved to the extent that carbon from carbon dioxide could be utilized to synthesize organic compounds.

At this point, autotrophy, as it now is know, became possible, autotrophy, in fact, may have evolved as a result of the exhaustion of the supply of preformed organic materials in the environment and the consequent necessity of organisms to synthesize the requirements themselves in order to survive. Implicit in this theory is the demonstrable assumption that autotrophic cells contain the most complex biosynthetic organisation found in living things and that heterotrophic cells are simpler in that certain biosynthetic pathways do not occur. After the evolution of photosynthesis, a constantly renewable source of the organic compounds necessary for heterotrophic cell growth became available. It become feasible that hose organisms whose environments provided a constantly available supply of a given compound could lose, through changes in their genetic material (mutations), the ability to synthesize that compound and still survive. Entire biosynthetic pathways may have been lost in this way; as long as such mutant organisms remained in an environment that supplied the necessary compound, the simplification in cellular organisation and the energy saved by using preformed cell components would have given them a competitive advantage over the more complex parents from which they were derived and permitted stabilization of the mutation within the cell type. A theory that the requirements of modern organisms for essential organic nutrients arose through the loss of synthetic abilities present in more complex parent organism was confirmed between 1940 and 1950 by the discovery that artificially produced mutant offspring of microorganisms can be readily obtained and may require the presence of one or more preformed organic compounds, which the parent microorganisms could synthesize.

Deficiency Nutrition

It can either be due to mal-or under-nutrition. Malnutrition refers to non-availability due to faulty planning of meals or faulty utilization of nutrients in the body. Under nutrition on the other hand is caused due to insufficient intake of food. Some of the most common conditions caused are night blindness, anaemia, beri-beri, scurvy rickets, goitere and protein-energy-malnutrition. These conditions can be reversed and cured if the specific deficiency of the nutrient is met. More than one nutrient deficiency may occur at one time if the diet on the whole is poor. Also certain nutrients have common food sources e.g., fresh green vegetables supply not only vitamins but also minerals. Absence of these in food will lead to multiple deficiencies. The cause of mal-or under-nutrition are ignorance, poverty, frequent infections due to in sanitary conditions and certain socio-cultural factors.

Protein Energy Under Nutrition

It results from lack of protein and calories in the diet. It is more prevalent in growing infants and young children when requirements for these nutrients are high. It causes loss of weight and growth failure. Two severe forms of PEU are Marasmus and Kwashiorkor. Both physical and mental development may be affected by them.

Marasmus is most commonly seen around one year of age. It is primarily the deficiency of calories. Clinical signs are nuscle wasting loss of weight, stunted growth, and loose wrinkled skin due to loss of sub-cutaneous fat which is specially obvious in the buttocks and backs of thigh.

Kwashiorkor occurs in older children in the age group of 2 to 4 years. This results form deficiency of proteins primarily. It is characterized by growth failure, muscle wasting and edema 9accumulation of water in body). The skin has dark brown patches resembling burns. The hair may become lighter in colour and sparse. The child shows apathy and is disinterested in surroundings.

Prevention

Breast milk alone is not sufficient after the age of 4 months. Proper weaning foods made from cooked cereals, pulses and vegetables *e.g. dalia, khitchdi*, soup etc. Should be given to the infant along with breast milk. Animal milk, fruits, eggs and flesh foods can also be gradually added to the diet of the infant. Remember child has a limited capacity to eat hence food must be given at frequent intervals. The child has low resistance and great susceptibility for diarrhoea. Hence we must use clean boiled water and clean bottle or spoon etc. to prevent the spread of any infection.

Deficiency of Vitamin A

- Bitot's spots, which are triangular foamy patches on the dry conjunctive.
- Night blindness or inability to see in dimlight.
- Dull, dry lusterless cornea as the deficiency continues. Ultimately cornea becomes soft which can lead to fatal blindness.
- Rough and dry skin that resembles spines.

Prevention: Vitamin A rich foods like green leafy vegetables, carrot, milk, cod liver oil, egg, liver etc. should be eaten regularly especially by young children. Another sure and easy way to prevent deficiency of vitamin A is by giving a massive dose of vitamin A every six months to all children from 1 to 5 years of age. This is called the Vitamin A prophylaxis programme of the government of India.

Vitamin D Deficiency: It causes rickets in children and osteomalacia in adults. In rickets bones become soft and bend easily due to improper calcification. The joints of bones become enlarged especially at the wrist and bending of ribs occurs. The bones cannot stand the weight of the body and this leads to bow legs and knock knees. Rickets occur in children who live in dark, crowded places and do not get much exposure to sunlight. Osteomalacia or adult rickets occur more in women who observe 'purdah' system. They hardly get any opportunity to expose themselves to sunshine and thus prepare vitamin D in their skin. Repeated, closely-spaced pregnancies put extra strain on the stomach. In osteomalacia also bones become soft and fractures occur easily.

Prevention: Enough exposure to sunlight is very important. None of the foods is rich source of vitamin D, Fish liver oils can be given to small children to provide enough vitamin d and Vitamin A. Adequate amount of calcium should be taken in diet to facilitate bone mineralization.

Deficiency B_1: This leads to disease called beri-beri. It is seen mainly in areas where people consume large amounts of milled rice as staple with hardly any protective foods taken along with it.

Beri-beri is of two types:

(1) *Dry beri-beri*: The patient loses appetite and becomes very thin. The central harmone system is affected. This leads to sensory loss (tingling sensation), motor weakness and tenderness of calf-muscles.

(2) Wet beri-beri Edema is prominent feature of wet beri-beri. There is cardiac involvement which may lead to circulatory failure and death. Infantile beri-beri leading to sudden death may occur in 2-5 months old infants who are born to mothers suffering from B-complex deficiency. Breast milk of such mothers is low in the said vitamin.

Prevention: Avoid over-dependence on milled-rice. Use of parboiled or hand pounded rice and other cereals like wheat should be encouraged. Include foods like pulses, whole wheat flour, meat, egg etc. in diet.

Deficiency B2 affects the eye, tongue and mouth. There is burning sensation in eyes. The tongue becomes majenta-red and the corners of the mouth are red and fissured.

Prevention: Use foods rich in vitamin B-complex i.e., milk, green leafy vegetables, whole grains and meat etc.

Deficiency B12

It is seen mainly among people who eat corn and jawar as staple in their diet. Deficiency of B12 causes pellagra. It is called a disease of 3 D's – diarrhoea, dermatitis and dementis. The skin is dry, sore and red. The areas of the body that remain exposed to sunlight like neck, backs of hand, forearms and dorsal of feet are affected the most.

Prevention: Like in B1-deficiency the diet consumed should be balanced. Consumption of other cereals should be encouraged in corn and jawar eating areas. Pulses, peanuts, liver, meat etc. are good sources of this vitamin.

Vitamin C Deficiency

A gross deficiency of vitamin C leads to disease called scurvy. The gums become spongy and swollen and bleed easily. Wounds take long time to heal and the joints become tender and swollen. The need for vitamin C is increased in infections life tuberculosis, measles and chicken pox.

Prevention: Regular consumption of vitamin C rich foods like guava, amla, green leafy vegetables, citrus fruits, sprouted pulses etc. helps in preventing scurvy.

Deficiency Iron

This leads to condition called anemia which means a low level of hemoglobin in the blood. The number and size of red blood cells decreases. Anemia is common in India especially among the women and children of poor classes. The important symptoms of anemia are weakness, fatigue, and breathlessness on exertion. These are all related to reduced capacity of blood to carry oxygen to various parts of the body: Pollar of the face, eyes and finger nails are common signs of anemia. Spoon shaped nails are seen in older children and adults.

Prevention: Regular consumption of iron-rich foods like grean leafy vegetables, meat, fish, eggs and whole grains prevent anemia. Control of hook-worm and other infestations will help prevent excessive loss of blood leading to anemia. Under the National Nutritional Anemia Prevention Programme (NNAPP) of Government of India iron and folic acid tablets are distributed to small children and pregnant women and lactating mothers through Maternal and child Health Centres (MCHC).

Iodine Deficiency

This leads to enlargement of the thyroid glands which is situated in the front of the neck. This condition is known as goiter. It is endemic in sub-Himalayan regions of India where iodine content of water and soil is low. Lately cases of goiter have been found in Delhi and other places also. Cretin are born to women who suffer from gross iodine deficiency. These infants show growth retardation and their mental faculties are sub-normal. Cretins are usually deaf and dumb. Goitre and cretinism can be prevented by adequate intake of iodine. One of the easiest and chest ways of adding iodine to diet is by using iodized salt, under the National Goitre Control project iodized salt is distributed in endemic and now even other areas of the country.

Nutrition Intervention Programmes

The government of India is running several nutrition intervention programmes for improving the nutritional status of the vulnerable groups. Integrated Child Development Service (ICDS) is a programme of Central government for better health an nutrition of preschoolers, pregnant women and lactating mothers. Immunisation, referral services (medical care), preschool education, nutrition supplements, nutrition and health education and safe water supply are its important components.

Nutritional interrelationships may explain the fact that the nutritionally demanding lactic-acid bacteria are able to coexist with the nutritionally nondemanding coliform bacteria in the intestinal tracts of animals. It is known that the bacterial flora of the intestinal tract synthesize sufficient amounts of certain vitamins (e.g., vitamin K, folic acid) so that detection of deficiency symptoms in rats requires special measures, and the role of rumen bacteria in ruminant animals in rendering otherwise indigestible cellulose and other materials available to the host animal is well-known.

Thus, personl weight is not necessary an indication of nutritive status. In the United States, malnutrition due to undernutrition is most likely to occur in infants, children, and adolescents, when nutritional requirements for tissue growth and development are high. Undernutrition may inhabit growth, delay nutrition, limit physical activity, and interference with learning. The cause of undernutrition are many; poverty and lack of nutrition education.

Food and Nutrition

Man can and does eat a variety of foods, of both plant and animal origin. Human diet is not restricted to any special category of food. Variety is, for him, the spice of life—more so in foods, than in anything else. This natural desire for variety is justified by the fact that no single food provides us with all the nutrients that we need. Cereals, like rice of wheat which form the staple food of mankind, supply us only with a fraction of our nutritional requirements. We have to supplement cereals with other foods that provide plenty of fats and proteins and minor quantities of a number of vitamins and minerals. This means that the larger our diet sheet, the better our health will be. This will become evident, if we analyze what nutrients our foods contain and in what proportion.

The nutrients found in foodstuffs may broadly be classified as (a) Carbohydrates, (b) Fats, (c) Proteins, (d) Minerals, (e) Vitamins and (f) Water. Proteins, fats and carbohydrates are called Macro Nutrients. Proteins (from are the most versatile elements in the body. They are the chief substances of the cells of the body. They form important constituents of muscles and other tissues and vital fluids like blood. Enzymes, which assist in the digestion of food, and anti-bodies which are the body defences against infections are also mainly protein in nature. The nutritive value of protein depends on the essential amino acid composition. Amino acids are the bricks with which tissue protein is built and replaced. There are some 20 amino acids commonly found in dietary proteins. Of these, 10 amino acids can be synthesized by the body itself, whether by mutual

Table 2.1: Protein Value of Indian Foods

Foodstuffs	*Biological Value*	*Protein efficiency ratio*
Rice	68	2.2
Wheat	65	1.5
Maize	59	1.2
Bengal gram	68	1.7
Red gram	57	1.5
Groundnut	55	1.7
Gingelly seeds	62	1.8
Egg	94	3.9
Milk	84	3.1
Meat	74	2.3
Fish	76	3.5

conversion among amino acids or acids cannot be so synthesized and have to be supplied through diet. These are called essential amino acids. Adults require 8 essential amino acids while children require 9 or 10. Fat, like protein, is a necessary ingredient in diet and is of value to the body in a number of ways. It is a concentrated source of energy and supplies per unit weight more than double the energy furnished by either protein or carbohydrates. Some fats, especially vegetable oils, provide what are called essential fatty acids, linoleic and arachidonic acids, to the body.

Table 2.2: Balanced Diet Composition

Foodstuffs (G)	*Vegeta- rian Account*	*Non- Vegetarian (g)*	*Vegetarian Calories*	*Protein*	*Non-Vegetarian (g) Calories*	*Protein*
Cereals	325	325	1150	29	1150	29
Dal & Nuts	100	50	320	22	160	11
Milk	200(ml)	100(ml)	235	8	117	4
Root Vegetables	150	150	145	2	145	2
Other vegetables	100	100	50	3	50	3
Leafy Vegetables	100	100	50	3	50	3
Fruits	100	100	80	-	80	-
Egg	(1no)	50	-	-	85	6
Meat/Fish	-	100	-	-195	18	
Fat	50	50	450	-	450	-
Sugar/Jaggery	30	30	120	-	120	-
Total			2550	64	2552	73

Fats that circulate in the blood are of many types—triglycerides, phospholipids, etc. The quantity and quality of fat consumed affects the level of cholesterol in the blood. Some fats like groundnut oil, sesame oil or safflower oil which contain a high proportion of poly-unsaturated fatty acids do not increase blood cholesterol levels greatly. Others like coconut oil, butter, ghee and hydrogenated vegetable oils (vanaspati) contain high proportions of saturated fatty acids and greatly increase cholesterol levels. It is also found that consumption of smaller amounts off at different times causes less increase of cholesterol than a large amount of fat taken at a time.

Carbohydrates include every kind of starch and sugar. Grain foods are largely composed of starch and foodstuffs like cane sugar and glucose are pure carbohydrates. They form the main source of energy for the body. Being a cheap source of energy, carbohydrates form the bulk of Indian diet.

A balanced diet simply means a diet that will supply all the nutrients necessary for the growth and development of the body. In India, a balanced diet has become an imperative since most Indians consume foods that provide more carbohydrates and fats than proteins. The table be gives the amounts of the various foods that will make up a balanced diet for the average Indian. The quantity of food varies according to age and the type of work.

Vitamins and minerals comprise what are called micro nutrients as distinguished from proteins, fats and carbohydrates which are called macro nutrients.

Vitamins can be broadly divided into fat-soluble and water-soluble vitamins. Vitamin A, D, E and K are fat-soluble vitamins. Vitamin C and B (including vitamins B1, B2 and other B-Group vitamins) are water-soluble.

The vitamins are necessary auxiliaries in metabolism.

They combine with specific proteins, as parts of the various oxidative enzyme systems which are concerned with the breakdown of carbohydrates, proteins and fat in the body. Thus, they are intimately involved in the mechanism which releases energy, carbon dioxide and water as the end products of metabolism.

A large number of minerals is present in the body and performs a variety of functions. Minerals account for about 4 per cent of the body weight. Calcium and phosphonus form about three-fourths of the minerals elements. Five other minerals—potassium, sulphur, sodium, chlorine and magnesium—account for most of the rest. Many elements are present in such minute quantities that they are called trace elements or micro-nutrients. Water is a vital constituent of diet. An average man contains about 45 litres of water (70 per cent of the body weight). The cells contain 30 litres. Three litres are in the plasma of th eblood, where the suspended cells make a total volume of blood upto 5 litres. The remaining 12 litres (45-33) fill the space between groups of cells. This is tissue fluid which bathes all the cells of the body.

Water is absolutely necessary for the digestion and absorption of the foods taken in. It is the great solvent and neutralizer in the body. It is the substance in which bodily chemical reactions take place. Water is the carrier or transporting medium for all nutrients and body substances. It regulates body temperature. It is the great purifying agent in the body and removes waste materials in the form of tear, perspiration, urine and faces. Watery substances act as lubricants in the body, especially in the joints. It is a part of all body tissues and fluids.

Acidosis, alkalosis and dehydration, oedema, fever, shock, uraemia and constipation are some of the clinical signs of inadequate salt and water in the body. Sources: The body obtains water mainly from the fluids we drink, from the solids we eat and also from the oxidation of energy foods. Fats and carbohydrates are oxidized in the body to carbon dioxide and water.

Cereasl like rice, wheat and millets, ragi, cholam and bajra form the main food in India. Cereals are rich in carbohydrates. They generally contain 6 to 12 per cent protein, but these proteins are usually deficient in the essential amino acid lysine. Rice protein, however, is richer in lysine than other cereals.

Most cereal grains are poor in mineral content and rice is especially poor. Ragi is, however, rich in minerals, especially in calcium, and bajra in iron. Whole cereal grains are important sources of B-vitamins but in milling, rice loses the outer layers containing thiamine. Paboled rice, even when milled, does not lose its thiamine content. Except yellow maize, which contains some amounts of carotene, no other cereal grain is a source of vitamin A or C.

Pulses or legumes as they are called, are rich in proteins. Pulse proteins, however, are of relatively low biological value because of the deficiency of the essential amino acid *methionine* but they are rich in *lysine*. Pulses are not rich sources of minerals but they are rich in B-vitamins. Dried pulses do not contain vitamin C but if they are geminated significant amounts of vitamin C are generated.

Most of the green leafy vegetables are rich sources of calcium, iron, carotene, vitamin C, riboflavin and folic acid.

Roots and tubers are rich in carbohydrates. But roots like carrot are also rich in carotene (Vitamin A); those like potato contain significant amounts of vitamin C, while roots like tapioca contain calcium also. Other Vegetables are those which do not fall into the category of leafy vegetables or root vegetables. These vegetables are shoots, like lady's finger, cucumber, tomato, bitter gourd, snake gourd, brinjal, etc. They are fairly good sources of vitamins and minerals.

Nuts and oil seeds are good sources of fat (oil), protein and minerals and fair sources of vitamins: e.g., groundnut and cashewnut. Fruits in general are rich in vitamin C, particularly, gooseberry (amla), guava (perakka) and citrus fruits. Yellow fruits like mango and papaya contain carotene and dried fruits like dates are sources of iron.

Fish and sea foods are rich sources of protein, B-vitamins and also minerals, especially calcium.

Fleshy foods are rich sources of protein and B-vitamins, especially B_{12}. They are generally deficient in vitamin A, but liver is an exception.

Egg is a rich source of all nutrients except vitamin C. Its protein is of high quality.

Milk & milk products. Milk is an ideal food for infants and young children and a food supplementary food for all. It contains all vital nutrients, except vitamin C and iron.

Food is the only source of energy for humans. This means that our dietary sheet must change according to our requirements of energy. "if food is to perform the functions in he body it is meant to, namely producing energy providing materials for body building, and regulating body processes, meals must be planned.

Good food selection, the cornerstone of good nutrition, must be learned as unfortunately there is no automatic built-in mechanism in human beings to direct the choice of foods which build healthy bodies and which keep them running satisfactorily from day to day.

The question what food we should eat and how much, depends on the amount of energy we need. Food energy is

Table 2.3: Height-Weight Ratio

Adolescents:

Boys			Girls	
Height (cm)	*Weight (kg)*	*Age (years)*	*Height (cm)*	*Weight (kg)*
112.4	19.2	5+	112.5	18.6
118.8	21.9	5+	117.8	20.5
123.2	24.3	7+	123.2	23.8
127.9	26.1	8+	127.2	26.0
133.3	29.2	9+	132.5	29.0
138.0	31.0	10+	138.2	32.6
142.7	34.0	11+	145.1	36.3
148.4	37.8	12+	151.5	42.5
155.0	42.4	13+	153.8	43.9
162.6	47.3	14+	154.5	45.0
165.5	51.1	15+	155.8	47.3
168.9	54.8	16+	155.8	49.0

Adults:

Men Weight in kg				*Women Weight in kg*			
Height		*Age*		*Height*			*Age*
cms	*20*	*35*	*50*	*cms*	*20*	*35*	*40*
148	42.7	47.6	50.9	148	38.6	44.0	47.1
153	45.4	50.4	53.5	150	40.3	44.8	47.7
158	48.6	53.5	56.3	153	41.9	46.6	49.5
163	51.1	56.3	59.4	155	42.8	47.7	50.1
168	54.0	60.1	63.7	158	44.9	49.5	52.1
173	58.1	64.0	68.3	160	46.0	50.6	53.0
178	61.9	68.5	72.4	163	47.3	52.1	54.9
183	66.0	73.3	77.6	165	49.1	5.1	57.3

measured in terms of heat units called calories. A physiological calorie, also called large calorie or kilocalorie (abbreviated as Kcal), is the amount of heat necessary to raise the temperature of one kilogram of water by one degree centigrade. One gram of protein or carbohydrates yields 4 calories. One gram of fat yields 9 calories while the same quantity of alcohol yields 7.

Food Digestion

Within a few minutes of being swallowed, some of the food is propelled into the first part of the intestine, which is called the duodenum, and the stomach is normally empty within two to three hours of a meal. The average time taken for digestion to be completed in the small intestine is approximately 12 hours. Food is propelled through the intestines by a regular series of muscular contractions, or peristaltic waves, which squeeze the intestinal contents like toothpaste in a tube.

- *Salivary gland*: Located in the cheeks, under the tongue and in the lower jaw, these produce saliva, a digestive juice which helps to lubricate food and break it down to simple sugars.

- *Oesophagus*: a muscular tube which carries food from throat to stomach. It is closed at each end by s sphincter, or ring of muscle.

- *Stomach*: A storage place in which food is chumed, and where the digestive process is continued by the mixture of acid and peptic enzymes secreted by glands in the stomach lining. Stomach acid also destroys bacteria that may have been swallowed with the food.

- *Liver*: The products of digestion (excluding fats) are absorbed into the bloodstream and carried along the portal vein to the liver. There they are stored, or used in the synthesis of chemicals needed by the body.

- *Duodenum*: The first 25-30 cm (10-12 in) of the small interesting, where to the mixture of food and enzymes from the stomach is added the digestive juices from pancreas, gall bladder and glands in the intestinal walls.

- *Pancreas*: This produces pancreatic juice which flows into the duodenum to help digest proteins, fats and carbo-hydrates. Pancreatic juice is produced continuously, but the flow is increased by the influence of hormones released when food enters the duodenum.

- Gall bladder: a pear-shaped sac about 10 cm (4 in) long. Situated under the liver, it stores and concentrates bile secreted by the liver. After a meat, the bite is released into the duodenum to help with the digestion of fats.

- *Small intestine*: A coiled muscular tube about 7 m (23 ft) long, made up of the jejunum and ileum. Here digestion is continued and the resulting products are absorbed into the blood-stream.

- *Colon*: A 1.4 m (4 ft. 6 in) long tube where water is absorbed to leave solid faeces—consisting of the remains of undigested food, cells shed from the intestinal lining, bile salts, and acids from the liver.

Guides to meeting nutrients

The Food and Nutrition Board of the National Research Council, National Academy of Sciences periodically publishes recommended dietary allowances for many nutrients. Their publication also includes estimated safe and adequate daily dietary intakes of some vitamins and minerals for which less research information is available. The recommended allowances are set for healthy persons living in the United States and include a margin of safety to cover the widely varying individual needs of members of the population. These standards serve as a goal for good nutrition and are most effectively applied in evaluating the dietary intake of population groups. Since food is our source of nutrients, nutritionists often start with foods when they teach people about nutrition. Foods have been grouped together on the basis of the major nutrients that they supply. Nutrients do not work alone but are interrelated in many processes involved in nourshing the body. Various foods, both within and between food groups, supplement each other in providing all of the necessary nutrients. Foods that are mixtures, such as stews, soups, casserole dishes, and certain bakery products, fit into food groups on the basis of the basic ingredients they contain. Food groupings and patterns of eating that provide an adequate diet will vary n many parts of the world. However, there are basic similarities among the common food groupings used in many nations of the world. Most groupings will include vegetables and fruits; cereals and breads or foods high in energy nutrients such as starch; and foods high in protein such as meat, fish, poultry, eggs, cheese, dry beans and peas, lentils, and nuts. In the United States, a daily food guide has been presented through the U.S. Department of Agriculture and has been adapted by various groups concerned with nutrition education. The food groups and recommended amounts in this daily guide are as follows:

Milk group: some milk for everyone. Children under 9 years two to three cups, 9 to 12 years three to more cups and Teenagers four or more cups daily.

Meat or Alternates group: Beef, veal, pork, lamb, poultry, fish, eggs. As alternatives, use dry beans, dry peas, nuts.

Vegetable-Fruit group: Citrus fruit or other fruit or vegetable important for vitamin C. Adark-green or deep-yellow vegetable for vitamin A at least every other day. Other vegetables and fruits, including potatoes Bread-Cereal group, whole grain, enriched, or restored. Plus other foods as needed to complete meals and to provide additional food energy and other food, values.

The milk group is our major source of calcium. It also provides high quality protein, riboflavin, phosphorus, and vitamin A (carried by the butterfat). The meat or meat alternates group supplies high quality protein, iron, phosphorus, thiamin, riboflavin, niacin, other B vitamins, and trace minerals. Vegetables and fruits contribute many vitamins and minerals. The food guide emphasizes vegetables and fruits that are valuable sources of ascorbic acid (vitamin C) and vitamin A. This food group also provides fiber that promotes motility and health of the digestive tract. The bread and cereal group furnishes worthwhile amounts of protein, iron, several of the B vitamins, and carbohydrates for energy. Suggested choices from these food groups should supply a normal healthy individual wit most of the recommended daily allowances of essential nutrients except calories. Additional amounts of the four groups, supplemented with other foods such as fats and oils, can make up the needed calories while supplying additional vitamins and minerals as well. Empty calories, food contributing calories only, should be used in only limited quantities in most dietaries.

Good food adds to the joy of living, by both its contribution to buoyant health and the pleasure of eating. Food, appropriately prepared, looks good and tastes good and is good for us. With the development of a greater variety of manufactured and convenience foods and their availability to manufactured and convenience foods and their availability to the consumer, it is important that both the food scientist and consumer carefully consider the nutritional a quacy of the consumer's usually diet patterns.

When foods spoil, they undergo chemical and physical

changes that may render to food inedible or hazardous to eat. The two chief causes of food spoilage are the growth of microorganisms, including bacteria, yeasts, and molds, and the action of enzymes that occur normally in the food. Additional causes of spoilage include non-enzymatic reactions in food, such as oxidation and desiccation (drying out); mechanical damage, such as brushing; and damage from rodents and insects.

Microorganisms

In order to grow or multiply in number, all microorganisms need a source of nutrients, sufficient moisture, a favourable temperature, and an appropriate pH. Because, in a consideration of food preservation, it is impossible to eliminate available food as a factor in microbial growth, attention must be given to the control of other conditions that encourage microbial growth.

Molds are multi-cellular, filamentous fungi usually giving a fuzzy or cottony appearance when they grow on foods. They may be white, dark, or of various colours. Spores are produced by molds, usually asexually, in large numbers for purposes of reproduction. They are small, light cells that are resistant to drying and are easily spread through the air to alight on any exposed food. Given favourable conditions and enough time the spore may then grow on the food. Molds are able to utilize many different kinds of substances, from very simple to complex, for food. Molds are able to utilize many different kinds of substances, from very simple to complex, for food. In general, they are aerobic, requiring oxygen for growth. They can also grow over a wide range of pH, from quite acid to fairly alkaline (pH 2.0 to 8.5). They grow most rapidly at temperatures of 20° to 35°C and in a moist, still atmosphere. However, they may grow with very little moisture. Low temperatures retard their growth but molds may still grow at ordinary refrigerator temperatures of 45 to 50°F. A boiling water temperature destroys both molds and their spores. Temperatures somewhat below that of boiling water (160° to 180°F will readily destroy vegetative mold cells and will also destroy spores if the temperature is maintained for a sufficient time. The time is variable, depending on other conditions. Some molds will not grow in bright sunlight but others grow in eight darkness or light. In general, molds require less moisture than most yeasts and bacteria, and because they are also adaptable to many conditions of acidity and temperature they are commonly involved in the spolage of food. Molds will grow on sweet foods, such as jellies or jams. They commonly occur on meats (even cured meats), on cheese, milk, and other protein foods. They also grow on fresh fruits, vegetables, and on cereal products. For many years it was thought that molds were probably not harmful. However, certain molds, such as Aspergillus flavus, growing on cereal grains and on peanuts heave been found to produce toxins that have caused illness and death in animals and humans. The to in produced by Aspergillus flavus is called aflatoxin but the term mycotoxin is used to designated toxins produced by any molds. Some molds play valuable roles in food production. Certain cheeses, such as Roquefort and Camembert, are ripened by molds. Molds are also used for the commercial production of some enzymes, such as amylase for bread making, and for the production of citric acid. They are also used in making certain Oriental foods, such as soy sauce.

Yeasts are unicellular plants, also called fungi. They are usually aerobic and may play both useful and harmful roles in foods. Yeast fermentations, chemical changes in which enzymes produced by the yeast cells break down sugars into smaller molecules, are important in the production of such foods as bread, vinegar, beer, and wine. Yeasts are also grown for food and for the production of some enzymes. Yeasts are undesirable when they grow and ferment fruits, fruit juices, syrups, honey, molasses, and the like. Moist, sugar-containing foods, especially those that are slightly acid, such as fruit and fruit juices, are particularly susceptible to spoilage by yeasts. The optimum pH for yeast growth is 4.5 to 6.5. Fermenting foods are full of carbon dioxide gas bubbles. Yeasts grow most rapidly at temperatures of 20° to 38°C. As in the case of molds, temperatures somewhat below the boiling pint of water may be adequate for the destruction of yeasts if the tie of heating is extended. Yeast growth is inhibited by low temperatures and may be checked entirely in a concentrated sugar solution (65 per cent or greater). The boiling temperature of water destroys yeast cells and spores.

Bacteria are of many types and are widely distributed in air, soil, water, and in foods. Some types of bacteria produce substances of desirable flavour and are cultivated for their beneficial action. The lactic acid of buttermilk, sauerkraut, fermented pickles, cheese, yogurt, and butter (when made from sour cream) is an example of a desirable flavour substance formed by bacterial action. However, other products of bacterial decomposition bring about the spoilage of foods, causing them to become inedible or even highly toxic. Under conditions favourable for their growth, bacteria multiply rapidly. Favourable conditions usually include 25 to 30 percent available moisture and temperatures from 20° to 55°C. Some types of bacteria have an optimal temperaure for growth that is above 45°C and are called *thermophilic*; those having a low optimal temperature, of 20° to 45°C are called mesophilic. If bacteria require air or oxygen they are called aerobic; if they do not require oxygen and grow better in its absence they are called anaerobic. Facultative bacteria are capable of growing either with or without free oxygen. Each bacterium also has its own optimal pH or degree of acidity for growth, but most bacteria grow best at a pH near neutrality. Heat in the presence of acid is highly destryctive to bacteria. Therefore, in acid foods, the temperature of boiling water maintained for a relatively short period of time is adequate for the destruction of bacteria; Foods of low acid content or high pH (those of lower acidity than is represented by a pH of 4.5) are more difficult to preserve than are foods with a low pH because bacteria and their spores are more resistant to destruction in these low acid surroundings. Some bacteria, such as those of the genera Bacillus and Clostridium, form endospores or spores. These spores are much more resistant to heat and other destructive agencies than are the vegetative cells. Bacteia in the vegetative state may be readily destroyed in moist foods at the boilding temperature of water for relatively short periods of time.

Enzymes

Enzymes are present in many foods that are commonly preserved in the home. Unless undesirable enzyme action is controlled or the enzymes are destroyed (Usually by heating), they may be responsible for certain unwanted chemical changes in preserved foods. All methods used for preserving foods are based upon the general principle of preventing or retarding the causes of spoilage- microbial decomposition, enzymatic and nonenzymatic chemical reactions, and damage from mechanical causes, insects, and rodents. When the growth of microorganisms is only retarded or inhibited, preservation is temporary.

When spoilage organisms are completely destroyed and the food is protected so that no other microorganisms are permitted to reinfect it, more permanent preservation is achieved. No method of food preservation will improve the original quality of a food produce. If a preserved food is to be satisfactory, then fresh, flavourful produced at an optimal stage of ripeness or maturity must be used. With chilling temperatures, the length of time that the food will remain wholesome varies with the temperature and with the type of food. In home refrigerators, at 7 to 10°F (45 to 50°F), most foods keep for a few days only. In cold storage warehouses the length of time is increased. Here the temperature is low and the humidity is controlled, both of which conditions favour preservation. Freezing may reserve foods for long periods of time provided the quality of the food is good to begin with and the temperature of storage is below the actual freezing temperature of storage is belong the actual freezing temperature of the food. Some microorganisms are destroyed during the freezing process and subsequent storage but the chief preservative effect of freezing lies in the inability of microorganisms to grow at freezing and below freezing temperatures. Enzyme action is also retarded at freezing temperatures. Enzyme action is also retarded at freezing temperatures. However, in certain products, such as vegetables enzyme action may still produce undesirable effects on flavour and texture during freezing. Hot temperatures preserve by destroying both microorganisms and enzymes. Yeasts, molds, and enzymes are readily destroyed at the boiling temperature of water. The heating must be maintained for a long enough time to permit all parts of the food to reach the necessary temperature. Heat penetration is sometimes slow in such foods as partially ripe pears or peaches. Bacteria are less readily destroyed than are yeasts, molds, and enzymes, the vegetative or active cells being more readily destroyed than spore forms. Many bacterial spores are very resistant to heat. Canning as a method of food preservation involves essentially the complete destruction of microorganisms an their spores and enzymes by high temperatures and then sealing to prevent the recontially sterilized. Pasteurization of food products such as milk and eggs that are to be frozen or dried involves use of temperatures that are lower than those required for sterilization. All pathogenic or disease-producing microorganisms are destroyed but not all of the other microorganisms present are eliminated. This is a more temporary preservation than is sterilization and canning.

Moisture Control

The reduction in moisture content is one of the oldest methods of preserving foods. As practically applied, the food is dried in the sun or by air current and artificial heat until the moisture content of the food is reduced to an amount tat will inhabit the growth of microorganisms. The actual percentage of moisture is variable but it usually under 30 percent. Some dehydrated foods, such as dried potato silences, may contain only 2 to 3 percent moisture. Foods, such as many commercially dried fruits with an intermediate moisture content, about 15 to 35 or 40 percent, may have low enough water activity for preservation yet are pleasant to eat directly without dehydration. Freeze-drying involves the removal of water from a product, while it is frozen, by sublimation under a vacuum. Sublimation means that ice is changed directly to vapour without going through the liquid stage. This is an expensive process because of the equipment involved. Therefore, it is more commonly used for the dehydration of relatively expensive foods, such as seafood and meats, that can more easily absorb the added cost than can less expensive products such as vegetables.

The common preservaties, sometimes called household preservatives, are salt, sugar, acid, spices, and smoke. The phenols of wood smoke exert the preservative action, gound cinnamon and cloves are more valuable than nutmeg and allspice in quantities that can be used without marring flavour, but spices themselves are often responsible for introducing bacteria into foods. Oils of spice are sterile and have a more inhibitory effect on microbial growth than do ground spices. Acids, such as acetic acid in vinegar, and salt are commonly used in pickling vegetables. In pickle and sauerkraut fermentations, lactic and other acids are produced by certain bacteria. Sugar in large amounts is used in the production of jellies, jams, and preserves. Other preservatives may be used in small amounts in the commercial processing of foods. The U.S. Food and

Drug Administration must approve any preservatives that are used in the foods entering interstate commerce. Thorough testing for safety is required of these chemical additives before they can be used. Foods produced and sold within a state come under the jurisdiction of state regulatory agencies. Benzoate of soda, used in very small amounts in some margarines, and sulfur dioxide, used to prevent the discoloration of dried fruits, such as apricots, applies, and pears, are examples of preservatives that may be added to foods.

Use of Ionizing Radiation

The radiation preservation of food is considered to be a "Cold" process because there is only a slight rise in the temperature of the food irradiated. Adverse changes in flavour and texture by heat ate thus avoided. Radiation at levels above I megarad (a unit for measurement of radiation) has the potential for use in preserving meats, fish, poultry, and other highly perishable foods for long term without refrigeration. Doses of radiation below I megarad may extend the refrigerated. Doses of radiation below I megarad may extend the refrigerated storage life of perishable foods, may destroy food poisoning salmonellae organism in frozen animal products, may destroy insects in cereal grains, and may extend the shelf life of fresh fruits and vegetables by destroying molds and yeasts. Radiation at lower levels may pasterurize (destroy pathogens and reduce the level of microorganism while sterilization (complete destruction of microorganism) occurs at high dosages.

When considering the wholesomeness of irradiated food it is necessary to be assured that (1) there is no radioactivity in the irradiated food; (2) all pathogenic microorganisms have been destroyed; (3) noxic radiation products are produced; and (40 there are no unacceptable losses in nutritive value. After many years of testing, an international review committee from the World Health organization has concluded that food products irradiated to an average dose of up to 1 megarad are wholesome. The U.S. Food and Drug Administration is working with industry and other interested groups on recommendations for the radiation processing of various foods.

Antibiotics Use

Many antibiotic substances have been tested on raw foods to determine their effect on the storage life of foods at refrigerator temperatures. Aureomycin (chlortetracycline) and Terramycin (oxytetracycline) have been found to be superior to most of he other antibiotics tested. These antibiotics were previously used in small amounts in the chilling tanks during poultry processing but are no longer approved for this purpose by the food and Drug Administration. They extended the shelf life of the poultry and were destroyed in cooking. Some experiments have combined antibiotics and heat treatments in foods in an effort to reduce the total heating time necessary for canning low-acid foods. Some antibiotics that have been tried without complete success are subtilin, nisn, and tylosin. Some of the problems involved in the use of antibiotics in food preservation include the need to prove the nontoicity of the substance and the possible developed resistance of microorganisms to antibiotics that are used over a period of time. The consumer may become sensitized to an antibiotic with undesirable results when it is present in a food he or she consumes. It is also possible that he or she may develop strains of microorganisms in his or her body that are resistant to the antibiotics used in the food so that when he or she needs an antibiotic still must be solved in the area of the use of antibiotics for food preservation. With the increasing complexity of our civilization, methods of food preservation will play an even more important role in feeding people all over the world. All foods are perishable to some degree and may begin to deteriorate immediately after harvest or gathering. Man's knowledge of the technology of food preservation, properly applied, has helped to control this deterioration and increase the general quality and economy of food. Many of the foods commonly used in the home are preserved by such processes as caning, freezing, and dehydration. The decision as to whether or not these preserved foods are to be processed at home or purchased already processed is an individual family decision. Many factors may influence this decision, including the availability, cost, and quality of raw materials and equipment; storage space; the time and energy available; comparative palatability and family preferences for the various products; and the possible enjoyment derived form these types of do-it-yourself projects.

Healthy practices and good personal hygiene should be followed by all who handle food. Food borne diseases can be consideably reduced if clean healthy practices are followed in the kitchen. Al fresh fruits and vegetables should be washed well to remove dirt, sand and pesticides. Dirty hands with sores or boils should not be used to take food. Also avoid coughing and sneezing on food. containers and cooking pots should be clean and good water must be used for cooking. Boil drinking water during the rainy season.

3

CHAPTER

Importance of Food Technology

Food science and technology applications must be further concerned with economics and marketing; food preferences of various populations; quality assurance and control; regulatory aspects dealing with safety, wholesomeness, and honest representation and the production of affordable, quality food on a world wide basis. Therefore, food science interfaces with and draws upon many disciplines, including chemistry, physics, mathematics, the plant and animal sciences, biochemistry, enzymology, microbiology, genetics, engineering, statistics, computer science, nutrition, toxicology, psychology, and law. Food science is concerned with food composition, which includes not only the kinds and amounts of food constituents (such as proteins, fats, carbohydrates, vitamins, minerals, emulsifiers, acids, oxidants, antioxidants, enzymes, pigments, flavours, and water) but also their physical and physiochemical arrangements.

The entire spectrum of food engineering is associated with operation and maintenance of food processing plants as well as sophisticated research involving process design. The applications of engineering in food handling, processing packaging, and distribution can be described in terms of unit operations. There are many different unit operations associated with the conversion of raw food materials to consumer products. The movement of foods and other materials within the processing plant requires the use of unique equipment and processes. For example, special sanitary pumps are used to transport liquid foods, and the material-handling equipment for solid foods requires careful design for product-contact surfaces. The importance of thermal treatments for food preservation requires that a broad range of heat exchange equipment be used. Heat exchangers for liquids are unique in terms of sanitary design and cleanability of surfaces following thermal processing.

A special component of thermal preservation is the design of thermal processes. Several unit operations involve heat transfer in order to achieve the desired preservation even though storage stability is not the direct result of thermal treatment. An excellent example is the freezing process, where removal of thermal energy reduces product temperatures to levels where deterioration reactions are significantly inhibited. Concentration processes achieve a degree of preservation by reducing the availability of water for deterioration reactions, although the primary aim is reduction of liquid-product mass and volume.

Although traditional concentration processes have used thermal energy to evaporate water, membranes of various types are now used to achieve the same results. The preservation of food products is achieved by reduction of the water content to low levels by means of dehydration processes which use thermal energy. These processes are applied to liquid foods and to products that are naturally solid.

These constituents determine the properties of colour, texture, flavour, nutritive value, and keeping quality of food. Each property may be grossly changed by processing. That is, processing may alter a food's cellular integrity and the states of colloidal dispersion, emulsification, or solution of its constituents (as well as its constituent interactions), and the susceptibility to deterioration by air, light, temperature, relative humidity, microorganisms, and natural food enzymes. Food science deals with many food commodities and thousands of derived products. These commodities are processed for many reasons, including preservation, creation of new product forms, improvement of sensory and nutritional qualities, convenience, and removal of natural toxicants. Common processes are heating, cooling, freezing, concentration, dehydration, fermentation, sometimes irradiation, and packaging. Each process can be further classified by method; dehydration, for example, may employ drum drying, spray drying, cabinet drying, tunnel drying, vacuum drying, foam drying, freeze drying, and osmotic drying. Each process utilizes unique equipment that requires optimization of variables to maximize product quality and minimize costs, and is capable of yielding product with distinct characteristics. Further, commodities are increasingly utilized for their constituents which are separated, extracted, chemically and physically modified, and then recombined into an endless variety of formulated and engineered foods that are indistinguishable from their source materials. This often requires the use of highly specific food additives to improve processing properties ad acceptance factors, including nutritional quality. Nutrient levels and nutrient availability from foods may be decreased or increased by handling and processing practices. Food science is also concerned with all aspects of food safety, including natural food toxicants, industrial contaminants, misuse of food additives, and microbiological contamination as well as methods for the detection, exclusion, inactivation, removal, and regulation of harmful substances.

Consumers also must be protected against economic deception and misrepresentation. Undergraduate and graduate degrees in food science are offered by universities around the world. Food scientists, food technologists, and professionals from related fields are employed throughout the food industry and by suppliers of equipment, ingredient, packaging materials, and other services, as well as by government and academia. Food scientists belong to many professional organizations; predominant among hem is the Institute of Food Technologists. This organization, whose membership is international, is an excellent resource for information on all aspects of food science.

While a variety of physical or chemical properties of the product components are used in the various separation processes, two of the most important processes are filtration and extraction. Filtration, a physical process, has several applications in addition to its use for separating product components. Extraction is most often designed to remove a specific or unique product component for use in a separate operation or product formulation. After separation, the final product is obtained through the use of a mixing process which includes a variety of equipment types. Finally, the extrusion process involves the use of both thermal and flow properties to achieve product preservation as well as some specified set of structural and textural characteristics. The importance of cleaning and sanitation must be emphasized due to direct relationships to final product quality. The required operations vary considerably depending on the type of product handled and the type of equipment used.

The processes required to manage the wastes generated during food handling, processing, packaging, and distribution are all similar, and many of the waste-handling and treatment operations are the same as those used directly with the food products. The final operation to which the product is subjected before distribution is packaging. The package barrier is important for maintaining food products at desirable quality levels. Food packaging involves the selection of equipment needed for placing the product in the package as well as the selection of packaging material needed to protect the product in an optimum manner. An engineering input food handling, processing, packaging, and distribution that is applied to almost all unit operations is process control. The use of instrumentation and associated electronic controls has a significant impact on the efficiency of all components of the food delivery system. Fluid foods with widely differing characteristics must be pumped between many different unit operations before a final product results. Some pumps are selected for a single application or duty, and others are used for various products.

Handing of Pumps

Sanitary pumps are designed for easy and frequent cleaning. They are easily dismantled by removing wing nuts by hand or by using simple tools. In addition, the units are mounted to pipelines with special clamps and disconnects designed for rapid breakdown. Pumps may also be designed for cleaned-in-place systems, which reduce the need for frequent dismantling. These self-cleaning units are constructed with grooves which route sanitizers and create turbulence to help dislodges solids. Sanitary pumps must be manufactured from a materials that are resistant to corrosion and the chemicals used for cleaning and sanitation. Pump rotors and casings are commonly available in stainless steel; rotors are also available in natural or synthetic rubber. Sanitary pumps should have no internal wear, and the lubrication systems for bearings and other moving parts should be completely sealed to prevent contact with the food being pumped. This is typically accomplished with single or double O-ring-type seals which may incorporate flushing systems for vacuum applications or when pumping hot fluids. Centrifugal pumps differ widely in size and internal design; however, they all have the same basic principle of operation. The pump consists of an impeller rotating within a casing and attached to a shaft that is driven externally by an electric motor. Liquid enters the pup at the center of the rotating impeller and is accelerated to a high velocity by the movement of the impeller vanes. The resulting movement—from the center to the outer edge of the impeller—greatly increases the kinetic energy of the fluid. Velocity is reduced when the materials is discharged by the vanes to the casing, which causes some of the fluid kinetic energy to be converted to pressure. This increased pressure causes fluid movement from the discharge section of the pump. Liquid is delivered from a centrifugal pump in a steady stream, that is, without pulsations. Wear is minimized because the pump has no internal rubbing part and clearances are relatively large.

Material handling is a term used to describe the movement of materials through various stages of processing. It includes movement of raw material from a supply location to a processing plant; movement of material through different stages of processing within a plant; and movement of finished product to a warehouse or to storage. In material handling it is imperative that the movement of a known quantity of material to a preselected location occurs at the desired time while maximizing the economy of space. Equipment used for the mechanical handling of materials may be classified as conveyors and elevators, hoists and cranes, trucks and pneumatic handling equipment.

Hydrocyclones (also known as liquid cyclones) are stationary devices that utilize fluid dynamic forces to separate solid from liquid or two solids of differing density suspended in a liquid. The most effective use of hydrocycones is in the separation of protein in a water suspension of starch in starch manufacturing. Wet milling of corn, primary separation of starch and protein is performed with large disk-nozzle centrifuges. The crude starch fraction (1.5-3% protein) is then counter currently washed by using small (0.4-0.6 in. or 30-15-mm diameter) hydrocyclones to remove most protein and other soluble materials (solubles). The smaller less-dense protein conglomerates remain in he overflow, while the heavier starch granules settle and exit the system in the underflow.

This step provides the necessary fluid volume for efficient hydrocyclone operation and helps to remove soluble protein and other solubles in the starch fraction. The overflow, containing protein, solubles and a small amount of starch, is used to dilute the feed on the previous stage. Recycling of the overflow to the previous stage washes the solubles and protein upstream to the overflow of the first-stage hydrocyclone. The first-stage overflow is recycled to the primary disk-nozzle centrifuges. The number of hydrocyclones stages in a starch washing system depends upon the ease of separation of starch from protein and the amount of wash water used. Some starches, such as potato starch, require only six to eight stages for adequate washing; other starches, such as corn or wheat, may require up to 14 stages. The number of stages can be reduced if the volume of wash water is increased. About 1.1-1.8 liters of wash water per kilogram of corn (0.13-0.22 gal per pound) is used for maize starch washing. Because he capacity of individual hydrocyclone (often referred to as a cyclonette) is only 3.7 to 5.7 litres (0.98 to 1.5 gal) per minute, cyclonettes are arranged in parallel in a housing. They share common inlet and outlet manifolds. The most popular assembly, known as a clamshell contains approximately 480 cyclonettes. Other assembly arrangements are available. Cyclonettes used in the starch industries are either 0.4 in. (10 mm) in diameter, used for small starch granules such as maize, or 0.6 in. (15 mm) in diameter, used for large starch granules such as potato. Two types of cyclonettes are used in a starch washing system. The A-type cyclonettes are 0.4 in. (10 mm) in diameter with a 0.1-in. (2.5mm) feed inlet, a 0.1-in. (2.5-mm) vortex finder opening, 1 0.090-in. (2.3-mm) heavy-fraction opening, and a cone opening, a 0.090-in. (2.3-mm) heavy-fraction opening, and a cone taper of 6°. This is the standard cyclonette used throughout most of the stages of starch washing. Approximately 60% of liquid flow goes to the overflow (lighter fraction) and 40% to the underflow (heavier fraction). The B-type cyclonettes are also 0.4 in. (10 mm) in diameter with similar dimensions, except that the cone taper is 8° and the heavy-fraction opening (apex) is 0.094 in. (2.4 mm) in diameter. About 70% of liquid flow goes to the light fraction, and only 30% goes to the underflow; therefore a higher starch concentration is obtained in the underflow. B cyclonettes are used in the final or last two stages of starch washing. The 15-mm (0.6- in.)

Hydrocyclones/liquid cyclones have no moving parts. They rely upon slurry velocity to create adequate centrifugal forces to accelerate settling of the heavier solids. Slurry feed pressures in the range 90-140 ib/in.^{2} (620-965 kilopascals) are commonly used in the starch industry for separating starch and protein. Centrifugal separation of starch from protein in hydrocyclones depends not only on density differences but also on other starch characteristics, such as shape and size of granules. Starch size, shape, and surface, characteristics can enhance or retard separation from the smaller protein particles. Larger granules are more easily separated. Because of differences in shape, surface texture, and density of starch granules in various starches, different lower limits of starch granule size may be effectively separated from the protein among different starches. For maize, granules less than 6 micrometers in diameter will have equal probability of going out in the overflow or the underflow. This lower limit is about 1 and 5 ì m for rice and wheat, respectively. The probability of a particle gong out with the underflow deceases with decreasing particle size for all products. Genetic variation in the starchy raw material, environmental conditions in plant culture, and post harvest drying of the starchy raw material can also affect starch protein separation.

Heating and Cooling

It is used to change the temperature of the food product and to change the phases present in the food (vapor, liquid, solid). Thus, preservation processes such as pasteurization, blanching, and canning are based on principles governing heat transfer, just as are drying and freezing processes. Heat-transfer operations are used to either remove or add heat in order to alter the physical, chemical, or storage characteristics of food products. An example of using heat input to change a food product is cooking to alter texture and develop colour and flabour. Heat removal is used to change physical form as in the production of ice cream or candies. Heat transfer by conduction, convention, and radiation are all employed in food processing. In the application of heat transfer, however, it is necessary to know the effects of temperature on rates of change of the physical and chemical characteristics of the food. Knowledge of food science and engineering leads to the optimum design of heat-transfer operations. The food industry relies extensively on heating and cooling processes (either indirect or direct systems) to control the quality and characteristics of food products. These systems are used with a wide variety of heating and cooling media to effect temperature and phase change. In the application of these methods, the safety of the consumer is of paramount importance. Secondary criteria as to the choice of methods include production rate, cost, energy efficiency, and waste generation. Heating and cooling methods applied to foods can be classified as either indirect or direct.

Methods

These methods are used, the food product does not come in contact with the material absorbing (cooling) or supplying (heating) the heat energy. The heat is transferred to (from) the product through a physical barrier such as a stainless steel plate or a tube wall for heating (cooling). For heating processes, the heating medium is generally hot water or steam, although other heat transfer liquids or gas flames may be use in high-temperature applications. For cooling processes, the cooling fluid is usually a commercial refrigerant cycled through a mechanical refrigeration unit. The simplest type of indirect heat exchanger is a kettle which holds the food product. The outside of the kettle may be heated by direct flame (radiation and convection heat transfer), or the kettle may have an outer wall crating a space through which the heating medium can flow. Kettles are used in batch heating medium can flow. Kettles are used in batch heating processes, and the product is usually mechanically agitated to increase heat transfer and avoid local excessive hot spots and burn-on (fouling). For larger industrial operations, liquid food products are heated or cooled in continuous-flow heat exchangers. These take a variety of forms, including one with a tube inside another (tubular exchangers) and flow channels created by several parallel, corrugated plates (plate-and-frame heat exchanger). Milk is an example of a liquid food that is heat-treated in either type of heat exchanger prior to packaging and distribution. For more viscous food liquids, such as starch-based puddings and candies and vegetables purees (baby food), a tubular-type exchanger equipped with a rotating axial scraper blade is used. The action of the scraper blade increases heat transfer by removing the layer of liquid immediately adjacent to the wall and thus minimizes burn-on.

Direct heating systems are not as commonly used as indirect systems in the food industry. In cooling applications, direct systems include cryogenic freezing (using, for example, liquid nitrogen, carbon dioxide, or a commercial refrigerant), liquid immersion freezing (that is, using aqueous solutions of glycerol or sodium chloride), and cooling with ice. The systems differ largely in their cost, rate of freezing or cooling, and effect on product quality. For heating, water, steam, and air are most frequently used as direct heating agents.

In each case, the heating fluid must be of food-grade quality. For water, this presents no major problem since potable water must be used in contact with food material. For air, this frequently requires some filtering treatment prior to contact with the food. For steam, this requires that the steam be produced with FDA-Approved boiler compounds. Steam which can be used in direct contact with food is called culinary steam and is frequently made by using boiler steam to make steam out of deionized potable water. When steam is used to heat food directly, the condensate that is produced dilutes the food product and it may be necessary to remove this water. Frequently this is accomplished by boiling off the water (flashing) in the cooling operation (for example, exposing the hot product to a partial vacuum). In steam heating, the steam can either be added to the product (a process called *steam injection*) or the product can be added to a steam atmosphere, a produces called steam infusion. Steam injection is the more popular in industrial method. Heat transfer by radiation is best categorized as a direct method. Electromagnetic radiation in the infrared region (1-400 micrometers) is readily absorbed by water and many of the organic constituents of food, resulting in heat transfer. Infrared heating is used extensively I the baking and roasting industry. Microwave and dielectric heating are accomplished by electromagnetic radiation in the radio frequency range. In dielectric heating, the product is placed between parallel electrodes, and the charge or the plates is oscillated at 1000-3000 MHz/s. For microwave heating, electromagnetic radiation in the above frequency range is generated in a magnetron tube and transferred to the product located in a cavity where the energy is absorbed.

Thermal Processes

This treatment accomplishes many objectives, including inactivation of microorganisms enzymes, or poisonous compounds and production of desirable chemical or physical changes in foods. When compared to typical engineering material such as metals or minerals, food is relatively susceptible to thermal degradation. Therefore, to produce nutritionally sound and microbially safe food products, heat treatment should be accurately controlled in order to accomplish its objectives. To assist in this control, the temperature responses of foods subjected to heat treatments are frequently estimated by using empirical or theoretical heat-balance equations.

Heat Treatment

It may involve application of heat indirectly, as in a tubular heat exchanger, or it may be accomplished through the direct contact of the heating medium with the food, as in the backing of bread in a hot-air oven. The principal operations involving heat treatment of foods are blanching, preheating, pasteurization, sterilization, cooking, evaporation, and dehydration. Blanching is hot-water or steam-scalding treatment or raw foodstuffs to inactive enzymes which might otherwise cause quality deterioration, particularly of flabour, during processing or storage. Most vegetables and some fruits are blanched before canning, freezing, or dehydrating. The commonly used types of equipment are rotary perforated drums, rotary screw conveyors or troughs, and pipe flume blanchers. Water is the predominant heating medium in drum and flume blanchers; steam is used in the screw-type blancher.

Food Microbiology

Food microbiology is a broad field that can include not only microbiology but also sanitation epidemiology, biochemistry, engineering, statistics, and mathematical modeling. It is a subdiscipline in the field of microbiology concerned with the study of bacteria, fungi, and viruses hat grow in or are transmitted by foods. While bacteria are frequently associated with food spoilage and food poisoning, some species preserve foods through fermentation or produce food ingredients.

Spoilage Organisms

People dismiss food poisoning as a minor annoyance. In reality, the suffering and economic. Losses stemming from food-borne pathogens are substantial, but they are often hidden. Annual economic losses from food-borne pathogens are extremely high. Salmonella, which cause an average of 40,000 cases yearly and 2000-3000 deaths in the United States, are responsible for about a third of these losses. Individual outbreaks of food-borne diseases can affect thousands of people. Many outbreaks are predictable and preventable through good sanitation, preservatives, thermal processing, and refrigeration. More than half, however, are of unknown etiology are poorly understood, and may be caused by so-called new pathogens.

Historical Pathogens in 1960, mot food-related illnesses were attributed to one of five major groups of pathogenic bacteria. These were associated with particular foods, commodities, or processes and were classified as infectious or toxin-producing. These five groups, described below, remain major causes of food-borne illness.

Shigella

Theprimry infectious bacterium associated with foods is Salmonella. These organisms cause gastroenteritis with symptoms of fever, diarrhea, and vomiting 12-36 h after ingestion. Salmonellosis is usually self-limiting, but it can be fatal in the old, Salmonellosis is usually self-limiting, but it can be fatal in the old, young, or medically compromised individuals. Salmonella are commonly found on meats, especially poultry and eggs. Salmonella are easily killed by cooking. However, item contacted by the contaminated raw meat can transfer the salmonella to food that is ready to eat (cross contamination) and cause illness. The seasonal increase in Salmonella isolations illustrates how food-borne illness increases in warm summer months.

Shigella are related organisms which produce a similar infectious syndrome. They are usually transmitted by a fecal-oral route or through feces-contaminated water rather than through foods. The most dreaded toxin-producing organism is Clostridium *botulinum*. It excretes a potent neurotoxin that causes weakness, double vision, slurred speech, paralysis, and often death if ingested. The vegetative reproductive form of C. *botulinum* is heat-sensitive, lives only in the absence of air, does not compete well with other bacteria, and is rarely a problem in fresh foods. *Clostridium botulinum* spores are killed only through severe heating, such as in canning. Historically, botulism has been associated with foods canned at home. If canned foods received inadequate heat processing, competing bacteria are killed, air is expelled, and the botulinal spores germinate. Fortunately, botulinal toxin is often destroyed by heat when the food is cooked before serving; hence the standard advice is to boil home-canned foods before eating. Modern commercial canning is designed to destroy C. *botulinum* spores. Reported outbreaks of botulism caused by pot pies, potatoes, and fried onions have been caused by temperature abuse, that is, the holding of foods at warm temperatures that promote bacterial growth. Clostridim botulium can also be a problem in processed meats, such as hams and sausages. In this case, its growth is controlled through the use of nitrite, salt, and refrigeration. One type of C. botulinum is associated with fish.

Clostridium Perfringens and Bacillus Cereus

These are spore-forming, toxin-producing bacteria that cause illness when foods are heated enough to kill competing bacteria but not enough to kill the spores. When large volumes of foods are prepared, cooked, and then kept warm until they are served, spores can germinate. In the case of C. perfringens, which is associated with meats, the ingested cells release toxin in the digestive tract, resulting in cramps and diarrhea. Bacillus cereus, found in meats, dried foods, and rice, produces two different types of toxins: the diarrhea toxin, which has an etiology similar to C. *perfringens*, and the emetic (vomiting) toxin, which causes symptoms similar to those produced by staphylococcal toxins.

This bacterium produces toxins that are very resistant to heat. Staphylococcus *aureus* is found in the nose and throat of many healthy people and is transferred to food by inadequate hygiene. When foods are temperature-abused, the bacteria grow and produce toxin. Subsequent heating of the food kills the bacteria but does not inactivate the toxin. The toxin causes severe vomiting and diarrhea from ½ to 4 h after ingestion. The microorganism grows well at salt and sugar concentrations that inhibit many competing bacteria. Foods high in protein, such as cured meats, custards, and cream-filled bakery goods, pose special hazards for staphylococcal food poisoning.

Microbial Ecology of Foods

Modern food microbiology views foods as habitats where different organisms compete for survival. The fact that there are 250 genera of bacteria and that only 25 of these (8 pathogenic) are found in foods suggests that foods provide unique ecological niches. Viruses do not reproduce in foods and are not competitors in this sense (the food acts only as a carrier). Yeasts and molds usually grow more slowly than bacteria and are rarely a problem in foods that support bacterial growth. Bacteria reproduce by binary fission; it takes only 20 doublings for one cell to yield more than 1 million cells. In environments where the doubling time is short, this occurs quite rapidly. Many preservation methods alter foods' environmental conditions in order to slow microbial growth.

Temperature

The most important environmental condition is temperature. Most of food-borne pathogens are mesophiles; that is, body temperature is optimal for growth. With a doubling time of 20 min at 98.6°F , one bacterium generates 1 million progeny in less than 7h; at 32°F the doubling time increases to 1200 min and the 1 million cell count is not reached for 16 days. Keeping hot foods hot (> 145°F) and cold foods cold (<45°F) combined with rapid heating and cooling to get rapidly beyond the growth-promoting temperature range (45-145°F), prevents most food-borne illnesses. Psychrophylic (cold-loving) bacteria such as *Listeria monocytogenes* are exceptions.

Acidity

A food's acidity, quantified as pH, is another major environmental factor. The pH range for bacterial growth is 4-9, with fastest growth at neutrality (pH7). Changing a food's acidity can change the rate of bacterial growth. Meats, fish, poultry, and most dairy products are near pH7, which is ideal for bacterial growth; fermented foods and fruits have pH less than 4. Many yeasts and molds grow in acidic environments and spoils acidic foods. The pH value of 4.6 has special significance because C. *botulinum* can grow and produce toxin above this value. Canned foods with pH above 4.6 are legally classified as low-acid and must be processed in retorts under steam at 240-280°F to kill C. *botulinum* spores. Foods with pH below 4.6 are legally high-acid and are processed in open pans of boiling water. In this case, C. *botulinum* need not be killed because it cannot grow at low pH.

Activity of Water

Water available for microbial growth, that is, water activity (a_w), is the third major factor influencing microbial competition. Water activity is the equilibrium relative humidity generated by a food in a closed chamber divided by 100 to give a 0 to 1.00 scale. Salad dressings and honey, which both contain 50% water, are microbiologically quite different. The dressing separates into a 100% free-water phase (a_w =) and supports bacterial growth, while the sugar in honey binds water so tightly that it is unavailable for microbial growth. Most bacteria grow only at q_w = 0.90-100. fresh meats, vegetables, fruits, and perishable foods have water activity in this range. Most yeasts can grow at slightly lower values. Staphylococcus aureus is the pathogen most insensitive to water; it grows at a_w = 0.86. Since no pathogenic bacteria grow below a_w = 0.86, this value has special significance in the regulations defining low-acid foods. Foods having an a_w value below 0.85 are legally considered high-acid, regardless of their pH. Most molds grow at aw values as low as 0.8 and compete well in foods such as flour, cakes, beans, rice, and cereals. Some xerophilic molds and yeasts grow at aw values as low as 0.6. Dehydrated foods, with even less available water, are completely recalcitrant to microbial spoilage.

Oxygen can be favourable, neutral, or inhibitory to bacterial growth. In one process, foods are first vacuum-packed to inhibit aerobic spoilage organisms and are then partially cooked. This environment is perfect for anaerobic spore-forming microorganisms. However, the Food and Drug Administration prohibits the use of this process because of the potential botulinal hazard.

Preservatives

Chemical preservatives also render food environments unsuitable for microbial growth. The oldest preservative is common table salt; at very high levels, it produces water activities that are inhibitory to microbial growth, although many organisms are inhibited by as little as 3% salt. Nitrites are used in cured meat as anticlostridial agents. Acetic, lactic, citric, benzoic, and propionic acids and sodium diacetate can also be added to foods as microbial inhibitors. Considering the low levels used, the long history of safe use, and the consequences of microbial growth, the risk: benefit ratio associated with chemical preservatives is very low.

Consumer preferences for fresh and natural foods make it difficult to alter anyone environmental factor enough to inhibit microbial growth, and so the trend is to use multiple barriers, or hurdles. This approach employs several inhibitors at suboptimal levels. For example, clostridia may be inhibited by 7% salt at pH 7.0 or 0% salt at pH 4.6, but a meat treated this way would be unacceptable, tasting either salty or acidic. However, 3% salt at pH 6 in the presence of nitrite at a concentration of 125 parts per million provides multiple barriers sufficient to inhibit the bactria and not impair flavour.

The demand for longer shelf life in refrigerated foods combined with their increased popularity has caused renewed concern about psychrophilic pathogens, such as *Yersinia enterocolitica*, and enterotoxigeic organisms, such as Escherichia coli and Listeria monocytogens. These bacteria grow most rapidly at 59-86°F and, at refrigerated temperatures, can successfully compete with the normal mesophilic bacteria, thus limiting the shelf life of refrigerated foods. Listeria cause special concern because they infect women and their unborn children preferentially.

Campylobacter jejuni is a pathogen that is responsible for more illnesses than *Salmonella* and Shigella combined. Ingestion of relatively small numbers can cause diarrhea, cramps, and nausea. This organism is microaerophilic (requires 5-10 % oxygen), is relatively fragile, and show a seasonal pattern of outbreaks similar to Salmonella. It is associated with raw meats and unpasteurized milk, and can be controlled by pasteurization, heating, and good sanitation.

Analytic Approaches

Microbial analysis of foods frequently requires "zero defects" in the absence of 100% testing. Legally, ready-to-eat foods must be free of *Salmonella*. This demands that the food microbiologist be able to detect one Salmonella among millions of innocuous bacteria in a pound of food. Moreover, all of the food cannot be tested because microbial analysis is destructive. Therefore, statistical sampling plans determine how many samples must be tested to have confidence that the whole lot is free of *Salmonella*.

In the classical methods fro counting microorganisms, a food or its hemogenate is highly diluted so that only 30-300 cells are transferred to growth media. After 2-10 days, each cell grows into a colony, and these are counted and multiplied by the dilution factor to estimate the number of cells in the food. Automated methods. Have been developed that measure growth products, bacterial deoxyribonucleic acid (DNA), or specific toxins; these methods dramatically reduce the analysis time and are rapidly replacing the petri-dish method.

A procedure known as hazard analysis critical control points (HACCP) can replace meant postproduction testing. This technique examines a food, its ingredients, and its processing to identify points critical to safety. These points are then heavily monitored during production; if they are maintained, a safe product results.

Beneficial Food-borne Organism

When certain bacteria grow in foods, they produce desirable flavors and textures, and may also inhibit pathogenic organisms. Most of these bacteria belong to the genera *Streptococcus, Lactobacillus, Leuconostoc, Pediococcus*, or *Micrococcus*. They are used to make fermented dairy products, meats, and vegetables, and to preserve food by converting the sugars needed by competing microbes to lactic acid, which inhibits their growth. These lactic acid bacteria are unusually tolerant of acidic environments. Acetobacter and Gluconobacter are used in the production of vinegar. Yeats, usually Saccharomyces, which produce ethanol and carbon dioxide, are used in the processes of brewing and baking.

Lactic acid coagulates casein, the major protein in milk, and this process is used to manufacture cheese. During the aging of cheese, bacterial enzymes generate characteristic flavours, allowing a wide variety of products to be made by using many different bacteria. The bacteria used can be indigenous to the milk, derived from a previous fermentation, or added as pure cultures.

Until the late 1960s, staphylococcal food poisoning was a major problem in certain meat products, such as bologna, pepperoni, and salami. Since acid production by indigenous bacteria is often unpredictable, it is now recommended that defined starter cultures be used to ensure that sufficient acid is produced early enough to prevent staphylococcal growth. A novel use for starter cultures of lactic acid bacteria is to prevent botulinal growth in bacon. A small amount of culture and sugar are added to the cured meat; if the bacon is temperature abused, the lactic acid bacteria grow and produce acid to inhibit botulinal growth.

Certain vegetables are preserved by fermentation Pickles are made by fermenting cucumbers; olives and many oriental foods are also fermented. During sauerkraut fermentation, the addition of 2.5%, which is tolerated by L. Brevis, and this bacterium brings the product to a final acidity of 1.7%.

Molecular biology have generated interest in applications to food processing. The most important contribution of biotechnology to food microbiology is the production of probes that detect pathogenic organisms much faster than conventional methods. For example, conventional methods require 5 days to confirm the presence of Salmonella in foods; probes that detect Salmonella-specific DNA or antigens can give similar results in 2 days. The dairy industry has benefited from advances in biotechnology by acquiring the ability to determine the genetic basis for the bacterial metabolism of lactose in milk and to stabilize it.

4

CHAPTER

Community Nutrition Education

Public Health departments conduct many service and educational activities on the local, state, and national levels. Public health nutritionists help survey community nutrition needs, plan nutrition components of community nutrition needs, plan nutrition components of community health programmes, and provide training, consultation, and teaching materials for public health workers in other specialties such as nursing and sanitation. Public health nurses work with families through various health services, help organize and conduct clinics, and teach community health classes. Other government health agencies working in specific community projects include those formed in response to the Economic Opportunity Act, such as Vista and other groups operating in poverty areas, the India Health Programme, and the School Lunch Programme. A host volunteer health agencies, such as he American Heart Association, American Diabetes Association, and the American Cancer Society, provide educational opportunities and materials through their local chapters. In some larger urban areas, nutrition committees have classes taught by local nutritionists, nurses and physicians. These are sometimes arranged through cooperation with the local adult evening school. There are nutrition consultation and diet counseling services provided by a staff nutritionist with educational materials developed and printed by community physicians and health workers. There are also professional workshops on specific health problems. Volunteer nutritionits and nurses also work worth local chapters of the American Diabetes Association in their annual diabetes detection drives, and they teach classes in the local adult evening and extension schools.

Community Education

Population and family patterns and in medical and allied scientific knowledge bring with them inevitable changes in society that directly involve the teaching of nutrition to patients. These changes are reflected in shifting emphases in medical care itself. Until very recent years, stress was almost exclusively placed on the cure or amelioration of disease by surgery and drugs. While advances in these areas continue to be made with great rapidity, there is also an increasing tendency to blend curative practices with disease-preventive, health-oriented primary care. Generally a more sophisticated, affluent society knows more, has more, and asks more than a simple culture. People seek more involvement in their own health care. As the population increases, the greater numbers of people also demand more efficient approaches. Attempts to meet these demands have taken many forms, including group medical practice by specialists, clustering of medical facilities, and health insurance plans. There has been pronounced change in the role of the community hospital. It is rapidly emerging as the community health center of the future. Within its environs, nutrition education is becoming recognized by professional workers and by the community at large as an essential aspect of education for total health. Although the concept of the community health center as a focus for the coordination of curative and preventive health care is not fully forced, it is develop in as a result of social pressures and corrected trends in American medicine. Increasing leaders in medicine and hospital administration voice these changes in direction'. Project studies and pilot programmes are indicating the needs, and as a result the gap between the curative and preventive health systems is closing.

These reports indicate that the curative system is doing more work in home care programmes, in coordinated activities with chronic disease hospitals and nursing homes, in health care financing, and in area-wide hospital planning. The preventive system is organizing its services for the delivery of general healthcare, care of the chronically ill, rehabilitation work and overall community health planning, and broad community health planning, and broad community health screening programmes. The great need felt by leaders in the healthcare field is for increased functional coordination between the two health systems. In some situations this coordination may be a blending of the community hospital and the local health department, and it may include parts of the local welfare agency. In other situations, services of the two systems could be coordinated in activities such as home care programmes, outpatient clinic services, and broad public community education programmes. Such coordination would prevent much costly and inefficient overlapping and fragmentation, such as now exist in many communities. Fresh vision in planning and in programme development would give needed vitality and human dignity to pressing community health needs. Among community health centres being developed in this country is the health education centre formed by a group of physicians in Oakand, California, the Permanente Medical Group, in conjunction with their affiliated community health facilities, the Kaiser Foundation Health Plan and Hospitals. A directing staff that serves as a model health team coordinates and administers a long range programme of health education. Expanded facilities, centrally located, provide space for individual staff offices and counseling rooms, small conference rooms for discussion groups, and a larger auditorium for meetings, conferences, workshops, and lectures. A library, an exhibit theater, and individual teaching machine booths are available. A longstanding activity of the medical group, its comprehensive multiphasic health screening programme, has been expanded and involves extensive data processing equipment.

These data provide a broad basis for continuing research in limitless numbers of health problems. The multiphasic health screening programme is a fundamental part of the expanded health education programme. Numerous primary care programmes similar to the Kaiser model have developed in other parts of the country. The community health centre provides varied opportunities for health education and care through its facilities ad personnel. The coordinated health team approach underlies the basic programme of a community health centre. Under the guidance of the physician, specialists in various areas of health care work together with the patients to explore needs and provide services for family-centered health care. Individuals may have personal conferences with members of the health team, such as physician, psychologist, nutrition it, nurse, or social worker. Instruction maybe given concerning some aspect of health care as the need for such instructions becomes apparent.

Dietary modification is high on the list of probabilities for such instruction. Team conferences, under the direction of the family internist and pediatrician, are held in which workers in relevant disciplines explore and coordinate plans for family health care. Studies such as those of Lewin demonstrate that persons are more likely to carryout a decision if they have participated in the forming of it than if the decision has been made for them by others. Small discussion-decision groups provide opportunity for persons to explore needs, to obtain information about health care, to learn whether alternatives are open to them, and to gain motivation and support for action. Such discussion-decision groups are proving effective instruments for the education of persons with common health problems. Patients with diabetes, obesity, heart disease, or peptic ulcer or persons wanting to improve their health by stopping the smoking habit have found positive direction and emotional reinforcement through discussion decision sessions. Well persons with common health interests, such as parents of young children, expectant parents, teenagers, or older persons, have taken a lively interest in learning and sharing in these ways. More structured classes in subjects related to various health needs also provide needed information in such areas as prenatal care, natural childbirth, infant and child care, and family planning. Other classes maybe provided for persons with heart disease, diabetes, peptic ulcer, renal disease, genetic disease, and other chronic or long-term problems. Classes in broad areas of health interest maybe planned as needed. These may being areas such as family meal planning and marketing; preventive family health care through wise use of available comprehensive health plans and group medical practice, human relations, or current medical research in a wide variety of areas. The possibilities are as broad as the need in the individual community. For effective teaching in such classes, the health worker will need to plan carefully. The teaching plan will include sound research and other preparation and plans for the creation of a learning situation, for the guidance of learning activities, and for helping each person who attends to apply the material to his individual situation so that he may translate what he learns into action. Various teaching aids may be planned, prepared, secured, and arranged. Equipment and classroom facilities will need to be checked. During the class the pace at which material is presented, flexibility, and group involvement will be significant factors. After the completion of each class and at the end of the series, a follow-up evaluation the light of the stated objectives will be essential as the basis for planning future classes or series of classes. Health education materials, books, pamphlets, leaflets, models, pictures, and charts in an organized health library under the care of a qualified librarian provide rich learning resources as a part of a community health center. An exhibit area where displays of visual and graphic materials related to various aspects of healthcare may be presented is another highly effective means of health education. Booths may be provided with individually operated devices such as teaching machines and recorded audiovisual materials. Persons may be use these as desired to obtain new information or to review certain health care principles and practices.

A number of lay organizations conduct health-related activities for groups of persons having special needs. An example is the excellent "Meals-on-Wheels" programme conducted in some cities by volunteers who prepared and deliver hot meals to persons in need of such service. These are usually patients referred by the physician of the community. They are for the most part persons who are chronically ill or who are undergoing rehabilitation and are often elderly and alone. In rooming houses and apartment districts food is delivered by couriers on a regular schedule for a nominal fee. Often this courier is the only person who visits the patient for days at a time; he or she is awaited eagerly each day and brings more than food into the patient's life. Other local professional organisations medical, nursing, dietetics provide health education in a number of ways. They sponsor workshops, participate in mass communication through such media as radio and television, and issue staff-written article for publication in newspapers and magazines. A unique activity of the American Dietetics Association, for example, is the "Dial-a-Dietitian" programme that has been established in many urban areas. Through a telephone-answering service, person may make inquiries about food and nutrition; dietitians return the calls and give information or clarify a confused point. A number of food industries sponsor research, provide nutrition education materials, and underwrite community nutrition projects.

Among these organizations are the National Dairy Council and its affiliated state groups and the National Livestock and Meat Board. In many counties a nutrition council hose members represent the various nutrition agencies in the community nutrition projects, among these organisations are the National Dairy Council and its affiliated sate groups and the National Livestock and meat Board. In many counties a nutrition council whose members represent the various nutrition agencies in the community coordinates the work of all of he represented groups. These nutrition councils plan and sponsor community health activities such as projects and workshops that may be carried out through the local high schools. They also develop adult conferences on nutrition and issue teaching materials. Information concerning nutrition education work in a community may be obtained by writing or telephoning one of the following sources:

(1) Agricultural Extension Service, usually located in the state university

(2) Home advisors or home economists in district agricultural extension offices

(3) Registered dietitians in local hospitals

(4) Clinical and community nutritionists in private practice

(5) Pubic health nutritionists in local health departments or clinics

(6) Nutrition instructors in high schools, colleges, and nursing schools

Teaching about Nutrition

Health teaching involves dynamic interaction between teacher and learner, health workers who would educate patients about nutrition and health will at frequent intervals reassess their own developing comprehension of he dynamics of human behaviour, of growth and development, and of learning. They will evaluate from time to time their own growth in recognizing the needs and perceptions of persons and their increased sensitiveness to others. Such appraisals will help to equip them with realistic self understanding. In testing one's own success as an educator in the special field of nutrition, the health worker will use the techniques of self-appraisal that have become stand-bys in other aspects of health care. These are have become stand-bye in other aspects of health care. These are the methods developed by such students of human interactions as Carl Rogers Abraham Maslow,' and Thomas Weiss,' The health worker will want to reread the findings and recommendations of these and other authorities and consider them afresh in their application to the complex field of nutrition and the teaching of nutrition to patients and to community groups. Food's most basic function is to provide nutrients to the body. Nutrients are the substances in food needed to support life functions. One vital way in which this is accomplished is by providing energy a that the body needs. This energy, produced as a by product of food consumption, is measured in calories. A calorie is defined as the amount of heat energy required to raise the temperature of one kilogram of water one degree Celsius. All foods have specific caloric values, and a given among of food will produce a certain number of calories when broken down by the body.

Carbohydrates and Proteins

Carbohydrates are found in food as *monosaccharide, disaccharides*, and *polysaccharides*. The disaccharides are sucrose, lactose an maltose. Many adults, especially those of Oriental and back ancestry, suffer from lactose intolerance. In other words, undigested lactose is not absorbed and remains in the gastrointestinal tract, resulting in bloating, a large amount of gas, and abdominal cramping. This malady can be treated through a diet that includes high protein, high carbohydrate, low to moderate fat, and high calories. The polysaccharides are comprised of many glucose molecules and are the following: (a) *glycogen*, (b) *cellulose*, and (c) *starch*.

Carbohydrates are broken down into glucose, and the metabolism of carbohydrates produces energy. Four calories are produced per gram of carbohydrates. If carbohydrates are not abundant in the diet, protein and fat have to be metabolized to produce needed energy. Carbohydrates must be constantly replenish in the blood, either by eating or by breaking down glycogen stored in the liver and muscles. Carbohydrates are important in a child's diet and should comprise approximately 58% of total calorie in take. Foods rich in carbohydrates include rice, spaghetti noodles, bread, breakfast cereals, and potatoes. Many vegetables, fruits and fruit juices also contain some carbohydrates. Although candy and cookies are good sources of carbohydrates; the refined sugar they contain contributes to tooth decay and gum disease and does not provide additional nutrients. If food such as milk, fruit, and vegetables are eaten, the individual should brush and floss after the meal. If he cannot brush immediately after meal, he should at least rinse out his mouth with water. Brushing he flossing before bedtime are especially important in reducing tooth decay. Frits, vegetables, and juices make healthier snacks.

Protein means "to come first." This suggests that proteins are essential nutrients. No organism can live and almost no biological process can take place without protein. Proteins provide four calories per gram. Protein should comprise about 12% of a child's total caloric intake. Most children require approximately 60 grams of protein daily. Milk and meat products are excellent sources of protein.

Poultry is another good source of this essential nutrient. If a person eats a *vegetarian diet*, enough protein must be ingested to support normal growth and development, especially in children. This is called complementary protein ingestion, a dietary strategy which ensures that each food supplies some amino acids that the others lack for example, peanut protein is combined with wheat, oats, corn rice, or coconut, and soy protein is combined with corn, what, rye, or sesame. Non meat sources of protein include soybeans, dried beans, and nuts. Central grains, vegetables, and fruits contain vegetable protein, which must be augmented by other protein sources, as in the tortilla and beans example mentioned earlier.

Fats, or lipids, are the most concentrated source of calories we ingest. Fasts provide nine calories per gram, as compared with four for proteins and carbohydrates. There are two types of fatty acids: *saturated* and *unsaturated.* The dietary sources of saturated fatty acids are animal fat, beef, butter, chicken eggs, and whole milk. Unsaturated fats are found in vegetable oils, such as corn, olive soybean, peanut, and safflower. The more saturated a fat is, the harder it is at room temperature. Polyunsaturated fats, such as linoleic acid, can reduce *serum cholesterol levels*. Fats are an important part of our diets. Their vital role is sometimes overlooked because of the association of fats with cardiovascular problems. However, fats serve several vital functions. The energy they provide spares protein for tissue synthesis. Fats also serve as carriers of the fat soluble vitamins A, D, E, and K. As food, they provide satiety, because the rate at which a meal is emptied from the stomach is related to the fat content. The higher the fat content, the slower the food empties form the stomach. Fats are an important part of all cells, membrane structure in the body, and tissues. Additionally, fats provide protection in the adipose tissue just under the skin. This layer of *adipose tissue* also helps in maintaining the body temperature at a constant level despite changes in the environment temperature. Similarly, fats provide a layer of protective shock absorbing tissue between the kidneys, reproductive organs, and other organs. They also provide padding for the cheeks, palms of the hand, and balls of the feet. Finally, fast make foods more appetizing and flavourful. Fats should comprise 30% of total caloric intake. Thee fats should be equally divided among polyunsaturated, saturated, and monounsaturated fats. The major food sources of fat are animal and vegetable fats, such a butter, cream, lard, and salad dressings. Olives and nuts also have a significant fat content.

Blood Cholesterol

Cholesterol is a vital part of the body, but too much of it can result in health risks. Cholesterol is a waxy, fatlike substance found mainly in the liver, kidneys, and brain. Most of the cholesterol is transported through the body as lipoprotein. There are different forms of lipoprotein, and they are classified by their density. The most important forms of lipoprotein, and they are classified by their density. The most important forms of lipoprotein are low density lipoprotein cholesterol LDL) and the high density lipoprotein cholesterol (HDL). High levels of LDL indicate a cardiovascular risk. Many blood tests will provide only a total blood cholesterol reading, but a more important factor is the ratio of total cholesterol to HDL.

Although the body produces more cholesterol than is ingested through foods, the blood cholesterol level can be positively altered through a healthy diet. Generally, foods of animal origin, such as eggs and organ meats, should be increased. These foods will increase the amount of fiber in the diet, which will aid in digestion, increase intestinal motility, and possibly further lower cardiovascular risk. High fiber diets are also beneficial in preventing constipation, obesity, hypoglycemia, and high levels of cholesterol in the blood.

Cholesterol strategy should consist of two prongs, one to reduce LDL and the second to raise HDL. Even alopaths say that "food is the best medicine for conquering cholesterol". It is believed that only in one out of five hundred cases, cholesterol levels cannot be corrected by diet regulation. Heart attack remains relatively unknown in Japan because the traditional Japanese diet keeps the cholesterol LDL levels very low. For reducing LDL levels, foods which have cholesterol should be avoided. Their list with cholesterol contents is given below. Secondly, it has been established that soluble fiber binds itself together to cholesterol LDl and gets eliminated along with that cholesterol. So the second part of that strategy is to take foods with soluble fibers. In-soluble fibers do not bind themselves to cholesterol and do not help I eliminating it. Oat bran, apples and dry beans have a fair proportion of soluble fibers and are, therefore, moderately effective in lowering LDL cholesterol.

Example of other foods with soluble fiber are corn, pectine found in the skin of citrus fruits and apples, sunflower seeds. Thirdly, some foods are known to lower LDL cholesterol levels. Such as foods containing vitamin niacine vitamin C, chromium, magnesium and soybean lecithin. Avoid coffee, smoking and saturated fats.

5

CHAPTER

HEALTH AND HYGIENE

Good health, one should eat clean and hygienic food. The various food materials such as fruits and vegetables should be washed properly with clean water before eating or cooking. This is necessary because fruits and vegetables should be washed properly with clean water before eating or cooking. This is necessary because fruits and vegetables brought from the market usually have a coating of poisonous chemicals called pesticides. They may also carry some microorganisms (bacteria, fungi) and worms or their eggs. Proper washing of fruits and vegetables removes all these harmful chemicals, etc. The washed fruits and vegetables should be stored in a clean, cool, dry, fly-proof and dust-proof place to prevent their spoilage. One should also protect these items from the cockroaches.

For keeping good health, one should maintain personal hygiene such as taking bath regularly with soap and water, changing clothes regularly and washing hands properly before taking meals. One should also do brushing and flashing of the teeth and cleaning of tongue daily to check one's foul breath. If we do not bathe every day or change clothes every day then due to dirty conditions, the growth of mico-organisms takes place due to which out body as well as clothes begin to give four smell. These microorganisms may cause many disease particularly those related to the skin and genital organs. It is also very important to wash our face and the hands properly with soap and clean water every time after visiting toilet or before eating the food. Unwashed and dirty hands lead to many diseases. Cutting nails regularly is also necessary, Since pathogens along with dirt tend to accumulate beneath the unkempt nails and may spoil the food items.

Domestic hygiene includes good habits of cooking food, storing food and keeping the house neat and clean. The kitchen as well as toilet, both should be kept clean and dry to check the growth of pathogenic microbes. Further, since tobacco and smoking tobacco in the form of cigarette, beedi and hooka. Drinking alcohol in the form of wine, whisky, beer or country-made liquor and taking narcotic drugs such as heroin and morphine, cocaine marijuana can cause many physical and mental diseases such as damage to the eyes and hearing capacity of ears. They also damage nervous system and cardiovascular system.

The part of hygiene that deals with the care of the body is called Persona Hygiene. The study of personal hygiene is important because it guides us to look after various parts of our body e.g., eyes, nose, teeth, skin, hair etc. It also answers questions like which certain habits are bad for health. Following regularly the rules of personal hygiene we are able to prevent ourselves from getting infections and falling sick.

Care of Tooth

Each tooth has a crown neck and the root. It is made up of a very hard substance known as the dentine which is protection on the outside by a very thin enamel. Inside, there is a hollow which is known as the pulp cavity. It contains blood vessels and nerves which enter through the root of its socket ad the crown is the part of which we can see in our mouth. The neck is the part between the crown and the root. When we eat food we chew it to break and grind it to smaller particles. Some of these particles stick in between the teeth. If they stay there for a long time they start to putrefy. Germs grow on these food particles which are putrefying, and damage the substance of the tooth. Thus the tooth starts decaying. This gives rise to pain and formation of pus for abscesses in the roots of the teeth. In order to avoid or minimize any damage to our teeth we must clean our teeth not only in the morning but also before going to bed and after every meal. Cleaning of teeth is beast done with a tooth brush which is neither too hard nor too soft. A medium hard tooth brush with a good tooth paste or a very fine tooth powder helps in keeping the teeth clean and sparkling white. Even when we take liquids like tea, coffee and soft drinks we must rinse our mouth thoroughly with clean fresh water.

The tooth brush must be washed clean after every use and kept covered in a glass jar. This protects it from insects crawling over it. Repeated use of a toothbrush damages its bristles hence it should also be changed from time to time. After brushing our teeth we must also massage our gums with the help of a finger. Regular massaging leads to strong healthy gums. Moreover the grip of the gums on teeth also remains firm. Besides cleaning and care a balanced diet, which is rich in calcium and vitamin C, is good for the growth and good health of our teeth. Starchy or sweet foods stick to our teeth and cause decay faster, while fresh acidic fruits and salads are good for the teeth. Eating extremely hot and cold foods and cracking of hard huts etc. also damage the enamel of our teeth.

Skin

The skin protects and covers the internal parts of our body. It contains millions of pores, most of them art the openings for the sweat glands and some for the oil glands. The sweat glands help in sweating and therefore in regulating our body temperature. The oil glands secrete oil and thus keep our skin firm, supple and smooth. If we do not clean our skin properly everyday dirt and dust which stick on the skin surface will block the openings. This leads to the blocking of the sweat and oil glands. Germs also settle easily on the dirty skin and cause many skin diseases. Dirty skin gives out bad odour and then people do not like to sit with us. Bathing is the best way to keep the skin clean. The soap used should be of good quality and should not irritate the skin. Depending on the season, the water should be warm or tepid. Such a water has the best cleaning effect on the skin. It also helps to increase the blood supply to the skin and activates the sweat glands. We must take at least one bath in a day, preferably in the morning and before our meals. A very hot bath, even in winter, is harmful as there is danger of exposure to cold. Cold bath may be taken by the young persons but it should be very short and quick. Such baths have a stimulating effect on the skin. In case the skin is dry or rough we may take an oil massage before the bath. The massage helps in promoting the blood circulation to the skin making it soft and smooth. After the bath the skin should be rubbed dry vigorously with a clean dry towel. This is very beneficial, as it dries and massages the skin. This improves the blood circulation to the skin and makes it glow.

Hair

Hair should also be kept clean, properly combed and dressed. Dirty hair leads to breeding of lice, falling of the hair and many skin diseases. Oily hair needs frequent washing and cleaning as dust and dir stick easily to the oil. Dry hair can be kept soft and glossy with an oil massage to the scalp before the head bath. We should wash our hair at least once a week with a good soft shampoo of vegetable cleaners like amla berries and soap-nut (i.e., reetha nut). We should brush our hair daily, for at lest five minutes, twice a day. This keeps the hair clean and look glossy. The brushing stimulates the blood circulation to the scalp which strengthens the hair roots. Brushes and combs should not be shared and must be kept clean by washing and cleaning them once every week. Besides a balanced diet, proper sleep and protection from strong sunshine are also essential for healthy and glossy hair.

Eyes

When we wash our face we must also clean our eyes and use clean cloth or towel to wipe our face and eyes. Dirty eyes can lead to eye infections which if not checked can spread to other people and can result in affecting the vision. Therefore all cases of sore eyes must be attended immediately. While working we should be careful that the light is good. Working in poor light strains the eye, causes defects in vision and accidents. The light should be bright but not excessive or cause glare. It should fall on our work and come from behind. Excessive light from causes dazzling. Effect which is harmful. If there are any defects in the vision we should see a doctor. He will help us to correct the defects.

Hands care of our hands is important because we do many things with them. For this reason our hands get dirty easily. Eating with dirty hands means taking in the dirt with the food. Hands must be specially cleaned with soap and clean water before preparing, cooking, serving or eating food. Other wise the germs of infectious diseases like cholera, typhoid and dysentery are likely to contaminate the food which we cook, serve or eat. Nails should be kept clean, trimmed short. Long dirty nails harbour disease causing germs of various intestinal parasites like hook worms, thread worms and round worms. Our nails should be cleaned with a nail-brush, soap and clean water.

Clothes should be clean and should not irritate the skin. Man unlike animals does not have any natural covering to protect himself from extreme colds, heat or variations of the atmosphere. Therefore he has to use clothes. Clothes protect us against the effects of wind, weather and injuries. They also make us look smart and beautiful. They should be loose enough to allow free circulation of blood and free body movements. They should as be porous, light and preferably made of cotton, so that there is free flow of air over the skin, and the sweat evaporates quickly. During the cold weather we should wear woolen clothes which help us to retain our body warmth.

Dirty clothes can cause irritation to the skin and skin infections. Besides cotton and wool, clothes are made of many other materials like silk, flax, rubber, leather and nylon or synthetics. Clothes made of nylon or synthetic materials are very easy to wash and dry. These can be stored in a very small space. But they do not absorb moisture, can cause skin problems in certain people and can very easily catch fire. Therefore, we should wear clothes which are not only clean but also suit our skin and protect us from climatic variations.

We must eat at regular meal times and in a happy environment. Our food must be prepared, served and eaten with clean hands and in clean utensils. It should be protected from dust and flies. We must eat a balanced diet which contains will the necessary nutrient for our body. This helps in proper digestion. We must not eat food which is impure, dirty or bought from unhygienic restuarants, hotels or vendors. It should be freshly cooked and not be sale or spoiled. Eating food under unhygienic conditions can result in stomach upsets, indigestion and diseases like dysentery, typhoid and cholera.

The process of digestion and absorption is over the residue of the undigested food material in the large intestine is waste and has to be thrown out of our body. This waste, if not removed from the body regularly, can cause harmful effects like headache, drowsiness, lack of appetite and indigestion. When this waste residue after digestion of food is not removed regularly we call it constipation. Constipation may be due to not going to the toilet regularly, intake of less water, lack of roughage or undigestible fibres our food, deficiency of Vitamin B and weakness of abdominal and intestinal muscles. We can remedy this by going to the toilet at the regular time everyday. Drinking several glasses of water a day, especially a glass early in the morning after waking up and one glass at bed time before sleeping, helps proper bowel movement. Besides, eating a diet which has plenty of fruits, vegetates and vitamins, regular physical exercise and never ignoring the call of nature etc. all help in regulating the bowels and avoiding constipation.

Bad posture can result in early fatigue, deformations of the body and defective vision. While working our shoulders should be up and spine erect. Stooping or bending over our work will cause cramping of the lungs, deformation of the spine and defects of the vision. While standing, walking or running not only should the spine be erect but the body weight should be resting on the balls of feet and not on the heels. Sleeping in curled up posture interferes with circulation, breathing and causes strain to the muscles. High pillows are bad for the beck, chin, spine and for circulation of blood to the head and the face. Regular exercise, done preferably in the morning and before meals, keeps our body strong, fit and in good working condition. It has a special effect on the respiratory, circulatory, muscular and nervous systems. We remain active, alert and relaxed in mind. We do not tire easily while doing work. Taking part in regular sports and outdoor games helps us to relax, make friends, cooperate and share thins with others. Exercises which are strenuous and done irregularly are harmful and should be avoided.

People who cannot sleep properly remain tired, unhappy and sick. Sleep is very important to give rest to our body and its various systems. It is only during sleep the body can relax, repair the worn and torn tissues and remove the waste products form the body. People who cannot sleep properly remain tired, unhappy and sick. The amount of sleep needed varies with age and occupation. Infants, small children and the sick need longer hours of sleep as compared with the adults who need only six to eight hours of sleep a day. Children need 10-12 hours. People who live in hot climate should take a mid-day map. It helps in refreshing them. We should sleep on a clean firm flat bed, placed in a properly ventilated room and away from disturbing noises.

Physical and hard labour we start feeling tired. This tiredness or fatigue is due to the collection of Carbon-di-oxide and waste products produced de to muscular activity which the circulatory system cannot remove quickly. Resting enables the circulatory system to remove this waste materials by required throwing it out of our body through our nose. Once this is done we are once again refreshed to do more work. Warm bath, light massage and sleeping for sometime also helps us to get rid of our fatigue. When we do the same type of work day in and day out we start getting bored and our mind stars getting dull. In order to avoid boredom and fatigue we must do some activity which is different from our daily routine and gives us pleasure and relaxation. Some examples of such activities are listening to music, singing, painting, reading, playing games and going for a walk etc.

Such habits start developing form early childhood and remain with us forever. Even bad habits can develop during this period and persist forever. We must be very careful not to develop habits which may be harmful to us and to those who live around us. Some of the habits which have to be prevented from being formed are described in the following paragraphs.

(i) Smoking

It causes irritation to the throat and wind pipe and results in cought. Inhablation of cigarette or bidi smoke for long leads to insufficient working of lungs, heart, digestive system and nervous system. It is very easy to develop diseases like pulmonary tuberculosis, or cancer of the throat or lungs and heart trouble. This also causes irritation to their respiratory tract. This means that even if people do not smoke themselves they become susceptible to the same diseases as those who smoke.

(ii) Alcohol

The effect of alcohol on the human body is harmful and therefore its intake should be avoided. It is a narcotic and brings about sleepiness and insensitivity of the nervous system. When we are under the effect of alcohol our body does network properly, and we any slow in reacting to the dangers around us. We cannot think properly and judge what is right and wrong. At times under the effect of alcohol we may even do wrong things. Since alcohol has fuel or energy value, doctors use it under strict conditions for medical treatment. The taking of opium and certain drugs is as dangerous and harmful as alcohol hence these too should be avoided.

Chewing paan or betel leaf is a common practice in India. It contains calcium and is said to have digestive properties. But it has more harmful effects than benefits. It causes is coloration of the teeth, dead taste buds and thickening of the tongue. The betel nut and tobacco used in it ca lead to ulcers in the mouth which can later become cancerous. People who continuously use paan spit frequently and dirty the place around them.

Thoughtless spitting on the road or streets is a bad habit. It not only spreads dirt but also disease specially when the sputum is infected with the germs. The sputum from the patient of Pulmonary Tuberculosis can dry and mix with the air. It can then settle on our food or be inhaled by a healthy person.

Environmental Hygiene

Human beings live, whether in villages or towns, waste is produced. This waste if not removed and disposed in a proper manner can cause soil contamination, pollution of ground water (i.e. from wells), breeding of flies and diseases spread by filth. Also birds and animals like dogs and pigs, who are in search of food will scatter the waste allover and make our surroundings look dirty. Waste is partly solid and partly liquid. Solid wastes which decay and putrefy easily are human body wastes, like urin and faeces; cow and horse dung; waste from meat shop; rotten fruits and vegetables; left over food etc. Wastes which do not decompose easily are ashes, house dust, pieces of wood, iron, glass, pieces of paper, tins, and broken earthenware *e.g.*, jars and pitchers.

Liquid Waste is urine and dirty water from homes and factories. Often we see people using the fields and drains to get rid of their body waste. This is very dangerous for our health. This leads to contamination of vegetables that grow in the fields, pollution of soil, water, air with dirt and parasites like hook worms, thread worms and round worms. We must always use special privies or latrines which should be fly proof, clean and which should not create any danger to soil or water nor spread of any bad smell. The ideal way to dispose human waste is through the water carriage system. But it is only available and possible where we have a good water supply. This system leads to the sewer system as in big towns like Bombay, Delhi, Calcutta, Madras etc. or it may lead to a Septic Tank in smaller places. The sewage is further treated and purified before discharging it into the sea or used for irrigation in the fields. The solid part obtained from this treated sewage is used as manure in fields. In case water carriage system is not possible then we have other types of latrines under the dry conservancy system. This system is supervised and managed by the municipalities. A pail is placed under a seat which receives the human faeces. By means of a trapdoor this pail can be removed, emptied in closed containers cleaned and replaced back. The excreta or faeses are then removed in closed containers or closed carts etc. to a place set aside for disposal. It can be disposed by burning, trenching or composting. Burning is ideal and the safest but it cannot be practiced every where. Trenching enables us to covert it (with the help of bacteria in the soil) into harmless non-smelling material and lastly composing helps us to convert all the solid wastes into manure. By mixing them improper quantities and keeping them inputs or special trenches for 4-6 months manure or compost is formed. This compost is of great value in growing crops. It preferred over the pail type because it does not give bad smell, flies cannot breed, hook worms cannot spread and if we construct them away from the wells or groundwater supply it does not cause soil or water pollution.

The liquid waste from homes like waste water from the kitchen and bathroom can be drained way to the fields for irrigation or into a nearby river or into the sea in coastal area. It should not be allowed to collect and stagnate in shallow areas because it will lead to breading of mosquitoes and spread of diseases like malaria and filarial. It will also stagnate and create bad smell. In every home and at public places we must have covered, rust proof dust bins into which we must throw the rubbish. These dust bins must be emptied and cleaned everyday. The contents of such dust bins are usually pieces of paper, waste from the kitchen, dried leaves, house and road sweeping etc. This waste or garbage can be buried in deep pits away from the homes, burnt or used for making compost or manure. In big towns and places this removal and disposal of garbage is done by the municipalities. Besides proper disposal of waste there are certain health habits which individuals should observe so as to ensure good heath for oneself as well as for other. Good health habits help to keep the environment neat and clean, thereby minimizing the spread of diseases.

Food Hygiene

Healthy practices and good personal hygiene should be

followed by all who handle food. Food borne diseases can be considerably reduced if clean healthy practices are followed in the kitchen. All fresh fruits and vegetables should be washed well to remove dirt, sand and pesticides. Dirty hands with sores or boils should not be used to take food. Also avoid coughing and sneezing on food. Containers and cooking pots should be clean and good water must be used for cooing. Boil drinking water during the rainy season. Food should be cooked at high temperature to ensure that all bacteria are killed. Cover all the food as dust and flies bring infection.

All perishable foods must be kept in a cool place or in the refrigerator. While eating raw vegetables and fruits be sure that it is clean and that the plate and knives etc. are also washed well. When tasting food use a spoon not your dirty fingers. Do not return the spoon into the bowl of food, keep it one your plate. Do not eat mouldy or foul smelling food, also avoid preserved foods from damaged and bulging tins. These foods are harmful for health. When eating out at public eating places, make sue that food is cooked well in clean kitchens and served under hygienic conditions. In he kitchen adequate storage facilities should be present so that all dry and wet ingredients can be labeled and stored away. These should also be protected from insects and pests. Wash you hands before you handle food. Leave the floor, sink and working surfaces clean before you leave the kitchen. These practices help in keeping the kitchen free from insects and pests.

Poultry and Swine Foods

Food gives us energy to work and play. It also gives us resistance against diseases. The main components of food are carbohydrates, proteins, fats, vitamins, minerals, fibre and water. Fruits, green leafy vegetables and other vegetables are rich sources of vitamins and minerals. Your diet should include cereals, pulses, vegetables including green leafy vegetables, meat, fish or eggs, milk and milk products, fruits and nuts. This choice of food would help you to have a proper growth and stay healthy. In this chapter, we will study the components of food, their sources and functions they perform in our body.

Most food items get spoiled after some time and may become unfit for consumption. Proper methods of storage of cereals, fruits and vegetables can help us to maintain their quality. In this chapter, you will also leărn how to preserve food items and ways to prevent their wastage.

Food is absolute necessity for sustaining body functions. Nutrients are the components of food that the body needs in adequate amounts for growth, to reproduce and lead a normal healthy life. All types of nutrient have their own functions to perform, but the different nutrients must act together. On the basis of many such studies, scientists have found that a balanced nutrition is essential for maintaining good health. A balanced nutritional status required that the quantity and the quality of food-intake of an individual should be sufficient to meet all the needs of the body. A balanced diet is that which provides the minimum daily requirement of various nutrients, that is, carbohydrates, proteins, fats vitamins and minerals.

Carbohydrates provide energy needed by our body. They are called energy-giving foods. Carbohydrates are mainly found in cereals and sugars. Fats are found in vegetable oils, nuts, milk and milk products, like ghee and butter.

Proteins help in the building of new tissues and maintenance and repair of existing tissues in the body. These are also known as micronutrients because our body requires them only in small quantities. Vitamins and minerals help in protection of body against diseases and hence they are also known as protective foods.

The evolution from small flocks to large commercial units after World War II was facilitated by rapid advances in the knowledge of nutrition, breeding, housing, disease control, and processing of poultry and eggs, and by improvements in transportation and refrigeration which made possible distant marketing of fresh products. Poultry eggs can be successfully incubated in fan-ventilated incubators by maintaining a temperature of 99.5-100°F relative humidity. Eggs must be turned during the first two-thirds of the incubation period to prevent adherence of the embryo to the embryonic membranes. The duration of incubation, under these standard conditions, for several types of poultry are: Chicken, 21 days; turkey, guinea fowl, peafowl, and most ducks, 28 days; most geese, 30 days; pheasants, Chukar partridge, and Bobwhite quail, 24 days; Japanese quail, 17-18 days; and Muscovy ducks and Egyptian geese, 35 days. Modern incubators are constructed of materials that can be effectively cleaned and disinfected and that provide good insulation of the chamber. Eggs are set in specially designed plastic flats which fit into channels in egg racks that move on wheels. The egg racks are equipped with mechanical systems to tilt the eggs 45°; turning is usually done hourly. Eggs are transferred from the setting trays into hatching trays 3 days before expected hatch. Hatching trays are held in specially designed hatching units much like setter cabinets. After the hatch is completed, the chicks are transferred to a conveyer belt for processing or directly into plastic boxes with absorbent paper pads or into disposable paper boxes with wood fiber pads. Chick servicing often involves sexing, vaccination, and beak trimming. A machine is available for injection of eggs at transfer; vaccines for protection of chicks against Marek's disease can be administered to the 18-day-old-embryos with improved early immunity. Usually, chicks are held at the hatchery prior to shipment to farms, starting early on the day after hatching. Specially designed delivery trucks for buses are used to provide adequate ventilation for chicks during shipment. Hatcheries must be carefully designed for proper sanitation, and adequate air supply to incubators and hatchers. Ventilation air must be cooled in very hot weather and warmed in cold weather. Most hatcheries add moisture to air with humidifiers. Hatchery ventilation systems are designed to prevent movement of contaminated air from the hatching room, chick processing area, or equipment washing area into the dean egg storage or setting rooms.

Breeding

Meat poultry is selected for good meat type, fast growth, disease resistance, and efficient conversion of feed to meat. Different strains of chickens are used for egg production. These are selected for high egg production, large egg size, and small body weight for better conversion of feed to eggs and good livability. The genetic stock used for modern poultry production is produced by highly specialised breeding companies. The body weights of meat and egg production strains are dramatically different. The slow growth and low body weight of the commercial Leghorn demonstrate why these strains have low meat value. Dual-purpose breeds or strains of poultry are no longer used expensively for commercial production. Instead, producers of specialty poultry and eggs (for example, free-range poultry) may still use traditional breeds such as New Hampshire red or Barred Plymouth Rock which were used in the past for both meat and egg production. Commercial poultry breeders usually sell parent stock chicks to hatcheries or integrated poultry companies. In most cases the commercial product consists of female and male parent lines which are crosses. The customer must continue to buy parent stock from the breeding company because the second generation from these stocks would not produce.

Nutrition

Poultry diets consist of common grains and protein sources with mineral and vitamin supplements. Animal or vegetable fats may be added to increase energy and reduce dustiness. Corn, grain sorghum, wheat, oats, and barley are often used for poultry feeding in the United states. Soybean meal is widely used as a protein supplement. Other important protein supplements are meat meal, fish meal, safflower meal, feather meal, and canola meal. Byproduct ingredients (for example, corn gluten meal or brewers grains) are also used in poultry diets when warranted by availability and price. Rations for poultry are typically formulated by computer programmes which compare ingredient costs with dietary requirements.

Swine Production

Swine, as nonruminants, utilize large quantities of concentrate feeds; it is estimated that 30 per cent of the maize grain produced is fed to swine. Swine can utilize only limited quantities of roughage in their diet. The United States produces about one-fourth of the world's hogs. The swine production industry has changed from the status of a supplement to farm income to that of intensified units in which swine production is a major enterprise. The total number of swine producers decreased by 80 per cent from 1950 to 1980, but the volume per unit is increasing sufficiently to maintain the total volume of production. More than 90 per cent of all hogs are from independent producers. The others are produced by the intensified methods of integrated enterprises in modern confinement facilities which require highly trained biological managers capable of applying the principles of breeding, nutrition, physiology, environmental control, and economics. The primary products of swine are pork, lard, hides, and innumerable pharmaceutical by-products. Pork and lard supply about 15 per cent of the total calories consumed as food in the United States. Pork is more successfully cured and stored than many other meats, and it is estimated that about 60 per cent of the swine carcass is cured by various methods.

Breeders of purebred, hybrid, and crossbred swine provide the seed stock for commercial hog production, and are entrusted with the responsibility of changing the carcass so that it better meets the preferences of consumers. 85 recognised Swine breeds in the world and perhaps more than 220 varieties recognized as breeds in certain geographical locations. The pure breeds of major importance in the United States include Berkshire, Chester White, Duroc, Hampshire, Landrace, Poland China, spotted Poland China, and Yorkshire. An example of a meat-type market-weight pig. In European countries, the landrace and Yorkshire breeds are most prevalent. Most commercial producers of swine practice a system of crossbreeding, mating individuals from two, three, or four different breeds, since crossbreeding increases the vigor and feeding efficiency of the offspring. Crossbred dams mated to a boar of a third breed farrow and wean large and heavier litters than purebred dams.

Nutrition

Diets used in feeding programmes in modern swine production units are scientifically formulated to ensure nutrition that is adequate for maximum rate and efficiency of weight gain and for quality of product. In highly mechanized units, mixing and distribution to feeders of diets are computer controlled. Cost of feed represents 50-75 per cent of the total cost of production in commercial swine units. The most critical nutritional period is during the first few weeks of the pig's life. Needs during the other periods of the life cycle—gestation, Lactation, growing, and finishing—are easily met by fortifying natural feedstuffs. Water, energy (derived from carbohydrates, fats, and proteins), amino acids (protein), minerals, and vitamins are essential. Water serves as a medium for digestion, absorption, transportation, and excretion of other nutrients.

Dietary requirements decrease from about 12 per cent of the live weight for young swine to 5 per cent for mature swine. Most of the energy need is supplied by dietary carbohydrate. Fat usually plays a minor role, but supplemental fat is frequently in diets for very young pigs and for gestating (day 100 to parturition) and lactating sows. In general, carbohydrates such as starch, dextrins, disaccharides (except lactose), and monosaccharides are equally metabolizable by a weanling pig.

Lactose is an excellent energy source for the baby pig, but may cause diarrhea in older pigs because of a developmental shift with increasing age in intestinal enzyme activities. Energy requirements are usually expressed as a daily need for total feed or digestible nutrients. Feed intake increases as nutrient requirements for maintenance and weight gain increase. Amino acids required for maintenance, growth, gestation, and lactation, are chemically linked as proteins in feedstuffs. An essential amino acid is one that swine cannot synthesize at a sufficiently raid rate to permit normal growth and activity. Ten of the amino acids in feedstuffs normally fed are classified as essential for growing pigs. Lysine and tryptophan are of most practical importance since most cereal grains (maize, sorghum, wheat) have low levels. Soybean meal is the most common dietary supplement used to correct the amino acid deficiencies in cereal grains. Weanling pigs have special dietary requirements. Cereal grains and soybean meal lack adequate quantities of vitamins and minerals; hence, practical diet normally are supplemented accordingly.

Table 15.1: Mineral and vitamin needs for weanling pigs

Mineral	*Amount*	*Vitamin*	*Amount*
Calcium, %	0.60	Vitamin A, IU/lb(IU/kg)	1500 (3300)
Phosphorus, %	0.50	Vitamin D, IU/lb (IU/kg)	150 (3300
Sodium chloride, %	0.35	Vitamin E, IU/lb (IU/kg)	5 (11)
Copper, ppm	4	Vitamin K, ppm	2.2
Iron, ppm	80	Riboflavin, ppm	2.2
Iodine, ppm	0.14	Nicin, ppm	17.8
Maganese, ppm	3	Pantothenic acid, ppm	11
Zinc, ppm	60	Choline, ppm	890
Selenium, ppm	0.15	Vitamin B_{12}, ppb	15

*IU = International Unit; ppm = parts per million; ppb = parts per billion.

Calcium, phosphorus, sodium, and chloride are normally added as ground limestone, dictacium phosphate or defluorinated rock phosphate, and trace mineralized salt. The salt serves as a carrier for trace minerals, including iron, copper, manganese, selenium, iodine, and zinc. The trace minerals may not always be dietary essentials since they ma be obtained form extradietary sources. Supplemental vitamins are most economically provided as synthetically produced vitamin supplements. Growth promotants (antibiotics and other antimicrobials) are regularly used in pig diets. Usually, the younger the pig, the greater the growth rate response. The amounts used in diets of finishing pigs and gestating and lactating sows should reflect the general health status of the herd. Supplements containing antimicrobials (such as chlortetracycline, oxytetracycline, penicillin, tylosin) are usually added to provide 10-20 ppm in the diet; copper sulfate is also often used in the diet as an antimicrobial.

The specific action of these feed additives has not been completely delineated, but in general, herd health has been improved and the pigs perform more nearly to their genetic potential. Most pig diets are mixtures and usually are self-fed to growing-finishing pigs. This ensures a "balanced" intake of nutrients by the pig. Gestating females are limit-fed liberal amounts to provide adequate nutrition for full milk production.

Mortality of piglets may reach 25 per cent or higher within the first three days after birth, usually due to crushing by the sow, enteric infections, or starvation. Modern climatically regulated farrowing quarters frequently have farrowing crates to help protect the newborn. A newborn piglet is incapable of maintaining body temperature, and is therefore dependent on supplemental heat from the environment. Other biological management practices for the newborn piglet include clipping needle teeth, applying antiseptic to the navel, and providing iron to compensate for its severe deficiency in milk. Since the pig has very limited ability to dissipate body heat by sweating, finishing pigs or breeding stock must be protected during periods of high temperature. Shades and water mists have been used in the past, but modern confinement buildings for finishing hogs and breeding stock minimize environmental extremes. The reduction of temperature extremes encourages more rapid and more efficient gains, particularly in finishing swine.

Diseases

African swine fever, which is similar in effect to cholera, but there is as yet no adequately effective vaccine or curative. Erysipelas, dysentery, letospirosis, atrophic rhinitis, pseudorabies, and transmissible gastroenteritis are some of the other important diseases. Several diseases can be prevented by use of appropriate vaccines or other medication, but specific control has not been realized for many diseases. Swine are especially subject to infestations with ascarids, which are parasites primarily of the intestinal tract that impair metabolism and growth. Following ingestion of the embryonated ascarid eggs by the pig, the larvae burrow through the intestinal wail and migrate through the body causing considerable damage to the liver and lungs. Passing from the lungs to the mouth, the larvae are ingested and develop into mature ascarids in the intestine. Such parasites are particularly prominent in tropical areas. The use of confinement facilities, particularly those with slotted floors, reduces the spread o disease and parasites and allows rapid removal of excreta from the pens, thereby reducing opportunities for contact with the many vectors of the diseases.

European countries where restricted-feed programmes are used, pigs of the same size will be considerably older. About 87 per cent of the market pigs in the United States are barrows (male pigs that were castrated at a young age) and gilts (a female that has not borne young), and the remainder are sows, boars, and stags (males castrated after becoming sexually mature). The market hogs move from farm to the slaughter plants through terminal public markets, country buying stations, and auction markets or by direct sale to the packer. Market grades of a slaughter barrows and gilts have been developed according to a scheme which places a premium on the four major lean cuts: ham, loin, picnic, and Boston butt. In addition, market grades penalize excess ft in the carcass.

Sheep

Sheep were possibly the first animals to be domesticated about 11,000 years ago in southwestern Asia, a time when sheep were closely associated with the religious, civic, and domestic life of the people. They are referred to more often in the Bible than any other animal. Wild sheep range over the mountainous areas of the Northern Hemiphere. They have long, curved, massive horns and mixed coats with a hairy outer coat and woolly undercoat. Although wild sheep vary in size, they are usually larger than domestic sheep and have shorter tails. They are most heavily concentrated in the warmer parts of the temperate zones and are found in greatest numbers in the Southern Hemisphere in Australia, New Zealand, South Africa, and South America. Other countries were there are high sheep numbers include the Soviet Union, China, India, Iran, Turkey and the United Kingdom. Sheep are more common in drier regions and at high elevations. Hair sheep are found in the wet tropics. Domestic sheep were first brought to the Americans by Spanish explorers.

Sheep were introduced into the English colonies almost as soon as they were settled. By 1840, New England and was the center for sheep production in the United States; the center moved westward to Ohio by 1850. This westward movement of sheep continued, encouraged by the availability of year-round grazing, and by 1860 there were many sheep in California and Texas. The sheep population reached a peak in 1884 with over 50 million head. Since then numbers have declined to under 11 million in the 1980s. Sheep are common in the north-central states and from Missouri to Virginia, but the bulk are in the western states and Texas. Sheep are called lambs until about 12 months of age, from which time to 24 months they are referred to as yearlings, and thereafter as two-year-olds, and so on. The female sheep is called a ewe and the male a ram or buck; the castrated male is called a whether. Sheep meat is called lamb or mutton depending on the age at slaughter: Young carcasses, where the forefeet are removed at the break joint or temporary cartilage just above the ankle, are sold as lamb; mutton carcasses are those of older animals where it is necessary to take the feet off at the ankle. Mutton is sometimes less desired, brings a lower price than lamb, and may be used in manufactured meats.

Fish

Fish farms a good resource of animal food. A large section of Indian population use fish as food. Fish is a rich source of protein. Fishes are aquatic animals and their production is called water agriculture or fish farming. There is a good scope of fish production in India. Our inland water areas of about 1.6 million bectares and our long coast line of 6500 kilometers provides a high potential for the production of fishes. The major sea food items include fishes (such as sharks, oil sardines, eel, hilsa, salmon, pophrost, etc.), oysters, musels, shrimps and lobsters. The inland water bodies such as ponds, lakes, rivers and streams are sources of freshwater fishes. These fishes may be captured directly from the island waters or they may be cultured in ponds. Our freshwater edible fish include cat fishes such as wallago, Mystus etc., Indian major carps such as Catla, Rohu, Mrigal and exotic varieties such as silver carp and grass carp. Catla is the fastest growing carp of great economic significance. With the introduction of new techniques of fish breeding (e.g. induced breeding), hatching and growing has resulted in another revolution, called blue revolution, in Indian. During last two decades production of marine fish is increased about 57 per cent but increase of fresh water fishes is about 167 per cent. The eggs (fish seed) are collected from nurseries and hatched in hatcheries. The hatched in hatcheries. The hatched young fishes are reared for meat production. Different types of fish hatcheries meant for the production of fishes, at small and large scales are available to fish farmers all over the country. The central Institute of Freshwater Aquaculture (CIFA), Bhubaneshwar, has made significant advances in breeding and rearing the air breathing cat-fish in a great part of country. Fishes have various predatory enemies. For example, water beetles, water bugs, frogs, snakes and birds eat small and big fishes. Most types of diseases of fish are mainly caused by viruses and bacteria. For example, IPN (Infectious Pancreatic Necrosis) and VHS (Viral Haemorrhagic Septicemia) are well known infectious diseases of the fish. The pollution of water also causes great harm to the fish. When a water body gets polluted, the fishes of all sizes die, all at one time. This forms one of the serious problem for the fish farmers.

Flavouring and Spice

Spices, a unique category of flavourings which are given preferred legal status because of the long history of their use in foods, are pungent or aromatic substances of vegetable origin used in foods at levels that yield no significant nutritive value. Flavour is the perception of those characteristics of a substance taken orally that affect the senses of taste and olfaction. The term flavouring refers to a substance which may be a single chemical species or a blend of natural or synthetic chemicals whose primary purpose is to provide all or part of the particular flavour effect to any food or other product taken orally.

Flavourings are categorized by source: Animal, vegetable, mineral, and synthetic. The sensation of flavour has a chemical basis that involves both taste and smell. The elements of taste consist of sourness, caused by hydrogen ions found in organic and inorganic acids; sweetness, caused by organic chemicals containing hydroxyl, carbonyl and amino groups, for example glycerol, sugars, amino acids, saccharin, hexamic acid salts; saltiness, a characteristic of sodium chloride, but also exhibited by other inorganic salts; and bitterness, which is caused by inorganic salts and some relatively high-molecular-weight organic compounds, such as alkaloids, for example, quinine, tannins, and sucrose octacetate. The taste-producing substances are usually nonvolatile. Sensations of pain, heat, and coolness are also caused by chemicals. Several fatty acid amides of vanilly lamine are responsible for the heat or bite in red pepper. Menthol produces a coolness at low concentrations in the mouth. The astringency that is produced by alum is also produced by tannins from tea and other botanicals. The smell (odor) of a food is judged by the nose as volatile components of the food enter either through the nostrils or through the mouth. The chemical constituents which cause the odor component of flavour therefore are volatile. No simple characterization of basic odors has yet been found such as is available for tastes. Attempts to reduce the thousands of complex identifiable odors to a simple classification have been made, but have not been widely accepted.

Types and Classification

Research involving the chemistry of natural products in the second half of the nineteenth century provided a nucleus of chemicals for use as flavouring ingredients. The reactions studied at that time (Knoevenagel condensation, knorr pyrrole synthesis, Perkins reactions and rearrangements, Kolbe-Schmitt reaction) produce the characterizing ingredients of many spices and fruits. Spices contain the largest concentration of flavour volatiles and were the first to be studied. This early work confirmed the presence of, and the structure of, vanillin in vanilla beans at 2 per cent concentration, eugenol in clove bus at 12 per cent, and cinnamic aldehyde in cinnamon at 1-2 per cent concentration.

The first half of the twentieth century brought a continuous effort to identify the flavourful volatiles in food by classical organic chemicl methods. The many ingredients in citus peel oils and noncitrus fruits began to yield their flavour secrets. Creative flavourists utilized this knowledge and filled in the gaps with information supplied by their noses and their palates. Reasonably representative flavours of the fruits became possible to produce. These fruits contained volatiles which effected their flavour at concentrations of 0.01-0.1 per cent.

The second half of the twentieth century, especially since the application of gas-liquid chromatography, has seen an explosion of information concerning the identity of the volatile components of all flavourful foods. The sensitivity of equipment for detecting ingredients and the speed with which equipment can identify these ingredients has confirmed the complex nature of flavour. Many of the volatiles in the less highly flavoured foods have been examined, isolated, and identified. As many as several hundred volatile organic chemicals have been identified in common flavourful foods. These components range from simple hydrocarbons to complex chemicals with sulfur or nitrogen. While many of these chemicals are not present in sufficient quantities to affect the flavour and some key ingredients have not yet been identified, flavourists have used this information in attempts to prepare artificial flavours. A so-called nature-identical chemical is self-defining. If the flavour of foods were due to stable chemicals, flavours could be made from natural-identical chemicals alone. But the natural flavours of strawberries, grilled hamburger, or roast beef are not stable.

Flavourings can also be classified by their physical form, as solids, liquids, or pastes. The form will be determined by the nature of the flavouring, and the form of food to be flavoured. In the United States most flavourings are processed, since undried herbs and fresh fruits for desired flavour effects are available only on a small scale. Therefore another classification is by method of manufacture. There is general agreement on the several commercial designations of flavourings, indicating the method of manufacture of each and the type of flavours which are available by using ingredients from each category.

Chemical synthesis or physical isolation and include such substances as vanillin, salt, monosodium glutamate, citric acid, and menthol. Artificial or natural, they are only occasionally used alone, and usually are compounded or blended with other ingredients or diluted to achieve a specific flavour character at a workable concentration. Powders are manufactured by dehydrating vegetables, such as onions and garlic, or concentrated fruit juices. These are single ingredients or blends of flavourful (sometimes exotic) foods, spices, and seasonings, some of which may have been derived by fermentation, enzyme action, roasting, or heating. They are usually designed to be added to prepared food at the table (for example, chutney, vinegar, soy sauce, prepared mustard).

Some are completely natural, while others are a blend of natural and synthetic ingredients. These are natural substances that have been dehydrated and consist of whole or ground aromatic and pungent parts of plants, for example, anise cinnamon, dill, nutmeg, and pepper.

Essential Oils

The volatile oils obtained from spices and other plant materials which have the characteristic odors of their sources. They are usually obtained by distillation, although the citrus peel oil are obtained by expression. Essential oils are used in confectionery and beverage industries, and in compounded flavours form any applications.

Anise one of the earliest aromatics mentioned in literature. The plant, Pimpinella anisum (Aiaceae), is an annual herb about 2 ft (0.6 m) tall and a native of the Mediterranean region. It is cultivated extensively in Europe. Asia minor, India, and parts of South America. The small fruits are used for flavouring cakes, curries, pastry, and candy. The distilled oil is used in medicine, soaps, perfumery, and cosmetics.

Cardamon a spice from the plant Elettaria cardamomum (Zingiberaceae), a perennial herb 6-12 ft (1.8-3.6 m) tall and native to India. The small, light-colored seeds, borne in capsules, have a delicate flavour. An important spice in the Orient for centuries, they are used in curries, cakes, pickles, and in general cooking, as well as in medicine. In India the seeds are a favourite masticatory.

Cinnamon is an evergreen shurb or small tree, Cinnamomum zeylanicum, of the laurel family (Lauraceae). A native of Sri Lanka, the plant is now in cultivation in southern India, Burma, parts of Malaya, West Indies, and South America. In cultivation the trees are cut back and long, slender suckers grow up from the roots. The bark is removed from these suckers, dried and packaged for shipping. Cinnamon is a very important spice for flavouring foods. It is used in confectionery, gums, incense, dentifrices, and perfumes. Cinnamon oil is used in medicine and as a source of cinnamon extract.

Clove is the unopened flower bud of a small, conical, symmetrical, evergreen tree, Eugenia caryophyllata, of the myrtle family. (Myrtaceae). The cloves are picked by hand and dried in the sun or by artifcil means. The crop is uncertain and difficult to grow. Cloves, one of the most important and useful spices, are strongly aromatic and have a pungent flavour. They are used as a culinary spice for flavouring pickles, ketchup, and sauces, in medicine, and of perfuming the breath and the air in rooms. The essential oil distilled from cloves by water or steam has even more uses. The chief clove-producing countries are Tanzania with 90 per cent of the total output, Indonesia, Mauritius, and the West Indies.

Coriander a strong-scented annual herb. Coriander is cultivated in many places throughout the world for both seeds and leaves. The two forms are quite different in taste from one another, and both are used for flavour in a variety of foods. Only one species. Coriandrum sativum, is cultivated. Coriander is a member of the carrot family, Apiaceae (Umbelliferae), and is closely related to other spice seed plants such as cumin, caraway, anise, dill, and fennel. A number of distinct cultivars have been developed. Some, with longer maturity times and resulting higher leaf yield, are grown for cilantro, also called Chinese parsley. Other seed-producing types, having a more uniform seed set and types that resist splitting, have been developed in the Society Union and India. The growing of cilantro from seed to a harvestable size takes 40-60 days, and full maturity as coriander 9dry ripe fruit) is reached in approximately 120 days. Coriander occurs as an erect herbaceous plant with one to many stems that reach about 4 ft (1.2 m) In height. When the plant is young, small deeply segmented leaves are formed, but as the plant ages the leaves become more and more divided until they become feathery in appearance.

Cocoa Powder and Chocolate derived from the seeds of the tropical tree *Theobroma cacao*, which grows within a narrow bet along both sides of the Equator. There are three basic varieties: Criollo, which was native to Central and South America; Forastero, which constitutes the bulk of the world supply and is mostly cultivated in West Africa and Brazil; and Trinitario, consisting of various hybrids. The seeds, contained in pods which grow on the trunks and lower branches of the trees, are surrounded by a mucilaginous pulp. They are whitish in colour and have no normal chocolate flavour. Each mature bean is about 2.2.5 cm in length with an average weight not less than 0.04 oz 1g). The shell is about 12 per cent of the total bean weight, the nib 87 per cent, and germ one per cent – the last being the point at which germination would have commenced in the live bean. The main constituents of the dried nib are approximately the following: fat (cocoa butter) 54 per cent protein 12-14 per cent starch, other carbohydrates, and mucilage

20 per cent tannins 6 per cent theobromine 1.3 per cent; caffeine 0.2 per cent and moisture 3-5 per cent. Good-quality beans show a brown or purplish-brown color and striations in the sliced cotyledon. Unfermented beans have a dense structure and slaty color.

A chocolate flavour, the beans are first subjected to a fermentation process. The pods are split open and the seeds and pulp laced in heaps surrounded by plantain leaves or in "seat boxes." Under thee conditions microbiological and enzymatic action occurs, with a rise in temperature to about 120°F. After 4-6 days, during which the beans are turned over, they develop a purplish-brown color, and the outer shell and nib become more distinct. The pulp liquefies and drains away, and precursors of the true chocolate flavour are formed. After fermentation the beans are sun-dried in shallow trays that are protected from rainstorms by sliding canopies; in very wet climates, such s that founding Cameroon, various forms of artificial drying are used. After drying, the product is described commercially a cocoa or cocoa beans and should have a moisture content of 6-7 per cent. A series of well-defined operations are used to produce good-quality cocoa or chocolate.

Machines by a combination of sieving and air elutriation, remove stones, sand, bag fiber, stalks, and immature beans. Without this treatment, grit would pass to subsequent processes, resulting in machine damage and poor-quality products.

Essential process the chocolate flavouris fully developed from the precursors, the shell loosened from the nib, and the moisture content reduced. There are many roaster designs. One type is a rotating drum with external heating, which may handle single batches or have a continuous throughput. Other roasters use high-temperature air passing through a continuous stream of beans. Roasting temperatures vary greatly, ranging from 200 to 300°F. The temperature used is related to the time of roasting and the type of product required. The shell should never be burned. In two-stage roasting, the beans are heated at a low temperature in a closed, moist atmosphere, and then a higher temperature and drying follow. After roasting, the winnowing process separates the shell from the nib.

The ideal is complete separation with full recovery of the nib, but in practice this is not possible. Winnowing machines have been greatly improved. A modern system uses a ban of vibrating sieves with an air lift to remove shell pieces at the discharge end of each sieve.

Dill

It is an annual culinary herb of the carrot family, Apiaceae. It supplies four products: dill seed oil, dill leaf oil, dill seed, and dill leaf. Although all of the dill grown in the United States is one species, Anethum graveolens, a slightly different species, A. *sowa*, is grown in Asia. In the United States, two cultivars are grown, Mammoth and Bouquet. Bouquet is a tetraploid cultivars that was developed by treating mammoth seed with colchicines and then selecting for shorter (2.5 ft or 0.6-1.5 m) and more compact growth habit. Mammoth is a taller, more robust plant growing 4-8 ft (1.2-2.4 m) tall. Other varieties exist, such as those developed in India and Russia, but are not extensively grown here. Dill can be grown in most soil types in all areas of the United States, but most of the production is centered in Oregon, Washington, Florida, and California. Flowering of dill usually occurs 60-80 days after planting, with hermaphrodite and later homogamous flowers being produced. Pollination is effected by insects—primarily bees and flies-but many other flying insects, including wasps, aid in fertilization. Dill seed oil is a pale yellow oil which is steam-extracted just prior to seed shatter, about 105 to 120 days after planting. Dill grown for seed oil production is either planted in rows and furrow irrigated or flat-planted and sprinkle-irrigated. Seeding rates vary from 4 to 20 lb/acre 93.5 to 18 kg/hectare). Most of this production provides oil used in the pickle industry for flavouring dill pickles. Dill leaf oil is little used, and relatively little dill is grown for this purpose. Dill seed is used as a spice, and large quantities of it are imported into the United States. India is the primary producer of dill seed for culinary use. Dill grown for leaf, often called dill weed, is cultivated in a slightly different manner. Seeding rates are 18-22 lb/acre (16-19 kg/ ha), and it is planted in the fall or early spring to retard flowering. Dill leaf I harvested 50-70 days after planting. In the United States, dehydration is accomplished with forced-air dryers. Weed control in commercial plantings is accomplished by use of herbicides, such as Treflan or Prometryn.

Fennel Forniculum vulgare, a culinary herb of the parsley family. It is grown for the dried, ripe fruits or seeds which are used in bread, pickles, liqueurs, and meat sauces and dishes. Although similar in odor to anise, fennel seed can be distinguished by its warm, sweet character. Fennel is one of approximately five species in the genus Forniculum. The plant is an erect, branching, short-lived perennial growing 3-5 ft high. The leaves are three-to four-pinnately compound, threadlike, and 1.5 in. long. Common giant fennel a close relative, grows twice as large but has no culinary use. The three fennel varieties of commercial importance are vulgare, dulce, and piperitum. The variety vulgare is grown for its seed and the essential oil, obtained by steam distillation and known as bitter fennel oil. The variety dulce (finochio or Florence fennel) is grown for four products; seed and leaf for culinary use, the enlarged leaf base for a vegetable, and for the essential oil from the seeds.

Fennel is native to southern Europe and the Mediterranean region and is presently cultivated as an annual or biennial plant in southern and Eastern Europe, India, Argentina, China, and Pakistan. The plants do best in a mild climate and on limey, well-drained soils with plenty of sun. Sown in early spring at 8-9 lb/acre (9-10 kg/ha) with rows spaced 2-3 ft (0.6-0.9 m) apart, the fennel plants are thinned to 8-12 in. apart when established. The ripe seeds are greenish gray and fairly hard. When the plants are harvested, yields are low the first season but increase to 700-1000 lb/acre (800-1100 kg/ha) by the second year. Fennel should be located away from dill to avoid the resulting flavour effects from cross-pollination. Though it is primarily a culinary herb, commercial interest in fennel also lies in its essential oil, bitter or sweet, for cooking medicine, perfumery, and as a masking agent for insecticides and room sprays.

Ginger

An important spice of condiment; also the plant from which it is obtained, *Zingiber officinale*, of the ginger family (Zingiberaceae). The plant is a native of southeastern Asia. It is an erect perennial herb having thick, scaly, branched rhizomes which contain starch, gums, an oleoresin (gingerin) responsible for the pungent taste, and an essential oil which imparts the aroma. The rhizomes, dug up after the aerial parts have withered, are treated in different ways to produce green ginger or dried ginger or dried ginger. Ginger is used in medicine, in culinary preparations (soups, curries, puddings, pickles, gingerbread, and cookies), and for flavouring beverages, such as ginger ale and ginger beer. The plant is grown in China, Japan, Sierra Leone, Jamaica, Queensland, and Indonesia.

The ohemical compound sodium chloride. It is used extensively in the food industry as a preservative and flavouring, as well as in the chemical industry to make chlorine and sodium. Historically, salt is one of the oldest materials used in people's food.

Salt was originally made by evaporating seawater (solar salt). This method is still in common usage; however, impurities in solar salt make it unsatisfactory for most commercial uses, and these impurities also lead to clumping. Salt, freshly produced from seawater evaporation ponds, may contain large numbers of halophilic (salt-loving) microorganisms. These occasionally cause spoilage of meat, fish, vegetables, and hides when salt has been used in preservation. In the United States refined salt is obtained from underground mines located in Michigan and Louisiana. Salt is usually handled during the refining processes as brine.

Vanilla

A choice flavouring obtained from a climbing orchid, *Vanilla fragrans*, a native of tropical American forests. The vanilla plant belongs to the orchid family and is indigenous to southeastern Mexico, where it was used by the Aztecs to flavour their cocoa. In 1510 *vagnuila* first appeared in Spain. Its fruits are pods called vanilla beans. Vanillin (4-hydroxy-3-methoxybenzaldehyde) is the principal component of vanilla, although other components contribute to the distinctive flavour of he extract compared to synthetic vanilla. When they are harvested, the beans contain no free vanillin; it develops during the curing period from glucosides that break down during the fermentation and seating of the beans. The sweating process consists of alternately drying he eans in sunlight and bunching them so that they heat and ferment. Seating boxes are used in Mexico., whereas the shorter Madagascar method starts out by wilting green pods in hot water and uses blankets on which the beans can first be spread out and later rolled up for the enzymatic reactions and fermentation to take place. Further curing and dehydration occur in a warehouse. Periods of 4 weeks to 4 months may be required to develop the proper flavour and reduce the moisture content of the beans sufficiently to prevent molding. Beans can be artificially dried in ovens, but frequently an inferior-quality product results. After curing, the pods are sorted into grades based on quality.

Fermentation of Food

Production of food with the aid of microorganisms, which

may be yeasts, molds, or bacteria. Well-known examples of such foods are bread, cheese, beer, wine, vinegar, some sausages, sauerkraut, yogurt, and cultured milk. This article deals with fermented foods produced and consumed in large amounts by millions of people in Africa and Asia. In Japan, for example, soy sauce (shoyu) is consumed at the rate of 11 quarts (10 liters) per capita per year, and annual production is close to 330,900 gallons (1,252, 600 liters). Production of miso and natto is in the range of 625,900 and 174,200 tons (567,800 and 158,000 metric tons), respectively. Fermented commodities include cereals such as wheat, rice, sorghum, corn; legumes, peanuts, soybeans, pulses; red meat, sausages, pork; milk; fish, shellfish; and plant juices. Fermented food is used as a staple, such as tempeh in Indonesia; as a condiment like soy sauce; as a coloring agent like the red rice used widely in the Far East; and as the bread like product produced in India and the Near East. The food may be a liquid like the fermented fish sauces of Indochina; a paste such as miso made from rice and soybeans in Japan; or a solid, like tempeh, made by the old fermentation of soybeans.

Fermented foods were developed in prehistoric times and are widely produced all over the world. Their continued used results form the mild biochemical changes produced by enzymes. For example, starches are broken down to the sugars required for a second fermentation. In soybean fermentations, protein yields amino acids, and lipases act on the oil. Fermentations produce vitamins and simple chemicals such as lactic acid; improve digestibility, odor, and flavour; change physical properties; and prevent spoilage. Among disadvantages of fermentation is the possibility of food poisoning due to bacteria or molds. Also, some fermentations are slow (taking up to 8-12 months), so e product is always lost.

Among the molds used in food fermentations are Aspergillus, Rhizopus, Penicillium, Neurospora, Actinomucor, Mucor,

Amylomyces, and Monascus. The yeasts incude species of Saccharomycopsis, Zygosaccaromyces, and candida. The bacteria and Bacillus and lactic acid bacteria, including Lactobacillus, Streptococcus, Pediocovccus, and Leuconostoc.

Inoculum

The inoculum or fermentation starter may be of four types. The substrate may be moistened, heatsterilized, and inoculated with a single orgnism. In the commercial production o red rice, a singles species of Monascus is used to inoculate rice, which eventually takes on a reddish-purple hue that parts color to meat and wine. In a second type, more than one strain of a single species is used. Koji is the mold preparation containing more than one strain of Aspergillus oryzae that produces enzymes on rice, what, or soybeans. It is used in a second fermentation to make various types of miso and shoyu. A third type of inoculum contains more than one species of microorganism. Ragi is an Indonesian culture used in various fermentations of rice or cassava. Known by different names in other countries, the dry powder contains Amylomyces, mucor, Rhizopus, yeast, and bacteria. Finally, some substrates contain a complex inoculum in which many different microorganisms of unknown identity are present. An example is nuocmam, a fish sauce. Small fish are packed with salt in earthen containers and allowed to ferment at room temperature for several months. The resulting liquid is removed and used as a condiment much like soy sauce. The salt prevents the development of food-poisoning microorganisms.

Applications

There are countless varieties of food fermentations in the world, sometimes known under different names in different countries and varying greatly in complexity. Of the following two examples, one is quick and simple, and the other slow and complicated. Tempeh is a made by a simple mold fermentation, which is being introduced in the West. Only soybeans are used as substrate. Dry earns are washed and soaked overnight at about 77°F. the seed coasts are removed, and the beans are boiled for 30 min, drained, cooled, and briefly dried. After inoculation with spores of a Rhizopus strain, the beans are incubated for 20-24 h at 88-89°F n plastic bags perforated for aeration. Acid may be added to control bacterial contamination. The fermentation produces a solid cake in which the beans are bound together with mycelium. The product, after being sliced into than pieces and fried in deep fat, is brown and has a nut flavour.

Misoc fermentation is a complicated two-step process. The product is used in seasoning and as abase for soups in the Orient. Polished rice is washed, soaked for 16 h, drained, steamed, cooled and inoculated with the mold *Aspergillus oryzae*. After about 2 days at 82°F with frequent turning, the moldy rice is called koji. Soybeans that have been crushed, soaked in water, drained, steamed, and cooled are mixed with koji, followed by the addition of 2 kg of salt for 15 kg of the mixture and an inoculum of special yeast and bacterial cultures. The mixture is allowed to ferment for 3 months or more and is mashed to a paste for sale.

6

CHAPTER

Environmental Hygiene and Sanitation

Disposal of Waste: Human beings live, whether in villages or towns, waste is produced. This waste if not removed and disposed in a proper manner can cause soil contamination, pollution of ground water (i.e. from wells), breeding of flies and diseases spread by filth. Also birds and animals like dogs and pigs, who are in search of food will scatter the waste all over the make our surroundings look dirty. Waste is partly solid and partly liquid. Solid wastes which decay and putrefy easily are human body wastes, like urn and faeces; cow and horse dung; waste from meat shops; rotten fruits and vegetables; left over food etc. Wastes which do not decompose easily are ashes, house dust, pieces of wood, iron, glass, pieces of paper, tins, and broken earthenware dog. Jars and pitchers. Liquid Waste is urine and dirty waster from homes and factories. Often we see people using the fields and drains to get rid of their body waste.

This is very dangerous for our healthy. This leads to contamination of vegetables that grow in the fields, pollution of soil, water, air with dirt and parasites like hook worms, thread worms and round worms. We must always use special provides or latrines which should be fly proof, clean and which should not create any danger to soil or water nor spread of any bad smell. The ideal way to dispose human waste is through the water carriage system. But it is only available and possible where we have a good water supply. This system leads to the sewer system as in big towns like Bombay, Delhi, Calcutta, Madras etc. or it may lead to a Septic tank in smaller places. The sewage is further treated and purified before discharging it into the sea or used for irrigation in the fields. The solid part obtained from this treated sewage is used as manure in fields. In case water carriage system is not possibly then we have other types of latrines under the dry conservancy system. This system is supervised and managed by the municipalities. A pail is placed under a seat which receives the human faeces. By means of a trap door this pail can be removed, emptied in closed containers cleaned and replaced back. The excreta or faeces are then removed in closed containers or closed carts etc. to a place set aside for disposal. It can be disposed by burning, drenching or composting. Burning is ideal and the safest but it cannot be practised every where. Trenching enables us to convert it (with the help of bacteria in the soil) into harmless non-smelling material and lastly composting helps us to convert all the solid wastes into manure. By mixing them in proper quantities and keeping them in pits or special trenches for 4-6 months manure or compost is formed. This compost is of great value in growing crops. Yet another type of latrine is bore-hole type. It is preferred over the pail type because it does not give bad smell, flies cannot breed, hook worms cannot spread and if we construct them away from the wells or ground water supply it does not cause soil or water pollution. The liquid waste from homes like waste water from the kitchen and bathroom can be drained away to the fields for irrigation or into a nearby river or into the sea in coastal areas. It should not be allowed to collect and stagnate in shallow areas because it will lead to breeding of mosquitoes and spread of diseases like malaria and filaria. It will also stagnate and create bad smell. In every home and at public places we must have covered, rust proof dust bins into which we must throw the rubbish. These dust bins must be emptied and cleaned every day.

The contents of such dust bins are usually pieces of paper, waste from the kitchen, dried leaves, house and road sweepings etc. This waste or garbage can be buried in deep pits away from the homes, burnt or used for making compost or manure. In big towns and places this removal and disposal of garbage is done by the municipalities. Besides proper disposal of waste there are certain health habits which individuals should observe so as to ensure good health for oneself as well as for others. Good health habits help to keep the environment neat and clean, thereby minimising the spread of diseases. It is the duty of each of us to be conscious of these good health habits and to pracise them in daily living.

Good Habits

The health and sanitation practices which all individuals should observe at home and in public places are given below:

- Keep the surrounding area clean by not throwing out the garbage indiscriminately here and there.
- Preventing water from collecting and stagnating at one place so as to prevent breeding of mosquitoes.
- No spitting on the roads and in public places.
- Covering nose and throat when sneezing and coughing.
- Not giving the sick persons's or patient's clothes to dhobi but disinfecting thematic home first.
- Avoiding crowds during epidemics.
- Not eating from hawkers who sell uncovered food

which is exposed to flies and dust.

- Washing fruits and vegetables before eating. These should be washed with potassium permanganate solution during an edpimic
- Not using public towels found in the bathrooms of redcurrants.

Human beings, all over the world, do not eat same type of food. They take a variety of food according to their taste, availability of raw materials ad climatic conditions of that region. For example, (i) fish is more readily available at seaside areas than in hills; (ii) our main food is rice or bred (*chapti*), people living in mountains prefer to eat chicken and meat. The eating of particular set of food items by a person always depends on the taste and availability of raw food materials is called food habits. It is better to change the food habits some times because always sticking to a particular food type of diet due to food habits may cause some deficiencies of essential nutrients and may lead to deficiency diseases.

7

CHAPTER

FOOD TOXINS

Natural poisons which have a great variety of acute and chronic pharmacological effects. Presumably many of these evolved in plants as protective mechanisms against animals feeding on them. Animals in turn have evolved elaborate biochemical reactions and cellular responses for disposing of the toxins or of at lest partially neutralising their effects. Man and many other animals have also learnt by experience to avoid eatings on of the foods containing potent toxins. Some of the most potent toxins are found in fungi which may contaminate otherwise healthy foods.

In the middle Ages suffers made pilgrimages to St Anthony's shrine. It is now known that rye is liable to infection with ergot, a rust or fungus which contains a number of toxic alkaloids. Bager, who with Sir Henry Dale elucidated their chemical nature and pharmacological action, describes in his book both the properties of the alkaloids and the history of the epidemics. Sir Edward Meflanby pointed out that outbreaks of ergotism have usually been associated with times of food scarcity. Deficiency of vitamin a and other factors may well contribute. Outbreaks of ergotism are still occasionally reported from Eastern

Europe, where rye is eaten. Again it must be emphasized that rye is a wholesome food. Poisoning results from its consumption only when he grain is infected by rust. In 1960 a widespread outbreak of a fatal disease characterized by acute enteritis and hepatitis occurred in England among young turkeys which had been fed a ration containing imported groundnut meal. The groundnuts concerned had been harvested, stored and processed under conditions of high humidity. The toxic factors were produced by Aspergillus flavous a mould contaminating the nuts. They are known as 'afltoxins'. Aflatoxins are now known to contaminate many human foods. Thus samples of cow's milk from a dairy frarm in Indian contained 24 p.p.m. Aflatoxins damage the liver ad lead to carcinoma in many animals, the toxic dose in monkeys being 025 mg.kg/day. Affatoxin B, 'Is probably the most potent known hepatocarcinogen, at lest in susceptible species such as the rat and duckling. There has been much conjecture about their possible role in primary carcinoma of the liver in man in Africa and Asia. They are of great Importance in animal husbandry.

The discovery of aflatoxins meant that mouldy food and fodder is not merey unattractive; it may be dangerous. There has followed a period of search for other potentially dangerous mycotoxins, which may be produced by moulds that can grow on foods. Sterigmatocystin from Aspergillw versicoloron maize is carcinogenic in animals but much less potent than the affatoxins. Patulin from Penicillium expansum, which is found in rotten apples and may occur in apple juice and cider, is also carcinogenic, and so are two toxins which Japanese workers have found on rice infected with Pinicikllum islandicum luteoskyrin and cyclochloratine.

The trichothecenes, produced by species of fusarium on mouldy cerels, appear to be responsible for the human disease alimentary toxic aleuklam Russia. Ochrotoxin from Aspergillus ochraceus on mouldy barley has been responsible for kidney disease in swine in Denmark; and zearalenone from Fusarium graminearum causes genital hypertrophy and reproductive difficulties in swine. The full list of my cotoxins is much longer and still being added to. It will take a long time to work our which are of importance in human disease. Meanwhile all mouldy food should be regarded with caution. It would be salutary for the enthusiasts of natural foods to ponder that mycotoxins are more likely to contaminate foods grown and processed without fungicides, presser-vatives and chemical additives. Tares is the traditional English name for the vetches and an old word used loosely for various pulses and legumes. In Biblical times they were poorly regarded. 'But while men slept, his enemy came and sowed tares among the wheat'. Why the sowing of tares was regarded as an unfriendly ac is not wholly clear. The tendrils by which these plants climb up the wheat stalks certainly hamper reaping. But they may also have been known to be nutritionally unsatisfactory. For a long time one species of tare has been deli-berately sown with the wheat by farmers in dry districts of many countries in Asia and North Africa where the rainfall is uncertain. The seeds are commonly sown mixed with what. If the rains are good the wheat overgrow the lathyrus of which little is harvested. If the rains fall and there is a poor crop of wheat, a useful harvest of lathyrus may be reaped. Eaten in small quantities, lathyrus seeds are a useful and valuable food. But if hey are the main source of energy (providing more than 50 percent), a severe disease of the spinal cord may result, causing crippling and permanent paralysis. An excellent account of the disease and the circumstances under which it aroses has been given by a soldier, General Sleeman. A eurotoxin has been isolated from seeds of Latyrus salivus and shown to by P-N-oxalylamino-l-alanine. This substance, known as BOAA, has been found in samples of seeds in amounts up to 2 g/100 g (Nutritional research Laboratories, Hyderabad, 1968). Other neurotoxins have been isolated from seeds of the common vetch (Vicia saliva). The relation between intakes of

BOAA and the clinical features of lathyrism has not been worked out.

In the and regions of North America, horses and cattle sometimes suffer from a neurological disease called 'loco', attributed to eating a particular species of legume, Asralagus mollissimus. There is a further possible explanation of the Biblical suspicion of 'tares'. The seeds of another plant Lolium lemulatum (which is not a legume) commonly get mixed with wheat grown in Ethiopia and Aden. These seeds when ingested produce a condition resembling alcoholic intoxication. The local name for this weed is miscara, and in English 'flax darnel'. Allied vetches, notably the sweet pea, Lathyrus odonatus, when fed to rats, readily give rise to a condition in which there is a marked disturbance of collagenous structures throughout the body, notably in skin and bones and known as osteolathyrism. Osteolathyrism or ocloratism has not been described as a natural disease of either man or animals and appears to have been produced only in laboratory studies.

Bengal and Bihar mustard oil is the chief cooking fat. In the same part of the world epidemic dropsy has been endemic for a longtime. In a series of investigations in which the clues were analysed in the best detective manner, Lal and his colleagues showed that mustard oil was responsible for this disease. The toxin was not present in the oil from the mustard seeds themselves, but in oil from the seeds of a poppy weed (Argemone mexicana). This weed commonly grows in the mustard crops. Its seeds contain an alkaloid, sanguinarine, which is toxic. Sanguinarine inhibits the oxidation of pyruvic acid and, as in wet beriberi, pyruvic acid may accumulate, in the blood of patients suffering from epidemic drops. Other edible oils, such as groundnut oil, can be contaminated with argemone oil.

Ciguatera is an old Portuguese word introduced in 1787 to describe poisoning that arose after eating fish from the

Pacific Ocean and the Caribbean sea. The clinical features are those of an acute neuromuscular disorder with weakness and sensory changes. Most attacks are of moderate severity and the symptoms clear up in a few days, but itching may persist for several weeks and occasionally widespread paralysis is followed by coma and death. Captain Cook describes a typical attack. 5th September, 1774, Cape Colnet, New Caledonia. 'This afternoon a fish being struck by one of the natives near the watering-place, my clerk purchased it, and sent it to me after my return on board. It was of a new species, something lie a sunfish with a large, long, ugly head. Having no suspicion of its being of a poisonous nature, we ordered it to be dressed for supper; but, very luckily, the operation of drawing and describing took up so much time that it was too late, so that only the liver and row were dressed, of which the two Mr. Forsters and myself did but taste. About three o'clock in the morning we found ourselves seized with an extraordinary weakness and numbness all over our limbs. I had almost lost the sense of feeling; nor could I distinguish between light and heavy bodies, of such as I had strength to move; a quart pot full of water and a feather being the same in my hand. We each of us took an emetic, and after that a sweat, which gave us much relief. In the morning, one of the pigs which had eaten the entrails was fund dead. When the natives came on board and saw the fish hang up, they immediately gave us to understand it was not wholesome food.'

A large number of species of fish may be poisonous. Some of these are always poisonous and others may usually be eaten with safety, but are poisonous at certain times of the year. Poisonous fish have usually been feeding on a coral reef; deep-sea fish are generally safe. The toxin or toxins responsible have to been identified. Fish become poinsonous because of factors in their environment which get into their food supply. Jardinhas suggested that the toxins may be organo-minerals. It is possible that natural disturbances in ocean beds may affect the amounts of trace elements in rocks and sediment which become incorporated into organic material and so into the algae and other basic components of the food of fishes.

A toxin, saxitoxin, may be present in plankton, particularly the dinoflagellate Gonyaulax tamarensis which is ingested by vivaleves such as mussles. The toxin is stable and remains in the tissues of the shellfish which appear to be resistant. It is not destroyed by cooking. Dinoflagellates at times multiply to such an extent that they may colour th esea and such 'ed tides' cause a heavy mortality among seabirds, especially shags. Mussels, a delicacy usually safe to eat, may then become toxic. These conditions occur occasionally off the eastern seaboard of the USA and Canada, and more rarely during summer off the coast of Britain between Aberdeen and Yorshire. People who are unfortunate enough to eat mussels at such a time develop neurological symptoms within 30 minutes: paraesthesiae, weakness of limbs, ataxia and vomiting. Death can occur form respiratory paralysis. Other toxins which may be present in seawater fish are described by Bagins *et al.*

Fishermen and their families around the Koenigsberg Haff in east Germany during the period between the First and second world Wars suffered outbreaks of acute paroxysmal myoglobinuria, preceded by severe pain in all muscles. Always on the day before an attack fish, usually eel or burbot, had been eaten. The condition became known as Haff diseases, German investigators concluded that the fish eaten contained a toxin which had entered the Haff with the effluent from nearby industrial works. However, a small outbreak in Sweden affected persons who had eaten burbot from a lake uncontaminated by industrial waste. Berlin sug thiaminase present in the fish the cause, but this seems unlikely. Haff disease is rarely reported nowadays and the toxin responsible remains unidentified.

Ackee fruit (Blighia saptida) grows profusely in Jamaica

and is eaten by large numbers of people, especially children. Yet it is widely credited with being responsible for a form of food poisoning, vomiting sickness' Dr Cicely Williams undertook an investigation of the disease for the Jamaican Government. She was able to study numerous patients and a few out breaks in detail. In some, the symptoms could be attributed to diseases such as meningitis, heavy ascarls infestation and dysentery. Other outbreaks might reasonably have been attributed to staphy local food poisoning. Yet there were several patients in whom no definite cause could be found, despite thorough investigation. A specific poison from the ackee fruit could not definitely ~ be excluded. She concluded that if such a poison were indeed responsible, large amounts would have to be consumed, and the patients must be peculiarly susceptible to the poison, probably because of their poor state of nutrition. Her report confirms previous statements that 'vomiting sickness' rarely occurs except in children who are gravely undernourished. Ackee fruit contains a water-soluble substance a-amino-9-methlene cyclopropanyll propionic acid that causes acute hypoglycaemia and is known as hypoglycin. This substance may well be responsible for many of the clinical features of vomiting sickness.

Brassica is a large genus which includes cabbages, mustard s and rapes. Rabbits and other laborator animals fed large amounts of the raw leaves develop goiter, which may also occur after feeding the seeds. This is due to the presence of glucosinolates and thiocyanates. Glucosinolates act on the thyroid gland like thiouracil by preventing the synthesis of thyroxine. Thiocyanates reduce he concentration of iodine in the thyroid gland. Some of the brassica, notably cabbage, are common human foods, but there is not evidence that when eaten in normal amounts, as part of a balanced diet, they are anything but beneficial.

Cycáds is a high incidence of a form of motor neurone disease and of a disease known as parkinsonism-dementia among the Chamorro people on the island of Guam and nelghbouring Mariana islands. It has been suspected that the traditional high consumption of the seeds of the cycad, Cycad circlinalis, might be responsible. Certainly cycad seeds contain a toxin, cycasin, which in experimental animals is a point heptatotoxin and also carcinogenic. Yet heptatic disease, including crcinoma, I only slightly more common in Guam than in the USA; feeding adult animals with cycasin has not produced neurological damage, and it has not been shown that the victims of amyotrophiclateral sclerosis have eaten more cycad seeds or prepared them in a different way from unaffected islanders.

Spices and flavouring agents contain volatile and essential oils and hydrocarbons which stimulate glandular secretion and may have a weak action on the nervous system. Many of them if taken in large doses have toxic actions. For instance nutmeg, mace and dill contain myristicin. In 1832, the famous Czech physiologist, Purkinje, ate three nutmeg seeds and became delirious and went into a deep stupor. Smaller amounts of nutmeg may cause vomiting and colic. Wormwood oil obtained from an African tree, Artemisia absinthium, with a sweet-smelling wood is used as a flavouring agent in the liqueur, absinthe and in vermouth arid other wines. Its active principle, thujone, stimulates the nervous system arid may cause convulsions. Worcester sauce contains acetic acid, black pepper, garlic and other spices. Several patients who had acquired the habit of' consuming up to one bottle a day have developed severe renal failure, and lit sonic cases renal calculi. Complete recogery may occur when the habit is given up. Some plant foods, including soya bean, contain traces of oestrogens, but the amounts are so small that no adverse effects follow the consumption of such foods. Larger amounts of oestrogens may be present in meat from poultry and other animals, previously dosed wit oestrogens to promote growth. Attention was first drawn to the antivitamns in veterinary practice. Cattle fed on spoiled sweet clover develop a haemorrhagi disease. This is due to the presence in the clover of dicoumarin, a substance chemically related to vitamin K. It produces haemorrhages by causing vitamin K deficiency in the tissues. It is easy to imagine that a dicouniarin molecule could block the action of a vitamin K molecule at the surface of an enzyme system. Synthetic analogues of diocuoumarin are used in clinical practice to reduce the liability to thrombosis. Natural substances can act as antivitamilis by preventing their asorption or by destroying them in the gut. For example in 1936 an outbreak of paralysis developed in silver foxeson a farm in the USA. The foxes had been fed on carp. The presence of a thiaminase was demonstrated in the flesh and viscera of these fish. Additional thiamin both prevented and cured the disease. Thiaminase has been found in several species of fish and also in bracken arid other plants it is inactivated by cooking. Thiamin deficiency due to consumption of thiaminase has not been reported in man. Fish is used as a food in zoos arid nature reserves, as well as III commercial animal production, and those who use it should be aware of the hazard from thiaminase.

Hallucinogenic substances

In 1676 British soldiers engaged in putting down a rebellion in Virginia ate a salad containing the Jimson weed Datura stramonium. Some of them were reported to have been turned into natural fools performing many simple tricks, but they remembered nothing of this when they recovered. The weed contains alkaloids, such as scopolamine which produce hallucinations. Cases of poisoning have been reported recently in 'beatniks' who have eaten the weed for its psychic effects. Children who taste the fruit of the weed may also be poisoned. In Britain an occasional error is the eating of the fly toadstool, Amanita muscaria. This contains muscarine, but only in small amounts. The characteristic symptom of po) I soning is cerebral excitement, which is due to mycetoatropine. Horne and McCluskle describe a young man who was admitted to a Glasgow hospital in a confused arid drowsy state. By occupation he way a salmon poacher and he and his brother used to cat deliberately A. muscaria, because they enjoyed the feeling of unreality and detachment which it gave. Others have become addicted, including apparently the Russian empress Catherine the Great. Far more dangerous is the Death Cap toadstool, *Amanila phalloides*. This is riot easily distinguished from the edible field mushroom *Agaricikv campesirs*. Elliot et al describe a severe attack of poisoning and also give notes on the identification of poisonous fungi. Their patient, a farer who had eaten *Amanita phalloides* in error, was actually ill when admitted to Cumberland Infirmary. He became unconscious. Had watery diarrhoea arid was jaundiced. After 48 hours his urine was suppressed, but with tire aid of the artificial kidney he recovered.

Acid Foods

Oysters, fish, all kinds of meat, chicken, eggs, grins, wheat, nuts (except almonds and brazil nuts), cheese, lentils, peanuts.

Neutral foods Milk, butter, vegetables oil, white sugar.

Naturopaths recommend spring water as a partial treatment in many seemingly unrelated disorders such as kidney stones, prostate enlargement, indigestion and fatigue. These have one possible common cause: over acidity Mineral water, which is rich in alkaline ions, can help to neutralize acidity and purify the body. In Europe, it is common practice to prescribe specific spring waters for specific disorders. Nutritionally speaking, the purpose of fasting is to purify the body by stimulating the elimination of waste substances. Water is a most important part of the process. At least 2 quarts (4 pints) a day should be drunk to help detoxification. Toxic waters accumulated in the body during years of careless eating and living impair the functions of cells and tissues and cause various chronic disorders. When they are eliminated, therapeutic and rejuvenating effects are experienced. Animals fast intuitively; whenever they feel sick, they stop eating until they feel better again. Fasting can be dangerous for people who have a heart or kidney problem, or diabetes. In fact, anyone with a health problem should seek medical clearance before going on a fast. Even without a health problem, fasting for more than three days should only be done under medical supervision. Weight loss is the immediate result of a fast. Up to 3 pounds can be lost during the first 24 hours, provided only water or non-caloric beverages are taken. If fasting continues, the average loss over the next ten days will be 2 pounds per day, the loss, however, is not all fat. Fat accounts for roughly a third of the loss, water for about half, and lean tissue for the rest. Apart from being useful for dieters, fasting can rejuvenate the body and also help to break self-destructive habits such as alcoholism and smoking," Fasting also stimulates the release of growth hormone, the hormone which strengthens our immunity to disease. Some German and Swedish health clinics use fating to treat virtually all degenerative diseases, from arthritis and atherosclerosis to digestive disorders and skin conditions. A distinction should be made between fasting and starvation, "Hunger pangs' are not a sign of true biologic hunger. They are merely gastric contractions which we interpret as hunger; they are a craving for pleasure, comfort and the relief of boredom and can be largely be alleviated by drinking water. Appetite and stomach rumblings cease after two to four days. Then follows a period of about three to four weeks when no hunger or fatigue are felt. This is true physiological fasting. However, when appetite returns, it is a natural signal to break the fast, or else starvation will set in and vital tissues will start to be dismantled to prcvide energy. "Why doesn't the body consume itself in fasting? Because as cells break down, they are very efficiently recycled. The products of cellular breakdown are used to build new cells. Protein levels in the blood of a group of people who walked 325 miles in 10 days while on a total fast remained perfectly normal. However, prolonged fasting on only water has its drawbacks. First, the body has less than 1,000 calories in reserve at anyone time; these are stored in the liver as glycogen and are used up in the first two days of fasting. The body then starts to break down fat for energy, converting it into ketone bodies, such as acetone, acetoacetic acid and betahydroxybutyric acid. These ketone bodies replace glucose as a source of energy, supplying 70 per cent of the body's requirements. The rest of the body's energy needs are derived from the breakdown of lean tissue." However, these processes lead to ketosis and acidosis unless some glucose is taken orally or by injection. Ketosis is characterized by slight nausea, a bad taste in the mouth and acetone ('pear drops') breath. Acidosis usually begins a few days after the onset of ketosis and can be very dangerous, especially in people susceptible to kidney malfunction or diabetes. An additional danger is that as fat is broken down, toxic residues are released into the blood. It is not commonly realized that body fat is a dump for toxins which cannot be dealt with by the liver, kidneys, lungs and skin.

Sodium and potassium are largely depleted during prolonged fasting. Potassium loss can average as much as 1,500 mg a day. This can cause severe deficiencies, which manifest themselves as weakness, lassitude, nausea and kidney problems. Significant amounts of potassium should therefore be taken while fasting. Fasts of one to three days do not normally require medical supervision, but it is advisable to check with a doctor first if you are in the slightest doubt about you r health. If you have never fasted before, start with a one day fast, and see how you feel. What fasts of one to three days achieve is cleansing and quick weight loss of 2 to 6 pounds. Fasting should not be thought of as deprivation, but as a positive act. It rests the digestive system and is a step towards improved health. On rising, only water should be drunk, preferably pure mineral water. It is permissible to squeeze half a lemon or an orange into the water. During fasting, symptoms such as slight fever or chilliness, dizziness or headaches, are not uncommon, particularly in people who have never fasted before. These normally disappear after a day or so. Bad breath, sore gums and a 'coasted' tongue are signs that wastes are being eliminated. Breaking a fast properly is of the utmost importance. Eating should be resumed gradually, depending on the duration of the fast. A day's fast can be broken by sipping a little milk, fresh fruit juice or some vegetable soup and then resuming the normal diet at the next meal. A two or three day fast should be broken by sipping moderately diluted milk, fruit juice or vegetable soup for at least a day. The next day light meals only should be eaten, preferably of fruit and vegetables (fresh orange nice, grapes or an apple for breakfast; fresh tossed salad, carrot sticks, whole bread and butter, and fruit for lunch; steamed vegetables or dried fruit for dinner). A safer and esier type of fast, rapidly growing in popularity, is the raw juice fst or juice therapy. In this regimen, only fresh raw juices of fruits and vegetables are allowed; no solid food is eaten at all. Juices provide plenty of natural sugars, vitamins, minerals and trace elements, an alleviate the stress which accompanies water fasting.

They supply the basic elements needed for body healing and cell rejuvenation," stimulate cleaning, normalize biological processes and, most importantly, eliminate the risk of ketosis or acidosis. As Dr Rangnar Berg Says: 'During fasting the body burns up and excretes huge amounts of accumulated wastes. We can help this cleansing process by drinking alkaline juices instead of water while fasting. I have supervised many fasts and made extensive examinations and tests of fasting patients, and I am convinced that drinking alkali forming fruit and vegetable juices, instead of water, during fasting will increase the healing effect of fasting. Elimination of uric acid and other inorganic acids will be accelerated. A juice therapy now becoming popular in many clinics is the 'grape cure', used to correct numerous disorders arising from toxic overload. Only fresh grape juice is permitted. However, a juice fast need not be restricted to one type of fruit or vegetable. In many sanatoriums, a cocktail of mixed fresh juices is served to achieve various therapeutic effects. Vegetables and fruits should be juiced just prior to their consumption. They must not be peeled or soaked in water. Various types of fruits and vegetables are used in juice fasting, depending on the desired effect. Common ones are apples, celery, carrots, parsley, beets, cabbage, broccoli and kale, Gayelord Hauser, the distinguished nutritionist, has created the "Gayelord Hauser Cocktail." This consists of equal amounts of celery, carrot and apple juiced together.

Classification of Distilled Spirits

Distilled spirits are classified according to (1) the raw material which has been fermented and subsequently distilled, such as grain, molasses, and fruit; and (2) the further treatment given the distillate to add specific flavours and aroma. These are referred to as compounded or flavoured spirits. Examples of beverages made from grain are whiskeys, vodka, and gin. Some types of vodka and gin are made from potatoes. Molasses is used for the manufacture of rum, and sugarcane juice for the Brazilian cachaca or pinga. Fruits are used for the preparation of brandies, and agave juice for Mexican tequila. The so-called compounded or flavored spirits are made from distilled spirits by the addition of sugar, essential oils, color, herbs, bitters, or other ingredients. Examples are English and Dutch gins, various liqueurs or cordials, absinthe, and aquavit.

Fermentation

When starchy materials are to be fermented, it is necessary to convert the starch to fermentable sugars first. This is done by the addition of amyolytic or disastic enzymes from malt or certain fungi. Once the starch has been converted to sugar, mostly maltose and glucose, it can be fermented by yeast to alcohol and carbon dioxide. When wine is distilled the fermentation is carried out by various strains of the wine yeast, *Saccharomyces cerevisiae* or its variety eJlipsoideus. With other sugar-containing substrates, special distillery yeasts may be employed, usually also strains of *S, cerevisiae*, or a natural fermentation by uncontrolled species of yeast is used.

Distillation Process is done in stills of various design. In a simple pot still very little fractionation, or rectification, is accomplished. When a still is equipped with rectifying column, fractions of much higher purity can be collected. Te batch-type distillation is becoming replaced more and more by continuous stills, especially in the production of grain alcohol or neutral spirits. Normally, three types of fractions are separated. A fraction with a low boiling point, the "heads," is rich in aldehydes and esters. The main fraction is ethyl alcohol and a higher-boiling fraction is rich in so-called fuseloils or higher alcohols. The latter consists of D-amyl-and isoamylalcohol, butyl-and isobutlalcohol, propanol, and others. Isoamylalcohol and maylalcohol are the principal ingredients offusel oil. The strength of the ethyl alcohol is expressed by the term "proof." In the United States 100 proof spirit is a spirit containign50% alcohol by volume at a temperature of 60°F.

Various types of distilled spirits are:

Brandies

Brandy is a spirit obtained from the distillation of wine or a fermented fruit juice, usually after aging of the wine in wooden casks. Cognac is a brandy distilled from wines made of grapes grown within the legai limits of Charente and Charente Inferieure Departments, the Cognac region of France. Armagnac is brandy made in the Department of gers, southeast of Bordeaux. Both types of brandy are aged for many years in oak before bottling. Before bottling, various lots are blended, the alcohol content is adjusted to 42-44% and if necessary, coloring matter such as caramel is added. Brandies distilled from grape pomace of the wine press are called *eau de vie de marc* in France and *grappa* in Italy. Spanish brandies are usually distilled from sherry wines and have a distinctive flabour. Quite different from cognac or armagnac. American brandies are primarily products of California and have a flavour different from the European brandies. Whereas in Europepot stills are most common, continuous stills are preferred in California. Apple brandy is called applejack in the United States and is called calvados in france. It is distilled from completely fermented apple juice and aged in oak barrels for 5-10 years; it has a distinct apple flavour. Other fruits from which brandy is made include black, wild cherries (kirsch or kirschwasser), plums (slivovitz from Hungary or Rumania, and quetsch or mirabelle from France), black betrries, and apricots. When stone fruits are used, some of the stones are broken or crushed and a small amount of the oil is distilled over with the spirit, giving the brand a more or les pronounced bitter almond flavor.

Whiskeys

These distilled spirits are made b distilling fermented grain mashes and gain the distillate in wood, usually oak, Examples are scotch whiskey, Irish whisky, Canadian whiskey, rye whiskey an bourbon whisky. Scotch whiskey is made primarily from barley. The barley is converted to malt by allowing it is sprout after which it is dried in a kiln over a peat fire. The malt absorbs some of the smoke aroma which is carried over later with the spirit distilled from it. The drying and roasting of the malt is to a large extent responsible for the flavour of the whiskey. After the malt is made into a mash, it is fermented. Distilled, and aged in oak casks. Thee are often casks in which cherry has been shipped. A Scotch blended whiskey may contain a certain percentage of grain whiskey besides malt whiskey. Irish whiskey is made from malt, unmalted barley, and other grains such as wheat, rye, and oats. The malt is not smoke-cured as in Scotland, and as a result the flavour of the resulting whiskey is different from that of Scotch whiskey. Many types of whiskey are made in the United States. Depending on the principal source of grain, whiskeys are classified as bourbon (corn orgrain), rye whiskey (rye), and others. Blended whiskeys are differentiated from straight whiskeys by a certain content of neutral spirits. American whiskey as are aged for a number of years in new charred white-oak barrels. In all types of whiskeys discussed above, the type and quality of the water used in the plant is an important factor in the quality of the finished product.

Gins

The flavour is imparted by distillation of herbs (distilled gin) or by adding essentials oils (a compounded gin). There are two principal types: English, or London dry, and Dutch (Jenever). English gin is made from pure neutral spirits, which are redistilled in the presence of juniper berries and small amounts of other ingredients such as coriander seekd, cardamon seed, orange peel, anise seed, cassia bark, fennel, and others. English gin is not aged. Dutch gin is made of malt. The flavouring ingredients are mixed directly in the mash, after which it is distilled at a rather low proof. Dutch gins are heavier in body and contain more fusel alcohols and other volatile compounds (congenerics) besides ethyl alcohol than does English gin. Some types of Dutch gin are aged. Dutch gin has a pronounced flavour of its own and is consumed straight, whereas English gin is usually used as an ingredient in cocktails.

Rum

The alcoholic distillate from fermented sugar cane juice or molasses is known as rum. Cuban rum is light-boiled and light-colored. The middle fraction of the distillation, known as aguardiente, is used for making rum. The aguardiente is aged in uncharred oak barriels; it is then decolorized, filtered, and supplied with some caramel to give it the proper color. Occasionally some fruit aroma is added. It is then aged for several more years. Jamaica rum is heavier-bodied and contains more congrenerics (fusel alcohol, esters, and aldehydes) than Cuban rum. Arak is a rum that comes from the island of lava. It is a dry, highly aromatic rum. A natural fermentation of the molasses by various species of yeast also contributes to the flavor of this drink.

Vodka

A product originally produced in Russia but now popular in many countries, vodka is usually made from wheat. It is highly rectified during distillation and thus is a very pure neutral spirit without a pronounced taste. It is not aged.

Cachaca or Pinga is Brazilian spirit made by distilling naturally fermented sugarcane juice in pot stills. It is high in congenerics and sold at various degrees of proof. It is usually not aged.

Pulque and tequila are of Mexican origin. A sweet sapis obtained from agave (century plant an American aloe) by removing the growing bud from about 3-year-old plants. The sap (aguamiel or honey water) is collected and fermented by natural fermentation and is then called pulque. Distilled pulque is tequila.

Liqueurs or cordials are alcoholic beverages prepared y combining a spirit, usually brandy, with certain flavourings and sugar. In fruit liqueurs, the color and flavour are obtained by an infusion process using the specified fruit and spirit. Sugar is added after the extraction is complete. Plant liqueurs are made by maceration of plant levels, seeds, or root with spirit and then distilling the product. Sugar and coloring matter are added after distillation.

VINEGAR

Vinegar, like wine and certain milk products, is one of the oldest fermented foods used by humans. Babylonian records indicate that vinegars prepared from wines and beer were widely used as early as 5000 B.C. It is a food condiment containing mainly acetic acid that is produced by the bacterial oxidative fermentation of various ethanolic solutions.

In the United States, white distilled vinegar makes up over 80 per cent of the annual production. The names for the different vinegars are based on the substrates from which they are made. These include the juices from different fruits, starchy vegetables, cereals, and distilled ethanol. Much of the white distilled vinegar is made from denatured synthetic ethanol. Nitrogen compounds, minerals, and other nutrients must be added to the alcohol medium to support the growth and metabolism of the acetic acid bacteria. Acetic acid or ethyl acetate are commonly used as the ethanol denaturants. Most other vinegars are made from ethanolic solutions generated by a yeast fermentation. Fruit juices usually contain sufficient concentrations of hexose sugars and other yeast nutrients to support yeast growth and fermentation. Cider vinegar is produced from yeast fermented apple juice, wine vinegar from fermented grape juice.

Other juices such as pineapple, orange, and pear, as well as sugarcane syrup and molasses, can serve as fermentation substrates. Vinegar is also produced from starchy vegetables such as potatoes and from cereals such as bareley, corn, and rice. Yeasts do not ferment starchtoethanol. And therefore the starch first must be broken down (saccharified) to simple sugars, mainly glucose. Mal vinegar is made from an infusion of barley malt and other cereals in which the enzymes in the malt have converted the starch to fermentable sugars. Balsamic vinegar from Modena, Italy, is a costly product that is highly prized by gourmets. The juice of Trebbiano grapes is concentrated about 30 per cent by simmering, then fermented by Zygosaccharomyces yeasts that tolerate high concentrations of sugar. A portion of the ferment is transferred annually to a succession of wooden cases, where the acetic acid fermentation and other enzymatic changes occur. The battery of casks may be 200 years or older; thus, the harvested vinegar is of great age. About 2 liters (2 qt) of vinegar are produced from 100 kg (220 lb) of the concentrated grape must. Vinegar sold in the United States must contain at least 4 g of acetic acid per 100 ml of solution (40-grain vinegar). Other federal specifications describe permitted color, odor, presence of trace metals, and alcohol content. Nondistilled vinegars possess distinctive colors and flavors that reflect the properties of the original substrate.

Bacterua

Acetic Acid Baceria belonging to the genus Acetobacter are primarily responsible for the vinegar fermentation. Four species are recognized; they are distinguished on the basis of nutrient requirements, production of brown pigments, and tolerance to ethanol. All acetic acid bacteria require oxygen for growth and metabolism. Gluconobacter is a closely related genus that also oxidizes ethnol to acetic acid. The genus is differentiated from *Acetobacter* by the fact that it cannot oxidize acetic acid to carbon dioxide and water. *Acetobacter* species carry out the latter oxidation, often after ethanol has been depleted.

The production of vinegar

The simplest fermentations are slow and inefficient but are relatively foolproof and utilize inexpensive equipment. Submerged fermenters produce 120-150 grain vinegar in minimal time. But they are expensive and system failures can occur. The fermentation is carried out in a large cask in which holes have been drilled to permit the introduction of air. Screens are used to prevent the entrance of fruit flies. The cask has a spigot for the withdrawal of finished vinegar, and the bung (stopper) contains a tube so that fresh wine or other substrate can be added without disturbing the film of vinegar bacteria. The fermentation is initiated by mixing wine with about 20 per cent fresh vinegar. Although the process is slow and the yields of acetic acid may be under 80 per cent.

Margarine

Hyppolyte Mege-Mouries invented marg in 1869 and won the prize offered by Louis Napoleon for the development of an inexpensive butter substitute. Margarine is now considered a food in its own right and is manufactured in form unknown to butter, such as plastic, soft, or fluid. However, the interrelationships is still acknowledged since margarine is colored, flavoured, fortified with vitamins, and otherwise formulated to have same or similar taste, appearance, and nutritional value as butter. An emulsified fatty food product used as a spread and a bakir cooking fat, consisting of an aqueous phase dispersed in the a continuous phase.

In 1977 the U.S Food and Drug Administrative revised and broadened its margarine Standards of Identity to confirm to the agreements reached by the Codex Alimentarius commission international body of food and legal authorities charged with the responsibility of unifying foods sold in international trade. Margarine produced in the United States must contain not less than 80% fat. The fats and oil must be edible but may be from any vegetable or animal carcass source, natural or hydrogenated. The required acqueous phase may be after, milk products, or solutions dairy or vegetable protein, and must be pasteurized. Milk may be cultured after pasteurization. Vitamin A must be added to yield a finished margarine with not less than 15,000 international units per pound (0.45 kg). Optional ingredients include salt or potassium check for low-sodium diets, nutritive carbohydrate sweeteners, fatty emulsifiers, antioxidants, preservatives, edible colours, flavours, vitamin d, acids, and alkalies. Margarines are formulated by blending two or more fats and oils in proportions designed to obtain the desired texture, consistency, a melting characteristics in the finished product. The various types of components include unhydrogenated or liquid, lightly, moderately highly hydrogenated oils. Meat fats are used in various bakery margarine formulations.

Margarine is produced in continuous-flow equipment oil blend containing the oil-soluble components is held in one supply tank, the aqueous components solution in another. The two component are premixed in appropriate proportions, emulsified, and pumped through an internal chilling unit used in the United States. The margarine emulsion is cooled rapidly in the votator a unit but it of soupy liquid. It is allowed to rest in the static B unit until it become firm enough to be formed into prints for subsequent wrapping. If the margarine is to be filled into 50-lb (22.7 kg) cartons or cans for b, use or into ½ - or 1-lb (0.23-or 0.45- kg) tubs as soft margarine for household use, a working B unit which whips the margarine before filling is substituted. Low-calorie spreads designed to resemble margarine contain only 60% fat. The higher level of aqueous phase in the product require addition of emulsion stabilizers.

Safety and Acceptability

Safety and nutritional value are the two major concerns in accepting SCP. Admittedly, microorganisms may produce toxins and sometimes cause nausea and adverseintestinl and skin reactions. However, to say that all SCP is alway's toxic is as erroneous as to say that it is not. Just as there are toxic and edible mushrooms, there are toxic and nontoxic strains of fungi, yeasts, bacteria, and alge. Actually, toxicity may be a less of problem than nutritive value. Problems concerning the nutritive value include the indigestibility of cell wall material and the excessive levels of nucleic acids. The high percentage of nucleic acids in yeast and bacteria is undesirable because in humans it elevates uric acid to levels associated wit kidney stones, gallstones, and gout. Consequently, wit some organisms extracting nucleic acids may be a necessary step in production of human food. Approval of any novel protein source requires complete information on its toxicity, acceptability, and technological usefulness (incorporation into traditional foods or fabrication of new foods). Evaluation of the product requires appropriate chemical analyses, microbiological examinations, safety evaluations, and studies of protein quality and consumer acceptance. Much progress has been made in solving SCP problems, though not without creating new ones. There are still several controversial issue on the wholesomeness and the nutritive value of SCP as a food. SCP must undergo stringent evaluation and all reservations on toxic and allergenic effects must be eliminated. Yet even if those reservations are eliminated, who basic problems remain: economic and acceptability. The economics of SCP production will be a key issue in determining its success. The price of SCP products must be able to compete with that of the traditional materials they replace. SCP processing requires large capital investments, and one of the factors affecting processing economics is the size of the operation. To be economically feasible, as SCP manufacturing plant would have to produce at least 100,000 tons of SCP per year. The estimated cost of such a plant would be about 20-70 million dollars.

Other factors that affect the economic feasibility of SCP include the availability and cost of raw materials, water, and land. Economics of SCP production would be markedly improved if microbial cell components other than protein could be used simultaneously or if the microorganisms were grown primarily for the production of some valuable metabolite(s) leaving the cell material as by-product. Thus far, SCP is a rather expensive source of protein. A pound of protein from torula yeast costs about two and one-half times as much as a pound of protein from defatted soy flour and about the same as a pound of protein from a soy protein isolate.

To meet the criteria of acceptability, SCP should be unequivocally safe and nutritions and approved by regulatory agencies. It also should have good flavour, texture, and overall consumer acceptance, whether used as a supplement or as an independent food. The development of positive lifetime eating habits amount children is a critical issue. A parent or teacher should not resort to using a punishment reward system when trying to get a child to eat. Nether should each mealtime become a war zone. The following suggestions may help in establishing the proper habits for children.

8

CHAPTER

Some Exercises and Yogasanas for Good Health

The body and for making it vigorous and agile, two types of exercises are necessary—one aerobic exercises which take more air and oxygen into the system so that various parts of the body can draw strength there from. Walking, running, cycling, swimming, skipping etc. are some of the examples aerobic exercises. Second are those exercises which not only strength and extend your muscles and joints but also massage your glands, sense organs and other parts of the body. In this category Yogasanas are the most important. Exercise improves the blood circulation and more oxygen burns away the toxicity of the blood. Digestive system is strengthened and the expulsion of toxins proceeds vigorously. All parts of the body, its sense organs and glands gain strength and becomes active. You must exercise for a minimum of three days a week and normally for six days a work. Exercise should be done in open air with half naked body. Exercise should be stopped about one hour before a major meal and should be started only after two hours of such a meal.

In the beginning take ten or fifteen deep breaths so that the different parts of the body get a notice of the coming activity. Rubbing various parts of your body with a rough towel also improves blood circulation and the skin becomes vigorous and beautiful. In some of the western countries this very work is taken by rubbing the skin with a dry brush. This can cause various problems also but there is no problem in rubbing the body with a dry rough towel. In the morning and at bed time, while changing clothes you may rub the body with a dry rough towel for 4-5 minutes each time. This will strengthen the nervous system also. A lot of research has been done in some of the western countries as to how much exercise you should do everyday and what type of person can be considered healthy. It has been found that if an adult can run 2.4 kilometers in 12 minutes, he may be considered a healthy person. In case of men above fifty and for all women, even covering. 2.0 kilometer in 12 minutes may entitle them to a certificate of health. The researchers on the basis of the oxygen inhaled in various exercises.

Table 8.1:
Maximum permisssable pulse rates

Age group	*Minimum required Pulse rate per minute*	*Maximum permissible pulse rate per minute*
20 year	100	150
30 years	100	140
40 years	100	135
50 years	95	130
60 years	95	120
70 years	85	110
70 years above	80	105

How much exercise should one do, this question can be looked at from a different angle also. Our oxygen intake is to a certain extent related to our pulse rate also. And the pulse rate goes up with exercise. If pulse rate is above a certain minimum only then that activity can be considered an exercise. Again the pulse rate should not go beyond a particular limit otherwise it may be dangerous. These two pulse a rates are given below for different age groups.

Persons in the above age groups have a normal pulse rate between 70 and 80 per minute. If while undertaking some activity, their pulse rate remains below the rte given in minimum required pulse rate, then that activity ma not be considered as an exercise. It is only when the pulse rate is above that of column I that you can be considered doing exercise. If you exercise for 20 to 30 minutes each day with a pulse rate above that given in minimum required pulse rate per minute, it could be considered as a adequate.

While exercising, keep your own body limitations in view. Do as much as is convenient to do. Then increase those distances, speeds and durations gradually. Your capacity will automatically increase with practice. If today you can cover 2.4 kilometers in 18 minutes and if you go out for a walk and run everyday, it is not difficult that you may start covering that distance in 14 minutes within a year and in 12 minutes within a year and a half. Walking is the best exercise.

Walking is like taking an internal bath. It is also a mental bath. Sights and sounds change as you walk. Your lungs take in fresh air and along therewith your mind takes in fresh thoughts and ideas. A new perspective continues to emerge. For exercise, walk continuously for 20 minutes at a stretch at least. Walk briskly and vigorously, breathing deeply and rhythemically in pollution free areas. Morning walks are the best. Emerson says in his journal of 1836, "In the morning a man walks with his whole body; in the evening, only with his legs". Nietzche says in his "Maxims and Missiles", "A sedantry life is the real sin against the Holy spirit. Only those thoughts that come by walking have any value." Walk, Walk, Walk you must. While walking, both your arms should continue to move in a natural manner. This movement strengthens the muscles of heart, lungs, chest and back. After walking, in importance come running, swimming and cycling. Any way, every exercise is good.

Yogasanas are the foremost amongst exercises for your muscles and joints and for massaging your other body organs. Yogasanas are for keeping the body healthy and mind peaceful. These asanas were developed thousands of years ago on the basis of the practice of centuries and are very useful for the physical, mental and spiritual development of man. Asanas provide exercise to the glands, muscles, ligaments and nerves, and help them to keep in good health. The objective of the Yogasanas is to make this physical body an appropriate temple for he abode of the soul.

Asanas may be practiced in the mornings or evenings on an empty stomach or after a drink of water, tea etc. Asanas should be practiced only after one hour of a refreshment or after three hours of a major meal. Asanas should be done in a clean airy place where there are no insects and no noise either. Spread a folded blanket on a level ground and practise on it. Facing east or north you benefit more from the electromagnetic system of the earth. During asanas always breathe through he nose. Never stop breathing. Always breathe normally unless otherwise directed. During asanas there should be no tension on your face or in other limbs. Breathing should not be laboured. It would be better if you do jalneti before starting asanas. Dress should be light, loose and airy. Basically, Yogasanas are considered to be 84 in number; but they have hundreds of variables. There is a fixed process for practising each asana.

The procedure of some of the important asanas in brief:

Padamasana

Stretch both the legs straight in front. Bend the left leg at the knee joint and holding the foot with the hands place it at the base of the right thigh with the heel being near the naval. Thereafter bend the right leg, holding the right foot and placing it over the base of the left thigh with the heel again being near the navel. Place both hands in gyan mudra on your knees. Keep the entire back straight and erect and neck and head in lien with it. The eyes should be closed but inwardly gazing at the tip of the nose. Those not used to sitting on the ground, will, in the beginning, feel lot of pain in the knees. With practice this pain gradually subside. In this pose also the body is relaxed. Mind is alert and attentive. Blood circulation improves in the spinal and abdominal regions. Cues stiffness of joints.

Vajrasana

Kneel on the floor, keeping the knees together and the feet about 40 cm (16inches) apart. Soles of the feet should face upwards. Buttocs should ret on the floor. No part of the body should be on the feet. Wrists should be on the knees with the hands in any mudra. Keep the back, the neck and the head erect and in one line. This pose may be practiced after the meals to remove heaviness in the stomach.

Sarvangasana

Lie on the back with hands by the side of the legs. Tighten the knees, palms facing downwards. Bend the knees and move the legs towards the stomach. Exhale slowly and raise the hips begin supported by the hands, with the arms bent at the elbows. Trunk should be perpendicular to the ground and the chin should be touching the chest. Hands should support the middle of the spine and the legs should be stretched straight with toes pointing upwards. Hold for four to five minutes. Gradually increase this time to ten minutes. Breathe normally, gradually slide down while exhaling. This is the mother of all asanas. It is good treatment for most of the common ailments. It brings back lost vitality. Due to the chainlock, nerves are smoothened. The system is freed of toxins and constipation vanishes. People with hypertension should first do Halasana before doing this pose.

Bhujangasana

Lie with the face downwards. Keeping the feet together, extend the legs. Knees should be tight and the toes pointed. Keep the palms on he ground near the pelvic region. After inhaling, press the palms and pull the trunk upwards. Keep the body lifted with the pubis in touch with the floor. The entire weight should be on the legs and palms. Contract the anus and buttocks and tighten the thighs. Breathe normally. Revert after thirty seconds while exhaling. This pose helps restore the position of the spinal discs.

Dhanurasana

Lie with the face downwards. Bend the knees upwards. Take the arms back and hold the left leg at the ankle with the left hand and the right leg with the right hand. Exhale completely, raise the knees above the floor pull the legs and lift the chest off the floor. Do not join the legs at the knees. The body takes the shape of a bent bow, the arms and hands acting like a bow string. Lift up the head. Pull it as far back as possible. The abdomen should bear the entire weight of the body on the floor.

Salabhasana

Lie with the face downwards. The arms should be stretched back. Simultaneously lift the head and chest, legs and arms off the floor. Only the abdomen rests on the floor. The ribs should not rest on the floor. Thigh muscles should be contracted. The raised legs should touch each other at the thighs, at the knees and also at the ankles. Keep normal breathing. Retain this pose as long as convenient. This pose is good for digestion and for reliving gastric problems; imparts elasticity to the spine, helps the slipped disc and the prostate glands.

Gomukhasana

Sit with legs stretched in front. Taking support by placing palms on the floor, raise yourself, bend the left leg backwards at the knee and sit on the left foot. Lace the right thigh over the left one with the right foot also going under the left thigh. Raise the right arms over the head, bend at the elbow going down towards the centre of the back. Lower the left arm, Bend this also at the elbow and raise the forearm up behind the back. Try to clasp the hands together. It will be difficult in the beginning but with continuous effort you will succeed. Keep the head erect. Practice for about 30 seconds in the beginning.

Paschimottanasana

Sit with legs stretched in front. Extend the arms and catch both the big toes between the thumb and the first two fingers of the two hands. Pull the head and the neck backward. Bend the elbows, bring the trunk forward and touch the knees with your forehead. Stretch the neck and the trunk so that you touch the knees with your nose and then with your mouth. After sometime, try to hold the sole of your feet with your hands and bring your chin to touch the knees. In the initial stage you could even rest the elbows on the floor while holding the big toes. While taking every nee step, first exhale. This pose helps all the organs of the abdomen, the whole spine and improves digestion.

Savasana

This pose appears to be very easy but in reality it is difficult to practice correctly. Lie on your back like a corpse, with your hands a little away from the body, with palms facing upwards. Keep the heels together with toes apart. Close the eyes. Start deep breathing but it should be fine and slow. During exhalations, there should be no feeling of warmth of the breath at the nostrils. Relax completely. The jaw should be loose. There should be no movement of the pupils of the eyes. Pacify the mind. Given auto-suggestions for inducing perfect relation. Stay in this pose for about 5 to 10 minutes. This pose removes the fatigue and quietens the mind.

Rest and Relaxation

Rest and relaxation is necessary for every physical being. Already discussed the subjects of nutrition, elimination of the reuse from the body and also about the exercise to invigorate it. But if you keep this body machine always on some job, it would not last long as an efficient unit. Now discuss how to rest the body for optimum results.

Sleep: is a natural attribute of the body. It is during sleep that the body refills the Aakasha element from the atmosphere. That element removes the fatigue. Body has three stages of waking, dreaming and deep sleep. A healthy body false asleep quickly. If it takes you long to fall asleep, then in all probability your body and mind are not altogether well. Their health will have to be re-established. If the sleep is full of dreams, it is indicative of the restlessness of the mind. Because of this restlessness, replenishment of the Aakash element is low and the body is not fully refreshed. The mind will, therefore, need to be rested and pacified. In deep sleep even the mind goes to sleep, thee is reformation of ells and the body becomes agile. Our objective should, therefore, be to go into deep sleep. The Aakash element's abode is in the inter celluar space. When you over-eat, the pressure is exerted to throw this element out of those infinitesimally small spaces. Under such circumstances there is no question of replenishment of that element. The result is that you do not get up from sleep, refreshed. Go to sleep at least two hours after the meal and let the dinner be light. Before going to bed wash your feet. Sometimes before sleep put your feet in hot water for sometime. This will induce sleep early and it maybe deep sleep. Due to the heat of the water. Inter cellular spaces expand and there is more room for the Aakash element to fit in. In the morning you will get up more refreshed. A hot bath before going to bed will induce similar result.

After lying down if you mentally recite the holy name, peace will come to you. If you directly link this recitation with inhaling and exhaling, deep sleep will not take long to come. Try it.

To induce sound sleep, take plain hot cup of milk before going to bed. This has been the age long practice in rural India. Dr. Julus Segal of the Institute of Mental Health U.S.A. has indicated that milk contains large amount of the amino acid Tryptophan. When this amino acid was, during research, given to volunteers, they fell asleep in quick time and spent longer period in deep sleep. Even animals have been given large does of this amino acid as a sedative. So take a cup of plain hot milk before going to bed. It will be emotionally soothing and is likely to help you in moving your bowels also easily. If milk is not your cup of tea, try herbal tea before going to bed. Goat milk has greater sedative effect than cow milk. A biomedical device called EEG records brain waves. When one goes to sleep, the rte of pulsations changes from 20 per second to 5 per second. When you dream, the brain wave pulsations increase to 10 per second. Less the number of pulsations, more is the rest left by your system. The brain pulsation decreases even with the closing of the eyes. In sleep, you must aim at deep sleep where the rte of pulsation is the lowest. A mild activity in the evening triggers the need for rest resulting in quick and good sleep. Sleep is therapeutic. When we sleep we give nature a chance to do its normalizing, harmonizing and balancing work, without interference form our conscious mind.

Tension is probably the most common probably the most common cause of poor rest. Have a simple stretch before retiring. Pull upwards with hands raised as if trying to reach the ceiling. Hold on to that position and tighten muscles for a few seconds. Push your shoulders back and hold there for a few seconds. Use other methods as indicated a little later to reduce tension before you actually go to bed. Your bed should be hard. Use only a hard mattress. These days you can get hard mattresses of even foam and coir. If that is not available sleep even on a wooden plank with a small cushioning. By so doing you will save yourself from back ache even in old age. In the natural way of sleeping, there is no place for a pillow. But if it is difficult for you to sleep without a pillow then reduce its size so that it is no thicker than your wrist. With a smaller pillow, at night there will be comparatively greater flow of blood towards you head thereby developing your intellectual capabilities.

You should avoid lying on your back. If you have every to sleep on your back, place some pillow like article under your knees. While sleeping, the pose of your body should be just like the pose of an unborn child in the womb of the mother. Sleep on your side with knees bent inwards. You should change sides at night. It is beneficial to sleep on your left side when you go to bed. It is the sleep that you get before mid-night that helps you the most. On waking do not rush out of bed. At that time blood circulation is concentrated towards the head. If your rush out, the blood has to rush from your head down to your legs and this can, sometimes, even make you feel dizzy. Before arising, yawn, stretch your legs, your arms, interlock your fingers and press. Take a deep breath. Move your shoulders, and toes. Even when you start a car, you idle the car for some time before taking off. It helps the engine of the car. Similarly you idle your own body for some time.

It helps the heart to adjust. How long is it necessary or appropriate to sleep? In this connection no definite indication can be given about the number of hours you must sleep. Much will depend upon the type of sleep you get. In deep sleep your battery gets recharged sooner and in dreaming the rte of recharging will be comparatively slower. Even then, under ordinary circumstances, for an average type of person, seven hours sleep is considered sufficient. Children need much more sleep and the old may not get even that much. Out of this, if you can sleep for about half an hour during the day, it has a very positive effect on your health and on your energy Bank.

Nature has given you a life force which is ever engaged in preventing disease and keeping you healthy. That life force stops working as soon as the body stress exceeds ordinary limits. This excess of stress, therefore, immediately creates symptoms of increase in blood pressure and heart rate, release of fatty acids and sugars into the blood stream, muscle tension or disturbance of digestive processes. Adrenal and thyroid glands which are always striving to maintain a constant environment inside the body are stimulated and create the above symptoms. It is consequently very necessary that ways and means of removing that stress and of relaxing the body may be found which remove that extra stress so that your life force may again become active and restore your health. You have first to create awareness of a problem, then find out what the problem is, think of the ways of solving that problem and then create a mental reassurance that it will be solved. Then alone you are on your way to removing the stress. Body stress is the creation of your mind.

So the first thing to do is to pacify the mind. If you sit for contemplation and mediation, the use of oxygen and the metabolic rate go down and the blood pressure also goes down. It has been noticed that those who regularly sit for medication, do not suffer distress. So meditate. Again, sit with eyes closed and dream yourself to be at a particular place, a place where you had been before and make a mental picture of all that you had seen and get the same joy again. Mentally transporting yourself in this manner will immediately reduce the tension. It is the nerve force which is the attribute of the mind in the same ay as the circulation of blood is of the physical body. When the nerves get soothened by re-enjoyment of a known type, stress is bound to disappear. Think of those person whom you love or who love you. Mentally be with them. Love them the way you would, if they were by your side and see its effect on you. Contract the muscles of the effected parts of the body and then relax them. Repeat a few times. Simultaneously breathe slowly and deeply. When a child is tense and cries, the mother takes the child and rocks it. If you have a rocking chair, get into that chair and rock. Rocking will reduce the tension.

Laughing boisterously is the best way of reducing tension. But may people cannot even think of laughing when they are tense. Laughing boisterously is the best way of reducing tension. But many people cannot even think of laughing when they are tense. Singing classical songs, singing devotional songs, reciting mantras, sitting in the company of saintly persons and even playing with beautiful children greatly reduce tension. Devotion to God and remaining silent for a period of time also reduce stress.

When the body is over wrought in any manner, take cool water or butter milk, and if you sip that water slowly, stress will decrease. Also by practising savasana, taking spinal bath or by keeping cold bandages on the forehead you can reduce tension considerably. Apply pressure on never endings such as exist on the tips of your fingers. Massage the web structure between the thumb ad the first finger of the left hand for some time. All thee helping reducing tension. Eating a whole apple has a soothing effect on the nerves because of the pact in which the apple rind contains. In today's world excessive stress is your greatest enemy. Past is gone and the future is uncertain.

9

CHAPTER

Suggestions and Preventions for Good Health

Good habits are valuable for maintaining good health. Such habits start developing from early childhood ad remain with us forever. Even bad habits can develop during this period and persist forever. We must be very careful not to develop habits which may be harmful to use and to those who live around us. Some of the habits which have to be prevented from being formed are described in the chapter.

During the day, when you are not doing anything special or whenever you are free, take special benefit of that leisure time in doing some light exercises, which are imperceptible, which reduce tension , which strengthen the muscles and which take only a few seconds each.

For example:

(1) While standing or sitting, draw the abdominal muscles in, tense them, keep that way for some time, even hold the breath for one or two seconds and then slowly and gradually relax them.

(2) Slowly lower the left ear so as to touch the left shoulder.

Then lower the right ear slowly so as to touch the right shoulder. Then raise both the shoulders slowly so as to touch both the ears, thereafter slowly take the shoulders down as far as be possible.

(3) Turn the head slowly from one side to the other.

(4) Move the shoulders forward, backward, upward, downward, and at times in a circular motion. Sometimes slowly and sometimes quickly. You can give similar exercise to your other limbs also. All possible variables need not be described here.

Preventing Cold

Once a cold has you in its grip, you can only take steps to make it more bearable. The main question, therefore, is how to avoid catching a cold.

1) The body should be maintained in an alkaline condition. It will then be resistant to cold causing germs which prosper in an acid environment. Excess of alkinlinity should also be avoided. Diet consisting of all kinds of meat, eggs, cereals, fats, oils, sugar is acid forming. So are plums, prunes, dried peas, beans and pulses. All other fruits ad vegetables and milk products are alkaline forming foods. Fatigue, worry, stress and all emotional upsets produce acid condition. A good alkalaizer is baking soda. Sip a few glasses of water with a tea spoon of baking soda added to it. This will help prevent a cold.

2) In cold weather dress appropriately. Do not carry wet clothing on your body. Take off heavy clothing soon on arrival back home.

3) On the very first sign of a coming cold, take mega doses of vitamin C. Some scientists swear by its efficacy in preventing cold.

4) Cleanse you nasal system with Jal—Neti and practise Nedi—shodhak pranayana every day as explained in detail elsewhere in this book. Yoga experts claim that if you action thee procedures every day, you will not catch cold ever. Practise Ujjay praynayam also.

5) Complete elimination also helps in fighting a cold. Take enema, if necessary.

6) Colds and flu generally start with a sore throat. To avoid a sore throat situation, gargle with saline water once or twice a day regularly during the dangerous period. Take honey with a tea spoonful of juice of fresh ginger. It improves throat condition. Beat white of an egg, if you are a non-veg, add to it lemon juice, honey and 2—3 drops of glycerine. It is a good expectorant for cough and cold. Take a tea spoonful of this two or three times a day. Take garlic, raw union, vinegar, honey and lemon. Put a small piece of crystal sugar in one side of your mouth and let its juice go in the throat will be lubricated and coughing will no be that uncomfortable. Press the middle pahaiange of the middle finger to set body electricity to work on the improvement of the throat. At night apply warm oil to the throat and a bandage around the neck. It will help the throat condition considerably. Look for knots on the arm bone in line with the thumb, within 25 cms (10 inches of the base. At night apply a little oil and rubhard that portion of the arm three or four times. Knots will be reduced and the throat condition will improve. Repeat two or three times.

7) Rest is important for preventing and even treating a cold. During rest, balance is restored to the nervous system. Fasting will also help. Drink lot of liquids.

8) Practice line mudra as detailed in the first chapter. It

will produce warmth and will help in fighting cold and cough.

9) With reference to the pressure points, press the joints near the ends of the middle fingers. This is likely to help you with your cough. Pressing the lower parts of the thumbs and the webs between the thumbs and the index fingers will also help infighting the cold. Also pres the points for lung, throat and pituitary glands.

10) To stop water flow, apply lightly coconut oil or any other light oil with the finger insider both the nostrils upto one or two centimeters. The flow is likely to stop immediately.

High Blood Pressure: Improper food and environment are the two main causes of high blood pressure. Lack of exercise, stress, obesity, smoking, diabetes and kidney malfunction can also cause blood pressure to rise. In body chemistry terms, imbalance in acid—alkaline ration causes high blood pressure. Blood pressure is higher in cold weather and lower in warm weather. When you go to higher altitudes, you blood pressure is likely to rise. Some of the common symptoms of high blood pressure are pounding headache, tension, insomnia, raised temple arteries, flushing of the skin, ringing in the ears, ankle swelling, heart palpitation and some times, even pain in he heart region. What actually happens is that arteries become narrow and hardened and the heart has to exert greater pressure to pump the same quantity of blood within the same time. Heart pumps the entire quantity of blood through the circulatory system once every seven minutes approximately. To maintain normal blood pressure, follow suggestions made hereunder:

1) Reduce salt intake. Salt increases the water retentive capacity of the body and that causes higher pressure. It can even cause edema. Do not, However, delete salt absolutely out of you diet.

2) Reduce sugar intake. Sugar is all calories. It adds to obesity and higher blood pressure.

3) Reduce food with higher cholesterol in your diet. Cholesterol adds to the deposits in the arteries, narrowing them still further and thus requiring the heart to pump blood at higher pressure. This will mean reduction in the intake of all kinds of meat, eggs, fish, processed cheese, whole milk, butter and other whole milk products.

4) Reduce food with higher uric acid content in your diet. If kidneys have more uric acid, the blood is not properly purified. This continues to lower the efficiency of the kidneys. Blood carrying all those impurities has to be pumped at higher pressure to complete one round within the normal time period. This should mean reduction in the intake of all meat, fish, kidney, beans etc.

5) Garlic is both a marveleous food and a miracle medicine. Doctors Bordia and Bansal have established that garlic juice reduces the cholesterol level in the human body and significantly reduces the blood pressure in hypertensive persons. Take crushed raw garlic every day. Gulp it down and follow it up with a glass of water. One or two cloves from a bulb should suffice. Fix your own dose on the basis of experience. Garlic normalizes the blood pressure, reducing it is case of hypertensive persons and increasing it in case of persons with low blood pressure. If for any reason you are unable to take raw crushed garlic, take garlic pills or garlic capsules. If you have hypertensive tendencies, garlic is the answer to your problem.

6) No drug treatment has ever arrested or cured hypertension. It must, however, be admitted that drugs do moderate the intensity of the affliction for the time being. It would be obvious, from the above discussion that for

a person with hypertensive tendencies, vegetation diet is better. With respect of food, attention may be paid to the following points:

(a) Vitamin B complex and calcium have calming and relaxing effect. Note the uses of vitamin E with respect to better circulation of blood.

(b) Soyabean lecithin lowers cholesterol. This is better than egg lecithin.

(c) Vitamin c also removes cholesterol from arteries and body organs.

(d) Potassium helps release the water from the body. It is found in abundance in green leafy vegetables, dried nuts & fruits and tomato juice. Extra zinc in the diet help slower blood pressure.

(e) Vitamin B6 lowers blood pressure by controlling the sodium-potassium balance.

(f) Cucumber, water melon and water melon seeds are good kidney cleaners. Parsley and asparagus also help clean kidneys to remove blood impurities. Blood pressure is thus reduced.

(g) Apple, grace and cranberry juices, apple cider vinegar in water, as also honey and lemon in water, help reduce blood pressure.

(h) Whey i.e. the scrum or watery part of milk that is separated from the coagulable part of curd especially in the process of making cheese, is very good for changing the intestinal flora for the better. It is rich in lactose, minerals and vitamins and acts as a mild laxative. It is good for reducing high blood pressure. In western countries powdered why is available form health stores.

(i) Avoid smoking. Tobacco constricts the arteries.

(j) Avoid heavy meals. Heavier the meal, the higher it takes the blood pressure.

7) Mud bath once a week helps in such cases. Mud bandage on heart region for about 30 minutes gives instantaneous results.

8) In colour therapy blue, green and yellow are the colours for hypertensives. Blue clothes, blue colour of walls and massage of blue charged oil over forehead beck and heart region helps. Taking green charged water on empty stomach and before meals helps reduce blood pressure.

9) Exercise is necessary for regulating blood pressure. Walking is the best exercise. Sometimes stand relaxed. Then contract all muscles for 5—6 seconds and let go. This instant exercise helps considerably. Brushing massage is a very important exercise which gives disproportion ate advantages. Body brush, a small spongy stone or the inside fibrous frame of a dried gourd may be used for rubbing the body. It will open all pores for elimination of toxins and for intake of oxygen. It will provide blood circulation even to the minor blood vessels near the skin and thus directly reduce blood pressure.

10) When blood pressure rises suddenly, take enema. The blood pressure is likely to come down within half an hour. Warm baths lessen the vescority of blood and thus lower blood pressure. Hipbath in cool water also helps.

Diabetes

Diabetes is a chronic degenerative disease. It is caused by disturbance of the metabolism of the whole body and of its hormonic balance. Diabetes mellitus, the commonly known diabetes, is of two types. Insulin dependent juvenile diabetes often occurs in children and young adults when the cells that make insuline stop working. Non insulin dependent diabetes occurs were body makes some insulin but is unable to use it effectively. When glucose is unable to enter the cells, it builds up in the blood stream. The tendency to develop diabetesis believed to be genetic, Type-II non insulin dependent diabetes has an incubation period of 15 to 20 years before it becomes manifest. Besides heredity, diet and obesity are the main causes of diabetes. Liver disfunction could either be the cause or result of diabetes. Pancreatic insufficiency, caused by stress, nervous exhaustion, consumption of refined food, coffee, alcohol and smoking are among the more common causes of diabetes. It is very important that level of sugar in blood stays relatively even. Too little starves the cells of energy and too much disturbs the body's chemical balance. Hypertension, high cholesterol and kidney disfunction are risk factors in diabetes.

Frequent urination, weight loss, fatigue, nausea, thirst and hunger are symptoms of Type-I diabetes. These and muscle wasting, dry skin, itching, tingling of hands and feed, blurred vision, slow healing of cuts and constant drowsiness are symptoms of Type-II diabetes. Natural approach for control of diabetes consists of activation of pancreas by providing proper nutrition, proper exercise, acupressure, hydrotherapy and colour therapy. Yoga asanas could effectively massage and lubricate pancreas into meaningful action. Internal Availability of insulin has to be supplemented by the intake of such foods which contain insulin like substances.

Avoid sugar, honey, sweets, syrups, glucose, jam and molasses. Also avoid ice-cream, cakes, pastries, sweet biscuits, chocolates, soft drinks, condensed milk, cream and fried foods. Roasted peanuts are not good. Raw peanuts could be taken. Salt intake should also be limited. Use of Caffeine and alcohol must also be reduced. Total caloric intake must be controlled. Dr. Charles Wellet believes that "Weight reduction can bring this incurable disease closer to complete remission than any medication." Dr. J. Anderson found that diets high in fiber lowered insulin requirements. Complex. Carbohydrates take longer to breakdown into glucose. The fiber slows that breakdown every more. There is thus a more gradual release of energy into the body.

Fat tends to block the natural action of insulin. Avoid saturated fats. Prefer skimmed milk. Use cottage cheese made at home. Use non-stick cooking utensils to reduce the use of fats.

Bitter gourd contains high dosage of "plant insulin". It is the best missile in food therapy for diabetes. Take its juice. Take it as a vegetable with seeds.

Fenugreek seeds are commonly used in India for controlling diabetes. Effectiveness of these seeds is mentioned in Greek and Latin Pharmacopoea and also in Ayurvedic literature. A tea spoonful of these seeds can be gulped daily with a glass of water.

Jambu fruit is very effective in preventing and treating diabetes. Off season, the stone of this fruit is powdered and can b taken 2-3 gms a day.

Garlic, soyabean and food rich in potassium also invigorate panceas. Grapefruit, onion, lemon, neem leaves, black gram turnips, Bengal gram, sauerkraut, Parsley tea, almond meal, artichoke, brewer's yeast, pectin, yogurt and butter milk are some of the other foods which help in controlling diabetes.

Vitamins A,B,C & E as also chromium help in this behalf. Exercise reduces the trigly cerides and LDL in the blood. When you exercise, you send oxygen to panceas also and thus you stimulate your pancreas to function better. Physical action burns blood sugar as fuel and lowers its body level. Walking is the best exercise. Heel toe walk and other exercises also help.

Hydrotherapy affords a thoroughly rational method of treating diabetes by increasing the effectiveness of pancereas and increasing circulation to the relevant parts of the body. Warm shower on abdomen, hot baths, heat producing stomach bandage, cold friction, sitz bath, cold friction bath, and hot and cold compress are some of the effective ways of hydrotherapic treatment. IN colour therapy, take green charged water in the morning on an empty stomach and before major meals. Orange colour breathing helps. Rub sun charged organge water on the abdomen and cover it with red colour cellophine paper. Sun charge leaves of jamun tree in green and organge bottles and take a teaspoon of each with orange charged water.

Under acupressure press points in the centre of the palms in alignment with the bottom of the ring finger and on the soles of the feet, on third from the base of the toe next to the big toe and two thirds up from the heal.

Meditaton, gogic nidra and other relaxation techniques assume importance in control of diabetes. To prevent foot trouble wash feet occasionally and keep them warm. Waabetics should keep their extremities warm. In case of cut to the skin, do not take it carelessly, proper skin care is very important for diabetics. Use fatted soaps so that the skin remains lubricated. Be specially careful about your eyes because blood vessels in the eyes are likely to show effects of diabetes early.

Arthritis

Arthritis is generally caused by deficiency of calcium, hydrochloric acid or malnutrition, by obesity, physical stress or glandular, insufficiency. Osteo arthritis is a wear and tear disease associated with aging. Some call arthritis a disease of toxicity, the remedy lying in fasting to eliminate wastes.

Rheumatoid arthritis is generally the result of allergy or hormonal imbalance or lack of raw foods in your diet. Chronic joint disability is caused by the degeneration of the joint tissues due to nutritional deficiency problem and these deficiencies generally arise when one or more glands are not functioning properly. Arthritis in some cases could be hereditary also.

Body has great need for calcium and calcium foods. Acid is needed to dissolve calcium so that it does not turn into deposits. Assimilation of calcium will not take place without the presence of acid in some form. Calcification takes place only when hydrochloric acid is low in stomach. Mega doses of vitamin C—ascorbic acid will make an appreciable difference, so will the taking of pantothenic acid (vitamin B5). The food should also be rich in calcium and vitamin D. Bone-meal tablets may be sucked. Other foods which help in protecting you form arthiritis are honey with lemon in water, honey and apple cider vinegar in water, bananas, brewer's yeast, wheat germ, pecans, avocados, cherries and cherry juice. Naturopaths have found that taking one tea spoonful of concentrated germfree dietry sea water from health stores also helps fight arthritis. Foods high in vitamin B6 and vitamin E or their supplements are also good for arthritis. So are grapes, grape juice and asparagus. Other nutritionists recommend deletion of tomatoes, egg plant, pepper and tobacco from the diet. Grape fruit juice may also be deleted from the diet, if you feel arthritis coming.

Special importance is given to the juice of both stalk and leaves of celery in countries where this is available It contains such minerals lack of which predisposes a person to arthritis. It has a high and special type of sodium content which breaks down calcium deposits causing the affliction. Celery juice, if unpalatable, could be taken with carrot juice. Cucumber juice is a good substitute for celery juice in countries where celery is not easily available.

Alfalfa is a potent detoxifier. Take alfalfa concentrate. It contains oil soluble vitamins, proteins and chlorophyll. Alfalfa tea made with the seeds, not the leaves, is specially recommended. Cook the seeds in an enamel or glass pan, not metallic, for half hour with the lid on. Let it simmer and not boil. After cooking, strain the liquid of a golden colour. Add honey to taste. Refrigerate and take 4—5 cups a day. Continue for 2—3 weeks at a time.

Exercises help considerably in keeping arthritis away. Walking is the best exercise for this purpose also. Swimming comes next. You should do flexibility exercises also including stretching of limbs and gentle movements. Arms may be extended and moved to provide motion to the shoulder joints. Wrists may be moved clockwise and counter clockwise. Similar motions my be provided to other joints also. Squeezing a wet towel or heavy cloth is also good for forearm muscles and elbow joints.

Many yoga asanas have curative effects. Sarvanagasana (whole body pose), Gomukhasana and Ardh Matsyendrasana which have been recommended for lung conditions may be done for the arthritis of the dorsal region including the lower back. Besides, Padmasana would also help. For arthritis of the shoulder joints, practice of Halasanas would also be effective.

Deep muscle massage is recommended in case of arthritis. Crippling problems are in the muscles and not in the nerves. Their degeneration is due to lack of circulation of blood. No muscle is dead as long as you live. Thee may have become fibrous because of the deprival of the blood as well as the ritual electrical energy. These muscles have to be massaged back to active life. Reach the muscles next to the bones by digging your fingers deep into flesh in the affected part. Work on them and press them into a mass as if you were preparing dough. Work across the muscles and not along them, with a deep motion. Pain will be caused but it cannot e helped. You have to bring the degenerated muscles into action.

Glandular insufficiency and hormonal imbalances are some of the causes of arthritis. Press the reflex buttons of the pituitary, pineal, gonad and the adrenal glands. Apply a steady pressure on those points with your fingers. Those points which are sensitive to the touch may be pressed again and massaged with the fingers. In case of the knees, feel soft spots above the knee, one of each side, where the knee bone ends. Press and hold with the maximum pressure for about five seconds each time. Now locate two press buttons at the indentation just below the knee bone, one on each side, and press hard for about five seconds with your thumb and middle finger. Repeat thrice. Apply these pressures almost daily in the beginning. As things improve, reduce the frequency gradually to once a week.

Hot and cold treatment has great relevance in cases of arthritis. If such a condition seems imminent use wet bandage therapy. First wet the cotton cloth bandage in hot water, rinse and apply round the affected part. Above this bandage tie a woolen dry bandage of that size tightly. After about four minutes remove them. Wet cotton bandage in cold water, rinse and tie round the affected part for two minutes, covered as before with the woolen bandage on top. Repeat hot and cold bandages for four or five times, ending with a cold bandage. Let the last cold bandage with a tight overlap of the woollen bandage remain in position for about half an hour while you go about your normal work within the house. This is a method of shock therapy in an attempt, among other things, to get the uric acid released. In those days take care of your food and take only such foods which are low in uric acid so that the body can take effective care of the uric acid thus released. Application of dry or wet heat to the affected parts also provides some relief.

The midst of action on all the above suggestions, please do not forget that "Mind Power" is really the main miracle medicine and wonder food for arthritis.

Asthma, Bronchitis and other lung conditions:

Respirator problems are, these days, being aggravated by air pollution. On the first appearance of the danger signal, preventive action may be taken on the following lines:

1. Ensure diaphragmatic brething as already discussed under the caption of "Aakash element". It merits repetition here. This system of breathing alone is natural and can be learnt from an infant in deep sleep. With every inhale the abdomen goes up and with every exhale it goes down. This alone will improve your respiratory problems by almost fifty per cent.

2. Do not sleep on the back or on the abdomen. Sleep on the side with knees drawn in i.e. In the pose of the unborn child in the womb of the mother.

3. Daily practise: (a) Jal—neti kriya, (b) Bhastrika pranayam, (c) Nadi shodhak pranayam and (d) Ujjayi pranayam. These practices will put the breathing papparatus of your body in good shape.

Exercises are Purse your lips as if you are going to whistle and exhale as slowly as possible. Empty yourself completely before inhaling deeply again. Practise for five minutes at a time.

- Blow up balloons. In the beginning blow slowly for four or five minutes at a time. Gradually increase the rate of blowing and the time.

- Lie on a slant board with head downwards for sometime. That helps reverse the pull of gravity on the entire body and allows better circulation of blood into upper parts of the lungs.

Yoga—asanasa are Sarvangasana for two or three minutes every day. Bhujangasana salabhasana Dhanurasana Arhd

Matsvaendrasan Pause for half a minute between one asana and the other. End up with Savasana.

The various pressure points in your body working as off—and—on switches of its electrical system. Human body is energy held together by the pranaas i.e. the life force. Pressure at certain points restores the energy flow to a particular body system or function. For improving lung condition, the following reflexes may be pressed.

(a) Point below the neck where the collar bone turns upwards. Press down and firmly inward thrice for five seconds each time. Follow this with a massage of that portion for 15-20 seconds.

(b) Two points on the temples between the eyes and the ears.

(c) Eight points on the back, four on each side on the vertebral column, the first two, just above the point where the first rib joints the vertebral column, the second two on the third rib, two centimenters each from the centre of the spine, the next two on the fifth rib about three centimenters each from the centre of the spine and the last two on the seventh rib about four centimeters each from the centre of the spine. The pair of opposites should be pressed at the same time. These pressures centered atone spot each will have to be applied by another person employing both the hands.

It is important to avoid tension, stresses and fatigue. Be relaxed, Remove other causes like smoking etc. If certain articles cause allergy, either avoid those or try to develop immunity.

Avoid starchy refined foods and cattle milk Reduce intake of acidic foods, fats, fried foods and heavy protein diet—Avoid foods rich in potassium also. These conditions may be caused due to nutritional deficiencies. In distress, for short time, high doses of vitamins A and D and of bonemeal have been found to be effective. Vitamin E helps improve the distribution of oxygen to various parts of the body vitamins E and C help to relax the muscle walls of the small bronchii. These two vitamins also help in removal of excess muscus. Vitamins E and C could be taken in high doses even for a few weeks at a time with good results.

Use of honey is very effective in such situations due to its moisture absorbing ability. It draws moisture and has thus fatal effect on germs. Venegar heals serious lung infection and so does apple cider vinegar. Grape juice eliminates effectively the excess mucus and phlegm. Use of garlic is extremely important for such conditions. If fresh raw garlic cannot be taken for certain reasons, it may be taken in the form of garlic pills or capsules. Dosage may be fixed by yourself on the basis of your body reaction. A healthy body taking appropriate quantity of garlic will not smell.

Cut thin slices of raw onion and spread honey on each of those slices. Cover them and let stand overnight. The resultant syrup taken a teaspoonful twice a day is known to help in asthamatic and other similar conditions.

Cranberries are also known to be of help in these conditions. Cook or mash them into pulp and take with warm water in sips. Asparagus also helps. Use cranberries and asparagus liberally. Turmeric is considered a wonder food for asthma by some ayurvedic practitioners. Take it with honey or warm milk. Sweet yogurt taken in the forenoon inhibits production of histamine which produces the symptoms of allergy.

Tea made from amla leaves and tenugreek seeds, raw banana cooked as vegetable, juice of red cabbage made into a syrup, saffron used in various preparations, figs and munaka, soybean milk, juice of bitter gourd all help asthmatics. Pineapple juice dissolves mucus.

Relaxing of the facial muscles relaxes the airway muscles. So just smile and relax your facial muscles. Inhaling certain vapours also helps. A combination of eucalyptus oil, peppermint and clove oil is said to be good. A few drops of this combination could be added to a vaporizer to produce a mist for inhaling. Diluted sea salt could also be added to the vaporizer.

Back Pain and Other

Pain is a distress signal from nature. On receiving the very first signal look for the cause. It could be either a soft bed, wrong type of chair, uncomfortable shoes or trouble in the feet, bad postures, lifting weights the wrong way, high heels which throw the spine out of alignment, stress, emotional problems or most important of all, poor nutrition or lack of exercise can also cause back ache. Take care of the following points:

a) Sleep on a hard bed. The bed should be firm enough so that the spine does not sage as you lie on it. These days you can get hard coir or foam mattresses. In western type beds a firm board can be inserted in between the mattress and the spring to give it the required hardness.

b) Sleeping posture should be correct. A chair that is too deep or too short in the set is not good for the back. One should be able to sit with one's back almost straight and perpendicular to the ground. Change your chair from time to time.

c) Check you feet. A minor foot problems such as corn can effect your walk and eventually your back. In correctly fitting shoes can cause many foot complaints to affect your walk and eventually your back. You should make it a point to shop for shoes late in the day. Your fee expand as much as half a size between morning and evening. Avoid wearing of high heal shoes which are not comfortable. Heals should never be so high as will keep the spine off the normal alignment.

d) Stress can cause back ache. When under severe stress, break off from whatever you are doing for fie to ten minutes and take a walk to stretch your muscles. Long drives are bad for the back. Stop oftener to relax in between. In case of emotional problems, meditation may help. While standing, head may be moved forward and downwards, then interlace your fingers behind the neck and slowly raise the head till you are looking straight upwards. Hold for 10-15 seconds. Repeat three to four times.

e) Even when the spine has been restored to the correct alignment, it may not be able to maintain and retain that alignment due to weak and floppy muscles. The weakness of the muscles and the tissues may be due to poor nutrition. To strengthen muscles and ligaments you need calcium, vitamin E and manganese. Vitamin C in 500-1000 mg per day and vitamin B complex also help. Take food rich in these vitamins and minerals.

f) Most of the back aches are due either to very stiff or very weak muscles. Exercise is needed to remove the stiffness and also to strengthen the weak muscles.

g) Yogasanas are eminently suited for this purpose. Sarvanagasan, Bhujangasana, Salabhasana Dhanurasana, ardh Matsyendrasana, are recommended in this behalf.

10

CHAPTER

SPIRITUAL DEVELOPMENT AND MENTAL HEALTH

Mental health very important for maintenance of physical health. If the mind is restless, agitated, perverted or perplexed, it canto provide proper guidance to the sense organs. Whole body system gets upset. Sage sage Patanjali has, in his Yoga Darshan, emumerated five ethical dicipines, 'Yama', and five rules of conduct, 'Niyama' which control the passions and emotions and keep a person in harmony with his fellowmen. All great men consider the following these rules and disciplines is necessary to keep the mind healthy and at peace with its environment. Not causing hurt or injury of any kind to any living creature in daily life by thought, word or deed is called non-violence. Violence is a state of mind. It arises out of fear, weakness, ignorance or restlessness. It is only when these defects are removed that non-violent state of mind could develop. Non-violence is more than a negative command not to kill or hurt. It has a wider positive connotation of love. One who has imbibed the spirit of non-violence opposes the evil in the wrong doer and not the wrong-doer. Non-violence brings with it freedom from fear and freedom from anger. When one believes that one is different from the physical body, then follows freedom from fear of death also. Non violence brings a state of mind where one accepts justice for a wrong done by oneself while for a wrong done by another, there is forgiveness. A spirit of love for everybody and everything results when you follow the ethical discipline of non violence.

Truth: it means perfect truthfulness in thought, word and deed and complete abjuration of falsehood. Strength comes when mind thinks thought of truth, tongue speaks words of truth alone and the whole life follows patterns of truth. Then whatever escapes the lips of such person becomes a fact, a truth.

"Asteya" – Non- stealing: freedom from desiring in thought, word and deed what others posses or enjoy is called "Asteya". From such a desire arises the urge to convert and then an urge to steal. One may reduce one's physical need to the minimum, believing that if one collects things one does not need, one is depriving others of the same and is, therefore, a thief, freedom from craving brings greater freedoms and all temptations are warded off. One who follows this discipline rigidly starts considering oneself as a trustee of all that one owns or possesses and starts using that wealth in the service of mankind.

"Brahmacharya": It means life of celibacy, self-restraint and of religious pursuits irrespective of the fact whether one is a bachelor or married. It also means a disciplined sex life but not the negation of marriage. In marriage one experiences more intimately human love and happiness .Divine love is an expansion of that. This discipline brings vigour to your body and lustre to your personality.

"Aparigraha" – non hoarding: Parigraha means hoarding and holding. Not to hoard or collect is Aparigraha. Sages contend that if one hoards or collect things, it directly implies that he has neither faith in himself in the munificence of God. In chapter 9 verse 22 of Gita, Lord Krishna assures the devotes,

" those who worship Me alone with single minded devotion

in a disinterested spirit and are ever united in thought with

Me, I bring full security to them. I shall supply all their

Wants and shall protect them for ever."

Similar guarantees have been given by other incarnations like Jesus Christ. Have we the faith and the devotion which bring such guarantees in their wake?

Rules of Conduct

Purity of body is essential for physical well being. The cleansing and purity of the mind is more important. So is the cleaning of the intellect of impure thoughts. Purity of thought, word and deed comes form the purity of food that is consumed and also from the purity of the means used for procuring that food. Purification by elimination of the unwholesome promotes happiness and one-pointedness f mind. Restlessness is replaced by detachment and the journey starts on the way to self realisation.

Contentment is that state of mind in which one fully accepts as adequate all the wealth, lands, food and glory etc. that are available at that point of time and does not yearn for more. One feels the lack of nothing. Desires are fully under control. This happens more often to motivated persons who are one pointed in pursuit of the final goal.

Concerted effort to achieve the ultimate objective of this life is called tapas. This effort may involve serious austerities and penance. Purification and rigid self discipline are necessary parts of this effort to achieve spiritual heights. Non violence and continence are the tapas of the body. Recitation of the glory of the Lord, speaking the truth and having a wholesome system of address are the tapas of speech. Developing a mental attitude wherein one remains balanced in joy and sorrow is the tapas of the mind.

Observance of these ethical disciplines and rules of conduct will purify the mind, give it added strength and will make it at peace with itself. Mental health will be established. Mind will then be in a position to make the best use of the life force in getting things done effectively by the physical body and by other parts of the astral body.

Food has great impact on your mental health also. The proverb "Thoughts are made of the food you consume" shall ever remain true. Pure and fresh natural food in its original condition is the best for your mental health.

Meditation: You have to bring the senses somewhat under control. Practice of the rhythmic control of breath, as indicated earlier, is to be followed by concentration exercises. Swami Vivekanand says, "if you concentrate your thoughts on the tip of your nose, in a few days you will begin to smell most beautiful fragrance—to show you that there are certain mental perceptions that can be made obvious without the contact of physical objects." The reaction of the senses to external objects may be stopped. The mind may be freed from intrusion due to your sensory activity. The mind may not stop experiencing external phenomenon but may experience it through its own power of concentration and not through the media of the senses. This obtaining of mental impressions, according to Swami Vivekanand, is the first psychological stage in the concentration of the mind.

It due course when the flow of concentration is uninterrupted that is the state of dhyana i.e., meditation. Uninterrupted flow of concentration for 12 seconds is called 'dharna'. When such a state of complete absorption lasts for 144 seconds, it is dhyana i.e. meditation. First decide on the object of meditation whether it be a deity or a thing. Next, you should gain so much knowledge about that object that you are appreciative thereof. Thereafter when you sit in meditation, you feel the presence thereof, then the mind becomes pointedly concentrated thereupon. This is followed by a feeling of void—a void in which the feeling of peace transcends all other feelings. The mind then becomes like a lake which is tranquil and without any ripples. Everything gets reflected as from a mirror. For meditation, sit in Padamasana (lotus pose), Siddhasana or Vajrasana in the way prescribed for practice of asanas. If you cannot squat comfortably, sit on a chair with a straight back and a firm seat. Practise Gyan mudra. Decide upon the object of meditation whether it be your own deity or a lotus, a rose, a bright spot, figure of aum, name of your deity or even some sound. Close your eyes and think of that object—always the same.

It would be better if the time of meditation and the place of meditation also remain the same. Practise Nadi shodha pranayam and then recite mentally the mantra i.e., the holy name, which you have adopted for yourself. Repeat it two or three times. Then practise Ujjayi pranayam and concentrate your mind on the tip of the nose and inhale and exhale. Thereafter keep the mind concentrated on inhales and exhales but let the thought be centred on your feet and let that centre of concentration travel upwards upto the top of your head.

Spiritual Development

Aim of this life is the riddance of all pain and unhappiness and the realisation of permanent bliss. This realisation can come only when you are in the human garb because only then one has the intelligence to discriminate. For consideration and study of this subject, it is necessary to know as to whom am I, what is the soul, what is this world and what are the obstacles and hurdles in the way of knowing thyself and how could those obstacles and hurdles be removed, so that one could have realisation of permanent bliss. Brahm is the divine source of the universe, the eternal spirit, and which, in common parlance, is called God. The essence of all Vedas is contained in Vedanta. Those who know have given the essence of the Vedanta in four

Sanskrit words which can be translated into the following four phrases.

Here the word "that" means Brahm, the divine source of the universe, the Soul force which is known by some as God, by some as Parmatma and by others as Parmeshwar, Wahe guru, Allah, Ram and by thousand and one other names. That supreme consciousness cannot be known through inert sense—organs. That Brahm is the Truth i.e. Existence, Consciousness and Bliss. It is complete in Itself and unique by Itself. There is no other force elsewhere. Everything partakes of it. It is realized by itself alone. It can not be known by the sense-organs in the same way as a mute water pump of iron cannot known or describe the electricity which runs it. The Guru i.e., the spiritual guide, preceptor and the scriptures say that you are the Suland with the help of the meditative and contemplative sight, the soul sees itself. If a person with eyes shows the moon to another person, the person can see that moon if he has the eyes but if he has defective eyes, he cannot see it In the same way the Guru and the Scriptures point towards the Soul, a contemplative pupil gets to know about it and become scapable of making others experience that phenomenon.

Shakespeare has very nicely sung in Hamlet:
"What a piece of work is man, how noble in reason,
how infinite in faculties.
In form and moving how express and admirable,
in action how like an angel.
In apprehension how like a god
the beauty of the world
the paragon of animals"

Pascal in his pansees has el described man, in his earthly form "for in fact what' is man in nature? A nothing in comparison with the infinite, an All in comparison with Nothing, a mean between nothing and everything." We have to rise and realize our position, realize ourselves. "Man is at the bottom and animal, midway a citizen, and at the top divine. But the climate of this world is such that few ripen at the top." We have to mentally move ourselves into such a climate that we ripen at the top and appear in our true Divine Form. When there is divinity all around, fountains of love play. There, Love encompasses everybody and everything. If nature teaches us to love our friends, the religion teaches us to love our enemies also. Bertrand Russell says, "to love is to give light with inexhaustible oil. Love should be a tree whose roots are deep in the earth, but whose branches extend into heaven. A poet says "that love for one, from which there doth not spring wide love for all, its but a worthless thin."

Desires produce likes and dislikes, pleasure and pain and keep him in bondage. Once these desires are obliterated, the entire world appears to him an image of God, his own image. Guru Nanak's simple dictum is that one who does not desire anything, is the king of kings. One goes from one birth to the other according to one's desires. According to the Hindu scriptures, one may be a very religious person, master of scriptures and a knower of all that is worth knowing but if he is seized of worldly desires, he shall never attain self realization. Worldly desires arise only so long as you believe all that you see as real. Once you consider the world as inanimate, unreal and without a power base of its own, then the desire for things of that world also disappears. If you get something without wishing for it, then the use of that thing does not create a bondage. So what is bad is the craving or desiring at thing and not the use of that. Desires are of three kinds. Some desire heaven or paradise after death. Some seek to be scholars and masters of scriptures and there are others who crave for wordly pleasures relating to the comforts of their bodies. All these three kinds of desires must be shunned. According to Valmiki Ramayana, desires are of only two kinds, namely desires which are pure and desires which are not pure.

The desire to attain self realization alone is considered a pure desire. All other desires are impure, including the one to get a place in heaven after death. The impure desires keep one in bondage. The great saint Ashtavakar says in his *Gita* that worldly desires formulate our world and cause our bondage. These must be relinquished.

To kill worldly desires and craving for worldly things, one has to seek freedom from passion and attachment. A human being on birth, comes alone and empty handed; on earth also, he goes alone and empty handed. Worldly belongings neither come with him nor go with him. These are acquired here. On death, he leaves even is physical body behind. Mandookyakarak scripture says that if something does not exist before birth nor after death, it does not have any reality in the present. It has no real existence of its own and is every changing and only appears to be true and real.

Ego:

One who believes that it is he who does, is vain and proud. In Gita, Lord Krishna say, "All actions are being performed by the modes of Prakriti. The fool whose mind is deluded by egorism, thinks, I am the doer". According to the Christian scriptures, "pridegoeth before destruction, and an haughty spirit before a fall" A sense of doing and enjoying distinguishes an egoist from others. Ego arises out of ignorance and is the root cause of all pain and sorrow. Ego covers up the sense of equality and destroys the sense of discrimination. Ego can be destroyed only by continuous contemplation of the Brahm.

11

CHAPTER

COMMUNITY HEALTH AND PERSONAL HEALTH

Community health and personal health both are important. Personal health is linked with personal hygiene. The term personal hygiene includes all those personal factors which influence the health and well-being of an individual. It comprises a broad range of day-to-day activities such as care of the body regarding bathing and washing, care of clothing, care of teeth, care of hair, care of feet and nails, care of posture, cultivating good habits regarding eating, diet, exercise, sleep, smoking, drinking and attitudes towards life. Any disruption of these activities may damages health. For example, neglect of oral hygiene may lead to tooth and gum ailments; neglect of personal cleanliness may lead to scabies, eczema and fungal infection; excessive smoking may lead to chronic bronchitis and lung cancer; and over-eating may lead to obesity. The practice of personal hygiene is largely a matter of individual responsibility or self-care. Since, the foundations of personal hygiene are laid in early childhood, the goal of community health should be to provide a broad range o relevant information about health, illness and disability, and ways in which individuals can protect themselves and improve their own health. In a way, the health of the whole community depends on the personal habits of various individuals who constitute the community. So unhygienic habits of individual persons can create problems for the whole community. This is because dirty habits of some of the individual persons make it difficult to maintain a clean and healthy environment. For example, a person may be perfectly healthy, always eating a balanced diet, having clean personal habits and lies in a neat and clean house. But if the neighbourhood of such a healthy person is made dirty, unclean or polluted ten this person cannot keep good health for a long time. So a person cannot stay healthy if his home is clean but his neighbourhood is dirty or polluted. Let us consider an example to see how this may happen? If other people living in the neighbourhood of a healthy person dump garbage and domestic waste water in open space, then disease causing germs and their vectors such as flies, mosquitoes, cockroaches, etc., will grow there and spoil the neat and clean surroundings. This will ultimately lead to disease in the healthy person living nearby. Also, if a healthy person is given polluted water infected with pathogenic bacteria or protozoans, then in spit of all other favourable conditions, the person cannot stay healthy. In fact, an important cause for the greater incidence of water-borne diseases in rural areas is that village people take their drinking supply from those ponds in which they and their cattle tae bath. By bathing and washing the pond water becomes infected with disease causing organisms such as bacteria, protozoans and eggs of worms. People cannot stay well under these conditions, so they fall ill.

Community health care means all such activities which contribute to the improvement and well-being of the health of people in a community. Community health care services are being provided in many parts of our country. These services are provided by the establishment of health care services such as primary health centres, district hospitals, community health centres, medical colleges, All Indian Institutes, Regional Hospitals. The functions of community health are:

(a) It provides clean drinking water.

(b) It provides good and efficient sewage disposal system.

(c) It provides a lot of clean air to the people by developing green open spaces such as public parks, gardens and playgrounds, around the human settlements.

(d) It provides the proper means of cleaning the areas a round the human settlements and maintains an effective garbage (solid waste) disposal system. It also manages the domestic effluents/waste. Thus, it prevents the development of breeding sites of harmful insects.

(e) It provides medical aid to people and vaccination to the children. For example, immunization of children against six major preventable diseases such as tetanus, diphtheria, whooping cough or pertussis, polio, measles, hepatitis and tuberculosis, can check the incidence of these disease.

(f) Different types of environmental pollution is managed by central and State Pollution Control Boards.

(g) It provides family planning advices and services.

(h) It prevents food adulteration.

(i) It tries to keep off school going children from malnutrition by providing nutritious food and milk to them. The care of pregnant women and children would contribute to the reduction of maternal and child morbidity and mortality.

(j) It educates the people to take care of various diseases before they go out of control. Indeed most epidemics are spread because of ignorance and careless handling of the diseases by the people.

12

CHAPTER

NUTRITIONAL DEFICIENCY

Malnutrition refers to non-availability due to faulty planning of meals for faulty utilisation of nutrients in the body. Undernutrition on the other hand is caused due to insufficient intake of food. Some of the most common conditions caused are night blindness, anaemia, beri-beri, scurvy, rickets, goitere and protein-energy-malnutrition. These conditions can be reversed and cured if the specific deficiency of the nutrient is met. More than one nutrient deficiency may occur at one time if the diet on the whole is poor. Also certain nutrients have common food sources e.g. fresh green vegetables supply not only vitamins but also minerals. Absence of these in food will lead to multiple deficiencies.

The causes of mal-or under-nutrition are ignorance, poverty, frequent infections due to in sanitary conditions and certain socio-cultural factors.

Protein Energy Under Nutrition

It results from lack of protein and calories in the diet. It is more prevalent in growing infants and young children when requirements for these nutrients are high. It causes loss of weight and growth failure. Two severe forms of PEU are

Marasmus and Kwashiorkor. Both physical and mental development may be affected by them.

Marasmus is most commonly seen around one year of age. It is primarily the deficiency of calories. Clinical signs are muscle wasting loss of weight, stunted growth, and loose wrinkled skin due to loss of sub-cutaneous fat which is specially obvious in the buttocks and backs of thigh.

Kwashiorkor occurs in older children in the age group of 2 to 4 years. This results form deficiency of proteins primarily. It is characterized by growth failure, muscle wasting and edema (accumulation of water in body). The skin has dark brown patches resembling burns. The hair may become lighter in colour and sparse. The child shows apathy and is disinterested in surroundings. Prevention Breast milk alone is not sufficient after the age of 4 months. Proper weaning foods made from cooked cereals, pulses and vegetables e.g. dalia, khitchdi, soup etc. should be given to the infant along with breast milk. Animal milk, fruits, eggs and flesh foods can also be gradually added to the diet of the infant. Remember child has a limited capacity to eat hence food must be given at frequent intervals. The child has low resistance and great susceptibility for diarrhoea. Hence we must use clean boiled water and clean bottle or spoon etc. Hence we must use clean boiled water and clean bottle or spoon etc. to prevent the spread of any infection.

Deficiency Vitamin A

The signs suggestive of vitamin A deficiency are:

- Bitot's spots, which are triangular foamy patches on the dry conjunctive.
- Nigh blindness or inability to see in dimlight.
- Dull, dry lusterless cornea as the deficiency continues. Ultimately cornea becomes soft which can lead to fatal

blindness.

- Rough and dry skin that resembles spines.

Prevention

Vitamin A rich foods like green leafy vegetables, carrot milk, cod liver oil, egg, liver etc. should be eaten regularly especially by young children. Another sure and easy way to prevent deficiency of vitamin A is by giving a massive dose of vitamin A every six months to all children from 1 to 5 years of age. This is called the Vitamin A prophylaxis programme of the government of India.

Deficiency of Vitamin D

It causes rickets in children and osteomalacia in adults. In rickets bones become soft and bend easily due to improver calcification. The joints of bones become enlarged especially at the wrist and bending of ribs occurs. The bones cannot stand the weight of the body and this leads to bow legs and know knees. Rickets occur in children who live in dark, crowded places and do not get much exposure to sunlight. Osteomalacia or adult rickets occur more in women who observe 'purdah system. They hardly get any opportunity to expose themselves to sunshine and thus prepare vitamin D in their skin. Repeated, closely-spaced pregnancies put extra strain on the stomach. In osteomalacia also bones become soft and fractures occur easily.

Prevention

Enough exposure to sunlight is very important. None of the foods is rich source of vitamin D. Fish liver oils can be given to small children to provide enough vitamin D and vitamin A. adequate amount of calcium should be taken in diet to facilitate bone mineralisation.

Vitamin B_1 Deficiency

This leads to disease called beri-beri It is seen mainly in

areas where people consume large amounts of milled rice as staple with hardly any protective foods taken along with it.

Beri-beri is of two types: (i) Dry beri-beri, (ii) Wet beri-beri.

Dry beri-beri: the patient loses appetite and becomes very thin. The central harmone system is affected. This leads to sensory loss (tingling sensation), motor weakness and tenderness of calf-muscles.

Wet beri-beri: Edema is prominent feature of wet beri-beri. There is cardiac involvement which may lead to circulatory failure and death. Infantile beri-beri leading to sudden death may occur in 2-5 months old infants who are born to mother suffering from B-complex deficiency. Breast milk of such mothers is low in the said vitamin.

Prevention

Avoid over-dependence on milled-rice, Use of parboiled or hand-pounded rice and other cereals like wheat should be encouraged. Include foods like pulses, whole wheat flour, meat, egg etc. in diet.

Deficiency Vitamin B_2

Deficiency of B_2 affects the eye, tongue and mouth. There is burning sensation in eyes. The tongue becomes majenta-red and the corners of the mouth are red and fissured.

Prevention

Use foods rich in vitamin B-complex i.e., milk, green leafy vegetables, whole grains and meat etc.

Deficiency vitamin B_{12}

It is seen mainly among people who eat corn and jawar as staple in their diet. Deficiency of B12 causes pellagra. Is called a diseases of 3 D's—diarrhea, dermatitis and dement is. The skin is dry, sore and red. The areas of the body that remain exposed to sunlight like neck, backs of hand, forearms and dorsal of feet are affected the most.

Prevention

Like in B1-deficiency the diet consumed should be balanced. Consumption of other cereals should be encouraged in corn and jawar eating areas. Pulses, peanuts, liver, meat etc. are also good sources of this vitamin.

Vitamin C Deficiency

A gross deficiency of vitamin C leads to disease called scurvy. The gums become spongy and swollen and bleed easily. Wounds take long time to heal and the joints become tender and swollen. The need for vitamin C is increased in infections like tuberculosis, measles and chicken pox.

Prevention

Regular consumption of vitamin C rich foods like guava, amla, green leafy vegetables, citrus fruits, sprouted pulses etc. Helps in preventing scurvy.

Deficiency Iron

This leads to condition called anemia which means a low level of hemoglobin in the blood. The number and size of red blood cells decreases. Anemia is common in India especially among the women and children of poor classes. The important symptoms of anemia are weakness, fatigue, and breathlessness on exertion. These are all related to reduced capacity of blood to carry oxygen to various parts of the body: Pollar of the face, eyes and finger nails are common signs of anemia. Spoon shaped nails are seen in older children and adults.

Prevention: Regular consumption of iron-rich foods like grean leafy vegetables, meat, fish, eggs and whole grains prevent anemia. Control of hook-warm and other infestations will help prevent excessive loss of blood leading to anemia. Under the

National Nutritional Anemia prevention Programme (NNAPP) of Government of India iron and folic acid tablets are distributed to small children and pregnant women and lactating mothers through Maternal and Child Health Centres.

Deficiency Iodine

This leads to enlargement of the thyroid glands which is situated in the front of the neck. This condition is known as goiter. It is endemic in sub-Himalayan regions of India where iodine content of water and soil is low. Lately cases of goiter have been found in Delhi and other places also. Cretins are born to women who suffer from gross iodine deficiency. These infants show growth retardation and their mental faculties are sub-normal. Creations are usually deaf and dumb. Goitre and cretism can be prevented by adequate intake of iodine. One of the easiest and cheapest ways of adding iodine to diet is by using iodized salt. Under the National Goitre Control project iodized alt is distributed in endemic and now even other areas of the country.

The government of India is running several nutrition intervention programmes for improving the nutritional status of the vulnerable groups. Integrated Child Development Service is a programme or Central Government for better health and nutrition of preschoolers, pregnant women and lactating mothers. Immunisation, referral services (medical care), preschool education, nutrition supplements, nutrition and health education and safe water supply are its important components. Nutrition education and nutrition programmes it is hoped that the nutritional status of the masses of this country will a marked improvement.

13

CHAPTER

FOOD PREPARATION AND HYGIENE

Food preparation means getting the food ready for eating. It is a skill that requires considerable practice. Food is cut, mixed and /or cooked in order to blend flavours, textures, colour and shapes. Food cooking is an art which requires thought, care, skill and planning. There are varies methods of cooking food, each one having its own advantages.

Whatever method of cooking is employed the following principles must always be kept in mind:

- To keep the flavour in e.g. when a piece of meat is fried, the flavour is kept in.
- To draw the flavour out e.g., when meat is chopped up and put in to cold water and cooked slowly, as in the case of mutton broth the flavour is drawn out into the water.
- To preserve the full nutritive value of the food—e.g. in steaming, vegetables retain the food values, whereas in boiling they lose their mineral and vitamin content in water in which the food is boiled.

Food is cooked by application of heat in any one or more of the following ways:

Heat Applied

Dry	Through water	Through Fat
- Baking	- Boiling	- Frying
- Roasting	- Sewing	- Sauteing
- Grilling	- Steaming	- Shallow frying
	- Cooking under pressure	- Deep frying

We take up each method of cooking separately let us understand the reasons for cooking our food.

(a) there are certain foods which are hard and thus difficult to digest, e.g. cereals, pulses, root vegetables etc. Cooking helps in softening them and making the nutrients present in them more available to the body.

(b) Cooking also helps in brining out and blending of flavours or various food items. Rice, dals, vegetables give nicer flavours when cooked. These stimulate our appetite and help in better secretion of digestive juices.

(c) Cooking also enables us to improve the appearance of food and add variety to it. Consider a raw and a cooked potato. It not only looks better when cooked but can be cooked in a number of different ways e.g. wafers, finger chips, boiled and mashed, cooked wit other vegetables, stuffed in paranthas etc.

(d) Cooking also helps in making food free from germs and improve its keeping quality e.g. milk stays longer when boiled or dried.

Methods of Cooking by Dry Heat

Baking is cooking by dry heat in an enclosed box called an oven. The air inside it is heated by gas or electricity and the food is baked. A few examples of baked foods are bread, biscuits, cake, baked pies etc. Baking is a slow method of cooking but food thus cooked is easily digestible ad there is not much loss of nutrients.

Roasting

Roasting is cooking by radiant heat. It is either done by placing food in a preheated oven or tandoor (earthen oven) or in hit sand or ash. Roasted chicken is prepared by smearing it well with fat and putting it inside an oven or tandoor. But peanuts, or popcorn are roasting in hot sand or on flame. Brinjals, potatoes etc. are roasted by burning them in hot ash.

While roasting, food is turned round constantly so that it is cooked from all sides. The free circulation of hot air helps in quick sealing of outer layer of food and thus preventing the juices from flowing out. Food thus prepared is not only nutritious but has a rich flavour.

Grilling is a method of cooking food by placing it on glowing fire or under the defector of an electric oven. The high heat is maintained through and food is turned round and round so that all sides are cooked evenly. *Tikkas* and *Sikkh kaboab* are grilled. Food cooked this way is tasty but often looses many of its important juices.

Heat Applied through Water

Boiling is cooking by moist heat. Food is placed in boiling water to cook. If the water in which the food is cooked is thrown away, then this is a wasteful method because while boiling most of the water soluble nutrients from food are dissolved in the water. The amount of water used therefore, must be just sufficient to cook the food and the pan must be covered while cooking. Lower the flame or stove when water boils and allow the food to cook slowly. When cooking coloured vegetables like peas, carrots, cabbage etc., cook it on high heat, slow cooking will destroy their colours and shape. Boiled food is light and is easily digested. All vegetables, meats, cereals, pulses etc. Can be prepared by this method.

Stewing means cooking of food in water for a long time on low heat. The pan is kept covered to minimize evaporation. Vegetables, fruits and meat can be cooked b this method. Cheaper, tougher cuts of meat can be softened by stewing. Food to be stewed should be cut in small pieces to get it cooked well. The water should be just enough and the heat provided should be slow and steady. This is an economical method of cooking. Less nutrients are lost as the gravy is served with the food.

Like boiling and stewing, steaming means cooking by moist heat. It differs from oiling and stewing in that the food does not come in contact with water. Food is cooked by the steam from boiling water. This can be done either by direct or indirect contact with steam.

Direct Method: The food is put into a steamer which allows steam to come in direct contact with it. The rack with small holes allows some of the nutrients to fall into the eater below, this water is thrown away therefore the nutrients are lost. Idlis and dhoklas are good examples of steamed food.

Indirect method: The food is placed in a vessel and covered. This is put into another vessel which has boiling water. The food is thus surrounded by steam and is cooked gradually. The full flavour and nutrients are retained in the food. Custards and puddings are steamed and are light and easily digestible. A double boiler is very handy for steaming by the indirect method. To prevent food from becoming sodden, cover puddings and meat with paper on which a thin layer of butter or ghee has been spread evenly.

Cooking under pressure: Whensteam is retained inside the cooking pot and is not allowed to escape during cooking it exerts pressure on the food and cooks it faster. This saves fuel and time and the nutrient losses are minimal. For pressure cooking, it is essential to have an airtight lid on the cooking pot and it should not be opened now and then. A pressure cooker is the device for pressure cooking. Since no steam is allowed to escape while cooking the water loss from the food is minimal. All pulses, cereals, vegetables and meat can be cooked in a pressure cooker.

While using a pressure cooker care must be taken to see that the cooker is only 2/3 filled. Since the water losses are minimal, the amount of water in the cooker should be just enough to cook the food. The fire underneath should be high till the pressure of steam is built up and then reduced to slow, till the food is finally cooked. The cooker should not be opened till it has cooked down. The time of cooking should be checked carefully and the cooker must be operated accordingly. Longer cooking than required will result in overcooking and spoiling the food completely.

The food coming in contact with it is very rapidly heated and its outer surface is hardened immediately, preventing any loss of flavours and juices. Only foods that take a short time to cook can be fried. Food prepared by this method is tasty but difficult to digest. Different ways of frying are:

(a) *Sauteing*—a small quantity of fat is used, which is just enough to be absorbed by the cooked food. The food has to be turned frequently. Vagatables are often cooked this way.

(b) *Shallow frying*—sufficient fat is n\used in the frying pan or tawa. Food is turned on both sides equally as is done in the case of parantha, omeletee and pancake. Extra fat should be drained by using brown paper.

(c) *Deep frying*—Deep fat frying is done in a Karahi or deep sauce pan. Enough oil or ghee is heated, so that the food is completely covered in it. Chips, bonda, pakoras, puris are foods that are deep fried. The fat must be hot enough when you put the food into it. If the food is put before that fat is hot enough, the fat will soak into the food and make it very greasy. If the fat is over heated, the food will get burnt outside but will be uncooked form inside.

Heat on Chief Constituents of Food

Proteins coagulate when cooked. The connective tissue is converted into gelatine which is soluble in later. These forms of protein are more easily digestible than the original forms. Over cooking of proteins hardens and toughens it thereby rendering it indigestible.

Carbohydrates

(a) Carbohydrates are classified into two groups—

(i) Starches (ii) Sugars

By the application of dry heat, starch is converted to "dextrin", a midway product between starch and sugar, and which is formed when bread is toasted. Moist heat causes the starch grains to well, the cell covering of cellulose to rupture and the starch to be released, which gelatinizes at the temperature below boiling point of water. Te degree of heat required to cook starch varied with the kind of starchy foods.

(b) Cellulose is softened by the application of moist heat.

(c) Sugar when heated in water dissolves, ten forms a syrup and upon further heating turns first into barley sugar and then into Caramel sugar.

Fats are easily affected by heat. If heated to a very high

temperature by a dry method of cooking as in roasting, they undergo partial decomposition. Fatty acid substances are produced, which are acrid in odour and irritating to the digestive organs. At too low a temperature, the food will not cook satisfactorily and fat will soak into he food, thus rendering it less easily digestible. It is, therefore, important when cooking fat to have the temperature sufficiently high in order to cook the food and avoid on the one hand excessive penetration to fat and on the other formation of acroline. Fat is ready for use when it is still and a slight blue fume rises from it.

All vitamins are generally affected by heat. Vitamin A is fat soluble and is destroyed by very strong heat. Vitamin B is also unstable at high temperatures, while Vitamin C is destroyed by even a little heat. Vitamin D which is fat soluble, it not affected by heat.

Minerals are not affected by heat but are soluble in water. If the water in which the food is cooked is discarded, the minerals are lost.

In order to save nutrients while you cook, remember these simple rules:

- Peel vegetables thinly. Peel potatoes and beet root after boiling.
- Wash vegetables before cutting to avoid loss of minerals and vitamins. Cut vegetables into large pieces. Use a stainless steel knife.
- Use the leaves of vegetables like radish, knoll and onions.
- Put vegetables into boiling water.
- Use just sufficient water for cooking.
- Use any excess water or stock for cooking some other

food.

- Wash rice only a few times or nutrients will be washed away.
- Use atta with bran and unpolished rice. The bran and outer covering of rice contain minerals, vitamins and iron.
- Avoid baking soda, it destroys the vitamins in vegetables. Keep the cooking pot covered while cooking.
- Avoid overcooking and serve food immediately after cooking pressure cooker saves time, fuel and money and food is more nutritious.

Suggestions for Vegetable, Meat and Fruit Cookery

Essential steps in achieving good results in vegetable cookery:

(a) You will need good vegetables to begin with. Then wash them thoroughly to free them from sand dirt.

(b) Cook vegetables only long enough to get them tender. Modern vegetable cookery requires shorter cooking periods than formerly were considered desirable. Long cooking destroys the crispness and freshness of vegetables, as well as much of their food value and colour.

(c) More minerals and vitamins will be retained if you cook vegetables with the skins on. When peeling is absolutely necessary do it after cooking.

(d) Never let vegetables stand in water.

(e) Such vegetables, as green beans, cabbage, carrots, peas, potatoes, and spinach may be suitable cooked by boiling or steaming. Almost all vegetables, but green ones especially, are at their nutritive best when served whole at once after boiling or steaming. Season vegetables well to make them tasty.

(f) Boiling vegetables use as little water as possible. Do not put the vegetables in until the water is boiling and remove them as soon as they are tender. With a heavy kettle and tight cover, less water is necessary. Strong-flavoured vegetables may be cooked in uncovered pans. This procedure allows some of the strong flavor to pass off with the steam. Green vegetables keep their colour better if cooked uncovered for the first few minutes.

(g) Some people use steamers and pressure cookers for vegetables. The pressure cooker is a great time saver.

(h) Save the water in which vegetables have been cooked and use it for soups, gravies, or sauces.

(i) If vegetables are to be cooked with meat, add the vegetables just long enough before the meat is tender so that they will be well done.

(j) When you stir them, you break them up and mix air in, and this destroys some of the vitamins.

(k) Serve raw vegetables frequently—at least once a day is a good rule. The use of raw vegetables seems to be increasing. Their flavour, colour, and texture are appetizing. Lettuce, young onions, turnips, radishes, cauliflower, water cress, spinach, and cabbage are all enjoyed raw.

(l) Make raw salad at the last minute. Vitamin C gets away very fast from foods that are peeled or cut. The finer the cutting, the greater the loss is.

Try cooking peas with a small chopped onion and a little

lettuce, seasoning and adding a little butter and a spoonful of hot ream to the liquid, for paneer with spinach, or peas with yolk of egg.

Ortry cooking a few young onions with peas and may be a spring of mint. Cook them in the smallest amount of water, with a teaspoonful of sugar. When done add a little butter.

14

CHAPTER

NUTRITIVE VALUES OF FOOD

Food has so many calories, proteins, vitamins, minerals, enzymes and natural glucose etc. but that does not mean that as soon as that food article goes within you, immediately that much energy is transferred to the various parts of your body. It depends upon your various body systems as to how much energy and other elements the can extract from that food and transfer to various systems of your body. Mind draws its power from the soul and directs all sense organs. Mind has not other power source of its own. It is, therefore, clear that it depends upon your physical, emotional, mental and spiritual levels of that time as to how much energy etc you can extract or draw from the food you eat.

Nutritive elements which are ordinarily present in various items are indicated in tables. This tables gives only the averages. The child inherits many qualities and defects of the mother. In the same way many deficiencies of the mother earth are found in the food produced therein. Consequently food grown in different types of soils under different conditions will have nutritive elements different from the averages indicated in the tables.

Table 14.1:

Excess of acid or Alkali of edible portion of some other foods

In 100 gms

Food stuff	*Excess acid akali*	*Excess akali*
Almonds	-	129
Apricots fresh	-	68
Apricots fresh	-	313
Asparagus	-	8
Avocado	-	57
Bajra	57	-
Barley	57	-
Beans kidney	-	30
Bitter gourd	-	14
Bread white	71	-
Bread whole wheat	78	-
Brocoli	-	58
Brussel sprouts	23	-
Cauliflower	99	-
Celery	-	67
Cheese	-	41
Cherries	-	70
Coconut fresh	-	70
Coriander leaves	-	147
Cornflakes	54	-
Corn-Marze	102	-

(Contd...)

Currants	-	12
Dates dried	-	110
Fenugreek	-	110
Figs dried	-	1009
Crapefruit	-	42
Grapes	-	27
Ice cream	-	6
Lemons	33	
Meats	51	-
Bacon	110	-
Chicken	107	-
Cod fish	55	-
Egg	110	-
Lamb	94	-
Pork	-	18
Molasses	129	-
Olives	-	45
Onions	-	15
Radish	-	27
Raisins	-	236
Rice	72	-
Soybean	-	52
Strawberry	-	27
Turnip	-	110
Walnut	79	-
Wheat	77	-
Wheat bran	-	44
Yam	-	80

Table 14.2: Values of Foods for Nutrients (Cereals and Pulses)

Per 100 gms

Food Item	*Protein mg*	*Fat mg*	*Minerals mg*	*Fiber mg*	*Carbohydrate mg*	*Energy K.cal*	*Calcium mg*	*Phosphorous mg*
Bajra	11.6	5.0	1.3	1.2	67.5	361	42	296
Barley	11.5	1.3	1.2	3.9	69.6	336	26	215
Beans	22.9	1.3	3.2	-	60.6	346	260	410
Bengal gram	17.1	5.3	3,0	3.9	60.9	360	202	312
Black Dhal	24.0	1.4	3.2	0.9	59.6	347	154	385
Corn	11.1	3.6	1.5	2.7	66.2	342	10	348
Green Gram	24.0	1.3	3.5	4.1	56.7	334	124	326
Moth Beans	23.6	1.1	3.5	4.5	56.5	330	202	230
Moth Beans	23.6	1.1	3.5	4.5	56.5	330	202	230
Oat Meal	1.36	7.6	1.8	3.5	62.8	374	50	380
Peas, Dry	19.7	1.1	2.2	4.5	56.5	31.5	75	298
Rice Milled	6.8	0.5	0.6	0.2	78.2	345	10	160
Rice Unpolished	7.5	1.0	0.9	0.6	76.7	346	10	190
Sorghum	10.4	1.9	1.6	72.6	349	25	-	222
Soybean	43.2	19.5	4.6	3.7	20.9	432	240	690
Wheat	11.8	1.5	1.5	1.2	71.2	346	41	306

Table 14.3: Values of Foods for Nutrients (Vegetables)

Per 100 gms

Food Item	*Protein mg*	*Fat mg*	*Minerals mg*	*Fiber mg*	*Carbohydrate mg*	*Energy K.cal*	*Calcium mg*	*Phosphorous mg*
Amaranth	4.0	0.5	2.7	1.0	6.1	45	297	83
Asparagus	2.5	0.3	-	-	4.0	23	24	60
Bamboo Shoots	3.9	0.5	1.1	-	5.7	43	20	65
Beet Root	1.7	0.1	0.8	0.9	8.8	43	20	65
Bitter Gourd	2.1	1.0	1.4	1.7	10.6	60	23	38
Brinjal	1.4	0.3	1.3	4.0	24	24	18	47
Broccoli	2.9	0.45	-	1.3	5.0	27	47	65
Brussel Sprouts	4.7	0.5	-	1.3	5.0	27	47	65
Broad Beans	4.5	0.1	0.8	2.0	7.2	48	50	64
Cabbage	1.8	0.1	0.6	1.0	4.6	27	39	44
Carrot	0.9	0.2	1.1	1.2	10.6	48	80	530
Cauliflower	2.6	0.4	1.0	1.2	4.0	30	33	57
Celery	0.8	0.1	0.9	1.2	3.5	18	30	38
Cucumber	0.4	0.1	0.3	0.4	2.5	13	10	25
Drumstick	2.5	0.1	2.0	4.8	3.7	26	30	110
Ginger	2.3	0.8	1.2	2.4	12.3	67	20	60
Goose Foot	3.7	0.4	2.6	0.8	2.9	30	-	80
Lady Fingers	1.9	0.2	0.7	1.2	6.4	35	66	56
Lotus Root	1.7	0.1	0.2	0.8	11.3	53	21	74
Mango Green	0.7	0.1	0.4	1.2	10.1	44	10	19

(Table Contd...)

Mint	4.8	0.6	1.9	-	5.8	48	200	62
Mutard	4.0	0.6	1.6	0.8	3.2	34	155	26
Neem Leaves	11.6	3.0	2.6	2.2	21.2	158	130	190
Onion	1.8	0.1	0.6	0.6	12.6	59	40	60
Parsley	5.9	1.0	3.2	1.8	13.5	87	390	175
Potato	1.6	0.1	0.6	0.4	22.6	97	10	40
Pumpkin	1.4	0.1	4.6	25		-	10	30
Radish	0.7	0.1	0.8	3.4	17	-	35	22
Radish Leaves	3.9	0.6	1.6	0.6	4.2	38	310	60
Spinach	2.0	0.7	1.7	0.6	2.9	26	73	21
Tomato	0.9	0.2	0.5	0.8	3.6	20	48	20
Water Cress	2.9	0.2	2.2	0.6	4.9	33	290	140

Table 14.4:
Values of Foods for Nutrients (Fruits and Nats)

Per 100 gms

Food Item	*Protein mg*	*Fat mg*	*Minerals mg*	*Fiber mg*	*Carbohydrate mg*	*Energy K.cal*	*Calcium mg*	*Phosphorous mg*
Almonds	20.8	58.9	2.9	1.7	10.5	655	230	490
Amla	0.5	0.1	0.5	3.4	13.7	58	50	20
Apple	0.2	0.5	0.3	1.0	13.4	59	10	14
Apricot	1.0	0.3	0.7	1.1	11.6	53	20	25
Apricot Dried	1.6	0.7	2.8	2.1	73.4	306	110	70
Avocado	1.7	22.8	1.1	-	0.8	215	10	80
Bael	1.8	0.3	1.7	2.9	31.8	137	85	50

(Contd...)

Banana	1.2	0.3	0.8	0.4	27.2	116	17	36
Cashew Nut	21.2	46.9	2.4	1.3	22.3	596	50	450
Cherries	1.1	0.5	0.8	0.4	13.8	64	24	25
Coconut	4.5	41.6	1.0	3.6	13.0	444	10	240
Coconut Water	1.4	0.1	0.3	0	4.4	24	24	10
Cran-Berries	0.4	0.2	-	-	12.0	48	7	7.5
Currants	2.7	0.5	2.2	1.0	75.2	316	130	110
Dates Dry	2.5	0.4	2.1	3.9	75.8	317	120	50
Grapes	0.6	0.4	0.9	2.8	13.1	58	20	23
Grape Fruit	0.7	0.1	0.2	-	7.0	32	20	20
Guava	0.9	0.3	0.7	5.2	11.2	52	10	28
Jack Fruit	1.9	0.1	0.9	1.1	19.8	88	20	41
Jambul	0.7	0.3	0.4	0.9	14.0	62	15	15
Lemon	1.0	0.9	0.3	1.7	11.1	57	70	10
Lichi	1.1	0.2	0.5	0.5	13.6	61	10	35
Mango	0.6	0.4	0.4	0.7	16.9	74	14	16
Water Melon	0.2	0.2	0.3	0.2	3.3	16	11	12
Orange	0.7	0.2	0.3	0.3	10.9	48	26	20
Orange Juice	0.2	0.1	0.1	-	1.9	9	5	9
Papaya	0.6	0.1	0.5	0.8	7.2	32	17	13
Peach	1.2	0.3	0.8	1.2	10.5	50	15	41
Pea-nut	25.3	40.1	2.4	3.1	26.1	567	90	350
Pear	0.6	0.2	0.3	1.0	11.9	52	8	15
Pine Apple	0.4	0.1	0.4	0.5	10.8	46	20	9
Pomegranate	1.6	0.1	0.7	5.1	14.5	65	10	70
Prunes	0.5	0.3	0.6	0.5	12.8	56	10	18
Straw Berry	0.7	0.2	0.4	1.1	9.8	44	30	30

Table 14.5:
Values of Foods for Nutrients (Miscellaneous)

Per 100 gms

Food Item	*Protein mg*	*Fat mg*	*Minerals mg*	*Fiber mg*	*Carbohydrate mg*	*Energy K.cal*	*Calcium mg*	*Phosphorous mg*
Cardamom	10.2	2.2	5.4	20.1	42.1	229	130	160
Chillies-dry	15.9	6.2	6.1	302	31.6	246	160	370
Chillies Green	2.9	0.6	1.0	6.8	3.0	29	30	80
Cloves	5.2	8.9	5.2	9.5	46.0	286	740	100
Coriander	14.1	16.1	4.4	32.6	21.6	288	630	393
Garlic	6.3	0.1	1.0	0.8	29.8	145	30	310
Pepper Dry	11.5	6.8	4.4	14.9	49.2	304	460	198
Tamarind	3.1	0.1	2.9	5.6	67.4	283	170	110
Turmeric	6.3	5.1	3.5	2.6	69.4	349	150	282
Beef	79.2	10.3	1.6	0.5	0.2	410	68	324
Biscuit	6.4	15.2	1.1	-	71.9	450	-	-
Bread	7.8	0.7	-	0.2	51.9	245	11	-
Butter	-	81.0	2.5	-	-	729	-	-
Cane Sugar	0.1	0	0.1	0	99.4	398	12	1
Cheese milk	24.0	32.0	-	-	-	384	800	-
Duck Meat	21.6	4.8	1.2	-	0.1	130	4	235
Egg	13.3	13.3	1.0	-	-	173	60	220
Fish	11.2	9.8	4.6	-	9.1	109	1606	253
Fish Oil	19.6	2.0	1.8	-	0.1	97	357	349
Fish Prawan	19.1	1.0	1.7	-	0.8	89	323	278

(Contd...)

Goat Meat	21.4	3.6	1.1	-	-	118	12	193
Honey	0.3	0	0.2	-	79.5	319	5	16
Leer	19.3	7.5	1.5	-	1.3	150	10	380
Mushroom	3.1	0.8	1.4	0.4	4.3	43	6	110
Mutton	18.5	13.3	1.3	-	-	194	150	150
Milk	3.2	4.1	0.8	-	4.4	67	120	90
Pork	18.7	4.4	1.0	-	-	114	30	200
Poultry Meat	19.0	7.0	-	-	-	139	15	-

The average weight of a healthy person will depend upon your age, height and body frame. If you are tall and have broad frame, then even with a heavy weight, you could be considered healthy, on the basis of the charts of a life Insurance Corporation, for various heights ad ages, two types of weights are given – one which is considered ideal for that age and height and the other is the maximum weight beyond which even a person of the broadest frame should be considered unhealthy. The extreme limits beyond which you should not allow your weight to go. It also gives you the ideal weight for your height and age. It is now for you to decide as to how much reduction in your weight is required and over what period is that reduction to be achieved. You, in your weight is required and over what period is that reduction to be achieved. You, in your particular situation, know the average daily calory requirement of your body and can calculate as to how many calories less your may take daily to achieve the desired reduction in weight. Then looking to the overall state of your health, and also to your own tastes, you may decide which food article in what quantity you can take every day to achieve the desired result. If some food article is good for your health but you dislike it, then with a sudden shift, your palate will not get that satisfaction and your body mechanism will not send out the requirement digestive juices and enzymes etc for digestion of that food. You will thus not benefit from the change over. Let such a change be gradual over a period of time so that your tastes change gradually and you gradually start liking those food articles which are good for your health. Reduction in quantities can take place soonest.

Acidic and alkaline Food: with increase of acidity in the stomach, many digestive problems arise. If care is not taken in this regard ulcers may even develop. It is consequently necessary that you should not eat such food which increases acidity in the stomach. Cereals, pulses and all types of meats and fish increase acidity when taken. And almost all vegetable sand fruits increase alkalinity in the stomach and so decrease the acidity. Lemon, Oranges, Malta, Grape fruit and other fruits which have citric acid, when taken, decrease the acidity in the stomach. Unboiled milk produces alkalinity and the boiled milk and its products produce acidity.

Cholesterol

Cholesterol is a waxy, yellow-white substance produced mostly in the liver. It is a master molecule which plays a vital role in all animal life. Cholesterols is an essential element in our cell walls. It is a building block which is used by the body for making other materials required for the running of the body factory. Cholesterol is essential to our survival. It is needed for the insulation of our nerves and for making cell membranes and hormones also. In a healthy human body cholesterol which is part of the brain, nerves, muscles and fat tissues, remains constant between 140-160 mg. About 20-25 mg of cholesterol remains active in metabolic processes in the liver, the intestines and the blood plasma. Cholesterol is added to the human body from the diet. It is absorbed through the intestines.

All shortfalls have not be made up by the body itself. Cholesterol levels below 200 mg are good, between 200-240 mg need watching and above 240 mg are high and need medical attention. High risk factors in case of cholesterol are almost the same as in case of heart attacks. These are, (a) heredity, (b) age, (c) male gender (d) smoking, (e) high blood pressure, (f) extreme oesity, (g) diabetes, (h) Lack of exercise resulting in low HDL. The protection to women is provided by the female hormone estrogen. After menopause, when the wastes are not eliminated with menses and when the estrogen supply decreases the risk of high cholesterol levels and of heart attack increase. Cholesterol is being constantly moved in the blood stream. It has three forms i.e., Very low density lipoproteins, low density lipoproteins and high density lipoproteins. Does not seem to effect the coronary health. LDL is the main culprit promoting deposits in the arteries and gradually blocking the passage for the blood. HDL seems to be protective and helpful.

Cholesterol strategy should consist of two prongs, one to reduce LDL and the second to raise HDL. Even alopaths say that "food is the best medicine for conquering cholesterol". It is believed that only in one out of five hundred cases, cholesterol levels cannot be corrected by diet regulation. Heart attack remains relatively unknown in Japan because the traditional Japanese diet keeps the cholesterol LDL levels very low. For reducing LDL levels, foods which have cholesterol should be avoided. Their list with cholesterol contents is given below. Secondly, it has been established that soluble fiber binds itself together to cholesterol LDl and gets eliminated along with that cholesterol. So the second part of that strategy is to take foods with soluble fibers. In-soluble fibers do not bind themselves to cholesterol and do not help I eliminating it. Oat bran, apples and dry beans have a fair proportion of soluble fibers and are, therefore, moderately effective in lowering LDL cholesterol.

Example of other foods with soluble fiber are corn, pectine found in the skin of citrus fruits and apples, sunflower seeds. Thirdly, some foods are known to lower LDL cholesterol levels. Such as foods containing vitamin niacine vitamin C, chromium, magnesium and soybean lecithin. Avoid coffee, smoking and saturated fats. For a healthy person LDL should be below mg and the total cholesterol divided by HDL should have a ratio of less than 4.5. The important thing is HDL.

The lower this ratio, the healthier is the whole system.

Table 14.6:

Cholesterol content in 100 gms edible portion of various foods in milligrams

Beef-lean	70
Brains raw	More than 2000
Butter	250 to 280
Caviar	More than 300
Cheeses Cheddar	100
Cottage	1 to 5
Cottage creamed	15
Cream	120 to 140
Cheese spreads	65
Chicken raw	60
Crab	125
Egg whole	550
Fish	70
Ice cream	45
Kidney raw	375
Lamb raw	70
Lard-animal fats	95
Liver-raw	300 to 425
Skim milk fluid	3Mutton 65
Pork	70
Shrimp	125
Fruits	nil
Vegetables	nil
Cereals	nil

Soybean: Manchuria's king himself used to do the first sowing of soybean in a colourful ceremony. Chinese called it the yellow jewel. It was the staple food of the whole country. For Japan, soybean is the "food both for body and soul was it plays an important spiritual role for them. They scatter soybean at home to ward off evil spirits and two welcome the Japanese new Year" Germans, during World War II, called soybean as the 'wizard bean'. Soybean came to Europe in 1907 and now about 60% of the world's soybeanis grown in America. It has been known India for about a hundred years but the campaign to popularize it started only in1962 through Gandhiji's writings.

Honey: This is such a wonderful viscous food, already predigested by the bees, that it is included amongst the five nectars by the Hindu scriptures which a state "Medicinal vegetation and juices maketh honey. It is like nectar. Honey is like the vital force. Honey is liketh cereals. Even gods take the honey with great relish" there is mention of honey in the Bible for more than sixty times. It is written about Lord Jesus Christ that "he shall have a diet of butter and honey. For this reason He shall abhore wrong and choose righteousness". In the Bible also honey is considered symbolic of soft sweetness. In the Holy Quran Surat Ei Nihal is specially about honey. It prescribes honey as very good for the health of humanity. According to the scripture Buddhacharya, Lord Budha instructed all his disciples to make liberal use of honey in their diet. For physical and mental development, you should also make greater use of honey in the diet of your families. Honey, when heated excessively, deteriorates in taste and if it is boiled, it becomes unfit for consumption. It should never be heated beyond 65°C. Instead of heating honey on fire, place the honey bottle in warm water and then raise its temperature.

Honey makes the body "disease free and beautiful". It adds to the intellect, contentment and bliss. It is a great medicine for all ailments of heart lungs and blood pressure. It reduces obesity. It cures constipation. Honey readily enters into the blood steam. If you are thirsty and have a dry palate, you will benefit by holding syrup of honey in the mouth for sometime. In rheumatic cases it helps reduce the uric acid. Persons who have cough, pneumonia or condition of the lungs may take one tea spoon of honey with as much of almond oil twice a day and one the a spoon of honey with warm water twice a day. This will bring them great relief.

Amla: Amla is a great fruit without an equal. Its fresh juice has twenty times more vitamin C than the fresh orange juice. Vitamins of many fruits get destroyed when cooked or heated but the vitamins of Amla remain almost intact even on cooking. The candy preserve of Amla is delicious, cool and very beneficial. Eating one or two pieces a day is most beneficial for your general health.

BIBLIOGRAPHY

Anderson, D., 1979, Practical Implementation," in Anderson, D. (Ed), *Health Education in Practice*, London: Groom Helm.

Bhattacharya, Shukla, 1991, *Project Nutrition, Health Education and Environmental Sanitation: An Impact Study*, New Delhi: National Council of Educaitonal Research and Training.

Chandramani, M., 1988, *Impact of Nutrition Education at Different Levels*, Ph.D. thesis in Education and Home Science, University of Madras.

Elder, John, 1991, "From Experiementation to Dissemination: Strategies for Maximizing the Spread and Impact of School Health Education", in Don, Nutbeam; So, Haglund; Peter, Farley and Per, Tillgren (Edited), *Youth Health Promotion from Theory to Practice in School and Community*, London: Forbes Publication.

Ministry of Health, 1956, *National Plan of Health and Physical Education*, New Delhi: Government of India.

Ministry of Health and Family Welfare, 1983, National Health Policy, New Delhi: Government of india.

National Council of Educational Research and Training, 1976, *Curriculum Guide on Nutrition, Health Education and Environmental Sanitation in Primary School*, New Delhi: NCERT.

Nutrition Foundations of India, 1984, *Nutrition and Health Education through the Rural School System*, Scientific Report No. 3. New Delhi: Nutrition Foundation of India.

Potdar, Raj Kumar S., 1989, *Mobilizing, Education to Reinforce Primary Health Care Through School Children s Change Agents and revitalizing School Health Education to Attain Ultimate Goals*: Health For All by 2000 AD., Ph.D. thesis in Education, SNDT Univeristy, Bombay.

Sapru, R and Pandey, D.C., 1988, *Evaluation of the Government of India's Intensive Pilot Project of School Health Services*, New Delhi : National Institute of Health & Family Welfare.

State Council of Educational Research and Training (SCERT), 1984-1989, *Annual Progress Reports for Implementation of Project NHEES*, Allahabad: SIE.

World Health Organisation, 1954, *Report of the Expert Committee on Health Education 1953*, Cited in Swe U Min, "Health Education in South East : An Overview and Future Perspective, Word Health Organisation, *Health Education Strategies in South East Asia*, New Delhi: Regional Office for South East Asia.

INDEX